KU-749-325

Microsoft Dynamics® CRM 2011

Step by Step

Mike Snyder
Jim Steger
Brendan Landers

THE IET LIBRARY
2 SAVOY PLACE, LONDON WC2R 0BL

1 1 JUL 2016
10813
+44 (0)20 7344 5461   ...usk@theiet.org

| SHELF | 681.3:002 SNY |
| LOC | KC |

10813

PUBLISHED BY
Microsoft Press
A Division of Microsoft Corporation
One Microsoft Way
Redmond, Washington 98052-6399

Copyright © 2011 by Mike Snyder and Jim Steger

All rights reserved. No part of the contents of this book may be reproduced or transmitted in any form or by any means without the written permission of the publisher.

Library of Congress Control Number: 2010941617
ISBN: 978-0-7356-4890-6

Printed and bound in the United States of America.

4 5 6 7 8 9 10 11 12 LSI 7 6 5 4 3 2

Microsoft Press books are available through booksellers and distributors worldwide. For further information about international editions, contact your local Microsoft Corporation office or contact Microsoft Press International directly at fax (425) 936-7329. Visit our Web site at www.microsoft.com/mspress. Send comments to: mspinput@ microsoft.com.

Microsoft and the trademarks listed at http://www.microsoft.com/about/legal/en/us/IntellectualProperty /Trademarks/EN-US.aspx are trademarks of the Microsoft group of companies. All other marks are property of their respective owners.

The example companies, organizations, products, domain names, e-mail addresses, logos, people, places, and events depicted herein are fictitious. No association with any real company, organization, product, domain name, e-mail address, logo, person, place, or event is intended or should be inferred.

This book expresses the author's views and opinions. The information contained in this book is provided without any express, statutory, or implied warranties. Neither the authors, Microsoft Corporation, nor its resellers, or distributors will be held liable for any damages caused or alleged to be caused either directly or indirectly by this book.

Acquisitions Editor: Todd Merrill
Developmental Editor: Devon Musgrave
Project Editor: Valerie Woolley
Editorial Production: Online Training Solutions, Inc.
Technical Reviewer: Jennifer Ford; Technical Review services provided by Content Master, a member of CM Group, Ltd.
Cover: Girvin

Body Part No. X17-37450

[2012-10-12]

Contents

Acknowledgments xi

Introduction xiii

    A Word About Sandbox Environments xiii

    About the Examples in This Book xiii

    Looking Forward xiv

Features and Conventions of This Book xv

Using the Practice Files xvii

Your Companion eBook. xix

Book Support xxi

    Errata xxi

    We Want to Hear from You xxi

    Stay in Touch xxi

    Getting Help with Microsoft Dynamics CRM 2011 xxii

    More Information xxiv

Part 1   Overview

1   Introduction to Microsoft Dynamics CRM   3

    What Is Microsoft Dynamics CRM? 5

    Microsoft Dynamics CRM Deployment Options 8

    Integrating with Other Microsoft Products. 8

    Logging On to Microsoft Dynamics CRM Online. 9

    Logging On to Microsoft Dynamics CRM 11

    Accessing Microsoft Dynamics CRM by Using
    Microsoft Dynamics CRM for Outlook 13

    Logging On to Microsoft Dynamics CRM via Mobile Express 15

    Key Points 17

What do you think of this book? We want to hear from you!

Microsoft is interested in hearing your feedback so we can continually improve our books and learning resources for you. To participate in a brief online survey, please visit:

microsoft.com/learning/booksurvey

2 Getting Around in Microsoft Dynamics CRM 19

Understanding the Microsoft Dynamics CRM User Interface 20

Using Views to Work with Data Records 24

Sorting Records in a View 25

Selecting and Refreshing Records in a View. 27

Editing Multiple Records in a View. 29

Using Quick Find to Search for Records in a View. 30

Setting a Default Personal View 32

Accessing Recently Visited Records and Views. 34

Using Lookups and Automatic Resolution 35

Setting Personal Options 39

Using the Resource Center. 41

Accessing Help in Microsoft Dynamics CRM 42

Key Points 43

3 Working with Accounts and Contacts 45

Creating an Account 47

Using Parent Accounts and Sub-Accounts 49

Creating a Contact 51

Why Is It Called "Parent Customer"? 52

Attaching Files to Accounts and Contacts. 56

Deactivating and Activating Records. 57

Sharing Accounts and Contacts with Other Users 59

Assigning Accounts and Contacts to Other Users 61

Merging Account or Contact Records 62

Key Points 65

4 Working with Activities and Notes 67

Sidebar: Creating Activities by Using Microsoft Dynamics
CRM Workflow. 68

Understanding Activity Types 69

Sidebar: Custom Activity Types 70

Understanding the Regarding Field 71

Creating Follow-Up Activities 76

Viewing Open and Completed Activities for a Record 78
Creating a Note 85
Managing Your Activities 88
Sending Direct Email Messages 91
Key Points 93

5   Using Microsoft Dynamics CRM for Outlook   95

Accessing CRM Records Within Microsoft Dynamics CRM for Outlook. 97
Accessing CRM Settings Within Microsoft Dynamics CRM for Outlook. 101
Synchronizing Contacts, Tasks, and Appointments 102
Creating and Tracking Contacts 105
Using the Add Contacts Wizard 108
Creating and Tracking Tasks and Appointments 112
Sending and Tracking Email Messages in Microsoft Dynamics CRM for Outlook .113
Deleting Records in Microsoft Dynamics CRM
for Outlook. 118
Going Offline with Microsoft Dynamics CRM
for Outlook. 121
Configuring Synchronization Filters 123
Key Points 126

Part 2   Sales and Marketing

6   Working with Leads and Opportunities   129

Understanding Leads and Opportunities 130
Creating a Lead and Tracking Lead Sources 132
Qualifying a Lead 134
Disqualifying a Lead 136
Creating an Opportunity 138
Using Opportunities to Forecast Potential Sales 140
Closing an Opportunity 144
Reopening an Opportunity 146
Converting an Email Activity to a Lead 148
Key Points 149

7   Using Marketing Lists   151

Creating a Static Marketing List 152

Adding Members to a List by Using a Lookup 155

Adding Members to a List by Using Advanced Find 157

Removing Members from a List by Using Advanced Find 159

Evaluating Members Included in a List by Using Advanced Find 161

Removing Selected Members from a List 163

Creating a Dynamic Marketing List 165

Copying Members to Another Marketing List 167

Creating Opportunities from List Members 169

Using Mail Merge to Generate a Word Document That
Includes List Member Information 172

Key Points 175

8   Managing Campaigns and Quick Campaigns   177

Creating a Campaign 179

Adding Planning Activities. 181

Selecting Target Marketing Lists. 183

Adding Target Products and Sales Literature 185

Relating Campaigns 187

Creating Campaign Templates 189

Copying Campaign Records 189

Using Quick Campaigns 191

Key Points 193

9   Working with Campaign Activities and Responses   195

Creating a Campaign Activity 196

Associating a Marketing List to a Campaign Activity 200

Distributing a Campaign Activity 202

Recording a Campaign Response. 206

Promoting a Campaign Activity to a Campaign Response. 207

Converting a Campaign Response 209

Viewing Campaign Results. 212

Viewing Specific Campaign Information 214

Key Points 216

Part 3 Service

10 **Tracking Service Requests** 219

Creating and Assigning a Service Request Case. 220
Configuring the Subject Tree. 224
Managing Service Request Activities 226
Resolving a Service Request Case. 228
Canceling and Reopening a Service Request Case 230
Key Points 233

11 **Using the Knowledge Base** 235

Creating and Submitting a Knowledge Base Article 237
Publishing a Knowledge Base Article. 241
Searching for a Knowledge Base Article 243
Removing an Article from the Knowledge Base. 245
Creating Article Templates. 249
Key Points 253

12 **Working with Contracts and Queues** 255

Creating a Service Contract. 256
Activating and Renewing a Contract 264
Working with Service Queues. 269
Key Points 275

Part 4 Reporting and Analysis

13 **Working with Filters and Charts** 279

Applying Filters to Your Data and Saving Filtered Views .280
Setting Additional Filters on a Saved View 282
Using Charts to Analyze Microsoft Dynamics CRM Data .283
Creating a New Chart. 288
Sharing a Chart 292
Key Points 294

14 Using Dashboards 297

Using Built-in Dashboards 298

Creating Additional Dashboards. 303

Editing Dashboards. 308

Setting a Default Dashboard 314

Sharing a Dashboard. 315

Key Points 317

15 Using the Report Wizard 319

Creating a Report with the Report Wizard 322

Modifying a Report. 328

Sharing a Report 332

Scheduling a Report 334

Categorizing a Report. 337

Key Points 341

16 Using Advanced Find 343

Performing Advanced Find Queries. 344

Organizing and Formatting Advanced Find Results 349

Creating and Sharing a Saved View 353

Using Advanced Filter Criteria. 356

Using Edit Multiple Records and Assign Multiple Records from Advanced Find . .358

Key Points 361

17 Reporting with Excel 363

Exporting Static Data to Excel Worksheets. 364

Exporting Dynamic Data to Excel Worksheets 368

Exporting Dynamic Data to Excel PivotTables 371

Sidebar: Advanced PivotTables 376

Uploading Excel Reports to the Reports List in Microsoft Dynamics CRM 377

Key Points 378

Part 5   Data Management

18   **Bulk Data Importing**   **381**

    Using the Import Data Wizard 382

    Importing Data with Automatic Data Mapping 388

    Reviewing the Import Status 391

    Updating Data by Using Data Enrichment 394

    Key Points 398

Glossary 399

Index 403

About Sonoma Partners 419

What do you think of this book? We want to hear from you!

Microsoft is interested in hearing your feedback so we can continually improve our books and learning resources for you. To participate in a brief online survey, please visit:

microsoft.com/learning/booksurvey

Acknowledgments

We want to thank all of the people who assisted us in writing this book. If we accidentally miss anyone, we apologize in advance. We want to thank these members of the Microsoft Dynamics CRM product team, Sonoma Partners colleagues, and friends who helped us at one point or another during the book project:

Andrew Bybee
Matt Cooper
Maureen Carmichael
Jim Daly
Stephanie Dart
Richard Dickinson
Neil Erickson

Abhijit Gore
Mahesh Hariharan
Steven Kaplan
Amy Langlois
Humberto Lezama Guadarrama
Nick Patrick
Manbhawan Prasad

Girish Raja
Derik Stenerson
Jason Tyner
Praveen Upadhyay
Sandhya Vankamamidi
Renee Wesberry

Of course, we also want to thank the folks at Microsoft Press who helped champion and support us throughout the book-writing and publishing process, including Devon Musgrave, Todd Merrill, and Ben Ryan.

And we want to thank Valerie Woolley for managing the editing and production process and ensuring a successful delivery of the book. We extend our thanks to Kathy Krause and the rest of the OTSI team who contributed to our book.

Last but not least, we want to thank Jen Ford. As the technical editor for the book, Jen worked around the clock to confirm the technical accuracy of the text. This included reviewing and testing all of our procedures and double-checking our facts.

Mike Snyder's Acknowledgments

I want to thank my wife, Gretchen, who supported me during this project. Writing this book required an additional time commitment above and beyond my normal work responsibilities, and I appreciate her support. Special thanks go out to Neil Erickson, Jason Tyner, and Praveen Upadhyay who helped set up and troubleshoot a bunch of environments of the Microsoft Dynamics CRM for Outlook client! Lastly, thanks to all of my coworkers at Sonoma Partners, who allowed me the time and understanding to work on this book.

Jim Steger's Acknowledgments

I would like to thank my wife, Heidi, for her continued support in this undertaking. I also need to thank Neil Erickson, Jason Tyner, and Andrew Bybee for all of their efforts with providing us the various software builds without which we would not have been able to finish this book so quickly. I also received input from numerous members of the Microsoft Dynamics CRM product team, and I want to extend my thanks to them as well. Finally, I wish to express my gratitude to my associates at Sonoma Partners for their assistance during this process.

Brendan Landers' Acknowledgments

I'd like to thank all the wonderful people that made the writing process possible, including my wife, Jennifer, and daughters, Caily, Shannon, and Cassidy, who allowed me the time to work on this project. Also, I'd like to thank all my colleagues at Sonoma Partners for their support during the writing process, especially Neil Erickson and Jen Ford who helped me work through a variety of challenges along the way.

Introduction

Welcome to *Microsoft Dynamics CRM 2011 Step by Step*! Most likely, your organization has implemented—or is considering implementing—a Microsoft Dynamics CRM system, and you're ready to learn more about what the software can do.

Whether you're a sales associate following up with your top accounts, a marketing professional reaching out to prospects and customers, a customer service representative resolving customer requests and issues, or an executive manager seeking to analyze and understand all of your organization's customer interactions, Microsoft Dynamics CRM can help you do business better.

The intent of this book is to show you how to use key features in the software to understand your customers better, increase sales and productivity, and improve customer satisfaction. It's important to note that Microsoft Dynamics CRM allows administrators to easily customize the forms, fields, and other options in the software, so some of the names used in this book might not match your environment.

A Word About Sandbox Environments

If possible, ask your system administrator about setting up a second Microsoft Dynamics CRM environment—often referred to as a "sandbox environment"—that you can use to step through the exercises in this book. A sandbox environment allows you to modify records without affecting the data in your live system. Your organization might already have a staging or test environment you can use.

About the Examples in This Book

The descriptions and procedures in this book are based on the default forms and views in Microsoft Dynamics CRM. As you'll learn in the chapters that follow, the software also offers several access options: CRM data can be accessed from a Windows Internet Explorer web browser, from Microsoft Outlook by using the Microsoft Dynamics CRM for Outlook feature, or from a mobile device such as a cell phone. Most of the screen shots and examples in this book show the web browser option.

Just like some of the forms, fields, and data described in this book, the security roles referenced throughout this book also might have been modified in or even removed from your system. If you do not have the access needed to view or assign security roles, talk to your system administrator about setting up a few roles for testing. For the purposes of this book, we assume that the default roles included with Microsoft Dynamics CRM have not been modified.

Looking Forward

Microsoft Dynamics CRM is a fluid system that can adapt as your business grows and changes. By using the step-by-step processes laid out in these pages, you can explore whatever options you need to match the software with your requirements. We hope you find this book useful and informative as your organization moves into the future!

Features and Conventions
of This Book

This book has been designed to lead you step by step through all the tasks you are most likely to want to perform in Microsoft Dynamics CRM 2011. If you start at the beginning and work your way through all the exercises, you will gain enough proficiency to be able to create and work with all of the common views and functionality of Microsoft Dynamics CRM 2011. However, each topic is self contained. If you have worked with a previous version of Microsoft Dynamics CRM, or if you completed all the exercises and later need help remembering how to perform a procedure, the following features of this book will help you locate specific information:

- **Detailed table of contents** Search the listing of the topics and sidebars within each chapter.

- **Chapter thumb tabs** Easily locate the beginning of the chapter you want.

- **Topic-specific running heads** Within a chapter, quickly locate the topic you want by looking at the running head of odd-numbered pages.

- **Glossary** Look up the meaning of a word or definition of a concept.

- **Detailed index** Look up specific tasks and features and general concepts in the index, which has been carefully crafted with the reader in mind.

You can save time when you use this book by understanding how the *Step by Step* series shows special instructions, keys to press, buttons to click, and other information. These elements are shown in the following table.

Convention	Meaning
SET UP	This paragraph preceding a step-by-step exercise indicates the practice files that you will use when working through the exercise. It also indicates any requirements you should attend to or actions you should take before beginning.
CLEAN UP	This paragraph following a step-by-step exercise provides instructions for saving and closing open files or programs before moving on to another topic. It also suggests ways to reverse any changes you made to your computer while working through the exercise.
1 **2**	Numbered steps guide you through hands-on excercises in each topic.
See Also	These paragraphs direct you to more information about a topic in this book or elsewhere.
Troubleshooting	This paragraph explains how to fix a common problem that might prevent you from continuing with an exercise.
Tip	This paragraph provides a helpful hint or shortcut that makes working through a task easier, or information about other available options.
Important	This paragraph points out information that you need to know to complete a procedure.
	The first time you are told to click a button in an exercise, a picture of the button appears in the left margin.
Ctrl+Home	A plus sign (+) between two key names means that you must hold down the first key while you press the second key. For example, "press Ctrl+Home" means "hold down the Ctrl key while you press the Home key."
Program interface elements	In exercises, the names of program elements, such as buttons, commands, and dialog boxes, as well as files, folders, or text that you interact with in the steps, are shown in **bold** characters.
User input	In exercises, anything you are supposed to type appears in **bold italic** characters.

Using the Practice Files

Before you can complete the exercises in this book, you need to copy the book's practice files to your computer. These practice files, and other information, can be downloaded from the book's detail page, located at

http://oreilly.com/catalog/0790145307552/

> **Important** This website only includes practice files to help you learn Microsoft Dynamics CRM 2011; it does not include the Microsoft Dynamics CRM 2011 software. If you don't already have access to the software, you need to purchase it. Alternatively, you could also access a free 30-day trial of the software at http://crm.dynamics.com.

The following table lists the practice files for this book.

Chapter	File
Chapter 3: Working with Accounts and Contacts	Orders1.xlsx
Chapter 18: Bulk Data Importing	ContactImport1.csv

Your Companion eBook

The eBook edition of this book allows you to:

- Search the full text
- Print
- Copy and paste

To download your eBook, please see the instruction page at the back of this book.

Book Support

Errata

We've made every effort to ensure the accuracy of this book and its companion content. If you do find an error, please report it on our Microsoft Press site at Oreilly.com:

1. Go to *http://microsoftpress.oreilly.com*.
2. In the Search box, enter the book's ISBN or title.
3. Select your book from the search results.
4. On your book's catalog page, under the cover image, you'll see a list of links.
5. Click View/Submit Errata.

You'll find additional information and services for your book on its catalog page. If you need additional support, please send an email to Microsoft Press Book Support at *mspinput@microsoft.com*.

Please note that product support for Microsoft software is not offered through the addresses above.

We Want to Hear from You

At Microsoft Press, your satisfaction is our top priority, and your feedback our most valuable asset. Please tell us what you think of this book at:

http://www.microsoft.com/learning/booksurvey

The survey is short, and we read *every one* of your comments and ideas. Thanks in advance for your input!

Stay in Touch

Let's keep the conversation going! We're on Twitter: *http://twitter.com/MicrosoftPress*.

Getting Help with Microsoft Dynamics CRM 2011

If your question is about Microsoft Dynamics CRM, and not about the content of this Microsoft Press book, your first recourse is the Microsoft Dynamics CRM Help system. You can find general or specific Help information in a couple of ways:

- In the Microsoft Dynamics CRM window, you can click the Help button (labeled with a question mark) located in the upper-right corner of the web browser window to display the Microsoft Dynamics CRM Help window.

- On the ribbon, you can click the File tab to access the Help button.

Microsoft Dynamics CRM Help is context sensitive, so the software will automatically try to access the portion of the Help content that is most relevant to the page you're currently viewing. For example, if you're viewing a lead record and you click the Help button located in the upper-right corner of the window, Microsoft Dynamics CRM automatically directs you to the Help topic titled *Work With Leads*. If you want to access the full Help documentation, you can click the File tab on the ribbon to access the Help button on that screen. After you click the Help button, click Contents on the submenu that appears.

If you want to practice getting help, you can work through the following exercise, which demonstrates two ways of locating information.

 SET UP Use the Windows Internet Explorer web browser to navigate to your Microsoft Dynamics CRM website.

 1. In the upper-right corner of the Microsoft Dynamics CRM application, click the **Help** button.

The Microsoft Dynamics CRM Help menu opens. Microsoft Dynamics CRM Help displays a list of topics related to the page from which you started the Help process.

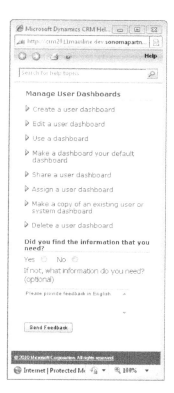

You can click any topic to display the corresponding information.

2. On the toolbar, click the **Show Contents** button. This button looks identical to the **Help** button.

The table of contents appears in the left pane, organized by category, like the table of contents in a book. Clicking any category (represented by a book icon) displays that category's help topics.

3. In the **Contents** pane, click a few categories and topics. Then click the **Back** and **Forward** buttons to move among the topics you have already viewed.

4. At the top of the **Microsoft Dynamics CRM Help** window, click the **Search for help topics** box, type *lead*, and then press the Enter key.

The Microsoft Dynamics CRM Help window displays topics related to the words you typed.

 CLEAN UP Close the Microsoft Dynamics CRM Help window.

More Information

If your question is about Microsoft Dynamics CRM or another Microsoft software product and you cannot find the answer in the product's Help system, please search the appropriate product solution center or the Microsoft Knowledge Base at:

http://support.microsoft.com

In the United States, Microsoft software product support issues not covered by the Microsoft Knowledge Base are addressed by Microsoft Product Support Services. Location-specific software support options are available from:

http://support.microsoft.com/gp/selfoverview/

You can also click the Resource Center link, typically found at the bottom left of the Microsoft Dynamics CRM application. Or you can access the same information via the Internet at:

https://rc.crm.dynamics.com/rc/2011/en-us/online/default.aspx

Part 1

Overview

1 Introduction to Microsoft Dynamics CRM. 3

2 Getting Around in Microsoft Dynamics CRM 19

3 Working with Accounts and Contacts 45

4 Working with Activities and Notes. 67

5 Using Microsoft Dynamics CRM for Outlook 95

Chapter at a Glance

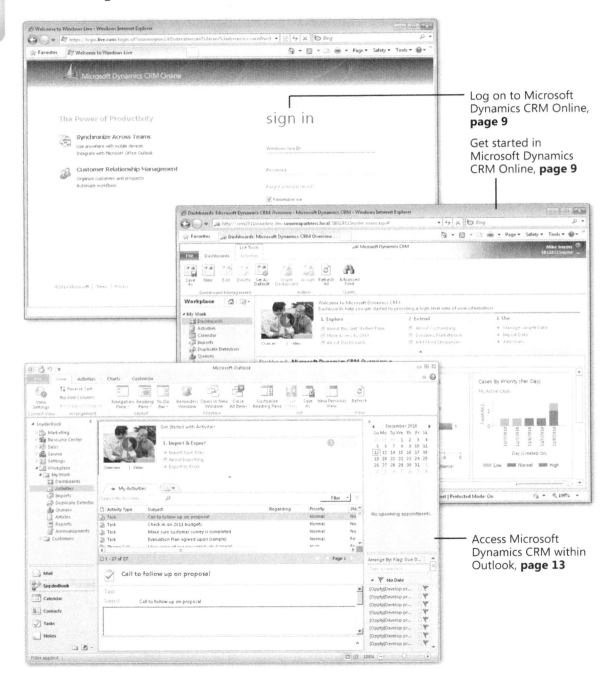

Log on to Microsoft Dynamics CRM Online, **page 9**

Get started in Microsoft Dynamics CRM Online, **page 9**

Access Microsoft Dynamics CRM within Outlook, **page 13**

1 Introduction to Microsoft Dynamics CRM

In this chapter, you will learn how to:

✔ Understand key concepts in Microsoft Dynamics CRM.

✔ Understand the three deployment models for Microsoft Dynamics CRM.

✔ Understand how other Microsoft software products integrate with Microsoft Dynamics CRM.

✔ Log on to Microsoft Dynamics CRM Online.

✔ Log on to Microsoft Dynamics CRM.

✔ Access Microsoft Dynamics CRM by using Microsoft Dynamics CRM for Outlook.

✔ Log on to Microsoft Dynamics CRM via Mobile Express.

Every successful organization relies on its customer base to sell products or services. Businesses that want to track and manage all of the various interactions with their customers frequently deploy a Customer Relationship Management (CRM) software system. With a CRM system, businesses can:

- Achieve a 360-degree view of the customer relationship.

- Automate common business processes to reduce manual tasks and common workflows.

- Deliver a more consistent customer experience by streamlining customer interactions.

- Enable executives to measure and report on key metrics related to their business so they can make better business and strategy decisions.

CRM software systems have been in existence for many years, but most of them earned a reputation for being difficult to use. Microsoft Dynamics CRM addresses the problems of previous CRM systems by providing an easy-to-use software application while still providing the flexibility and the technical platform that most businesses require. Microsoft Dynamics CRM works with most of the software products that businesses use today, such as Microsoft Outlook, Microsoft Word, and Microsoft Excel. Users do not need to learn a new software application to capture and work with Microsoft Dynamics CRM data; they can continue using the productivity tools they are comfortable using for other day-to-day business functions. The latest version of Microsoft Dynamics CRM includes new features such as visualizations and a revamped user interface designed to make the end-user experience as friendly as possible.

In this chapter, you will learn the core concepts of Microsoft Dynamics CRM. You'll also learn the different ways you can access Microsoft Dynamics CRM and other Microsoft products that integrate with Microsoft Dynamics CRM.

> **Tip** Many of the examples in this book use the sample data utility that Microsoft Dynamics CRM includes. You do not need to use this sample data, but you might find it useful for your training or testing purposes. Contact your system administrator to install the sample data.

> **Practice Files** There are no practice files for this chapter.

> **Troubleshooting** Graphics and operating system–related instructions in this book reflect the Windows 7 user interface. If your computer is running Windows XP and you experience trouble following the instructions as written, refer to the "Information for Readers Running Windows XP" section at the beginning of this book.

> **Important** The images used in this book reflect the default form and field names in Microsoft Dynamics CRM. Because the software offers extensive customization capabilities, it's possible that some of the record types or fields have been relabeled in your Microsoft Dynamics CRM environment. If you cannot find the forms or fields referred to in this book, contact your system administrator for assistance.

> **Important** You must know the location of your Microsoft Dynamics CRM website to work the exercises in this book. Check with your system administrator to verify the web address if you don't know it.

What Is Microsoft Dynamics CRM?

Microsoft Dynamics CRM is a business software application that allows companies of all sizes to track, manage, and report on customer interactions. Microsoft Dynamics CRM is part of the Microsoft Dynamics brand, which offers multiple software products to help businesses automate and streamline various operations, such as financial analysis, customer relationships, supply chain management, manufacturing, inventory, human resources, and so on.

Microsoft Dynamics CRM includes the following three main modules:

- Sales
- Marketing
- Service

Within each module, Microsoft Dynamics CRM lets you track various types of customer information, as outlined in the following table.

Sales	Marketing	Service
Accounts	Accounts	Accounts
Contacts	Contacts	Contacts
Leads	Leads	Service Calendar
Opportunities	Marketing Lists	Cases
Marketing Lists	Campaigns	Knowledge Base
Competitors	Products	Contracts
Products	Sales Literature	Products
Sales Literature	Quick Campaigns	Services
Quotes		Goals
Orders		Rollup Queries
Invoices		Goal Metrics
Quick Campaigns		
Goals		
Goal Metrics		
Rollup Queries		

Your company might want to track only some of this data about your customers, and some of these might not apply to your business. Even though Microsoft Dynamics CRM includes only these three modules, many companies extend the software to track other types of related data such as projects, status reports, events, facilities, and so on. The flexibility of the Microsoft Dynamics CRM platform allows businesses to capture almost any type of data related to their customers. In addition to managing customer data, you can use Microsoft Dynamics CRM to capture information about your prospects, partners, vendors, suppliers, and other related parties.

> **Tip** When businesses use Microsoft Dynamics CRM to track non-traditional sales, marketing, and service information, you might hear people refer to the term xRM. This term refers to using the flexible and extensible application framework of Microsoft Dynamics CRM to create line-of-business applications. xRM is not a separate product but rather a description of how businesses might use the Microsoft Dynamics CRM system to track non-traditional CRM data.

Microsoft Dynamics CRM is a web-based application that is built on the Microsoft .NET Framework technology platform. Because of its native web architecture, Microsoft Dynamics CRM can be accessed through the Windows Internet Explorer web browser. In addition to the web user experience (also known as the *web client*), another possible access point for Microsoft Dynamics CRM is through Outlook, if your administrator installed the Microsoft Dynamics CRM for Outlook software on your computer.

> **Troubleshooting** Because Microsoft Dynamics CRM for Outlook is optional software, you might not be able to access Microsoft Dynamics CRM through Outlook. If you are not able to use Microsoft Dynamics CRM for Outlook, contact your system administrator about getting it installed on your computer.

The Microsoft Dynamics CRM for Outlook software comes in two different versions:

- **Microsoft Dynamics CRM for Outlook** This version is designed for use with desktop or notebook computers that will remain connected to the Microsoft Dynamics CRM server at all times.

- **Microsoft Dynamics CRM for Outlook with Offline Access** This version is designed for users of laptop computers who must disconnect from the Microsoft Dynamics CRM server but who still need to work with Microsoft Dynamics CRM data when they are offline, just as they use Outlook for email management, contact management, tasks, and appointment management while working with no access to the Internet. The terms used by Microsoft Dynamics CRM to refer to the processes of connecting and disconnecting from the server are *going online* and *going offline*. The offline-enabled version of Microsoft Dynamics CRM for Outlook lets you work with Microsoft Dynamics CRM data offline; the software will synchronize your changes with the main database when you connect to the server again.

> **Tip** When we refer to Microsoft Dynamics CRM for Outlook in this book, we are referring to both the standard and offline versions. The two clients offer nearly identical functionality except that the version with offline access allows users to work while disconnected from the Microsoft Dynamics CRM server.

You can access almost all of the Microsoft Dynamics CRM system functionality from either the web client or from Microsoft Dynamics CRM for Outlook. Therefore, you can decide which user interface method you prefer to use to access Microsoft Dynamics CRM. Microsoft Dynamics CRM for Outlook also allows you to synchronize your email, tasks, contacts, and appointments from Outlook into your Microsoft Dynamics CRM system.

Beyond the computer, you can also access Microsoft Dynamics CRM from a web-enabled mobile device such as a cell phone, by using the Mobile Express module. Mobile Express allows you to access the same data that you can access from the web and Microsoft Dynamics CRM for Outlook clients, but Mobile Express delivers streamlined and simple web pages that are specially formatted for handheld devices. This mobile access to Microsoft Dynamics CRM can prove very handy if you need to perform common tasks such as looking up a phone number or street address of a contact while you are away from your computer.

> **Important** In order to access Microsoft Dynamics CRM via Mobile Express, your mobile device must have Internet access and Mobile Express must be enabled for your system.

Microsoft Dynamics CRM Deployment Options

Microsoft Dynamics CRM is unique in the world of customer relationship management because it is one of the only applications that offers businesses several choices for installing and deploying the software. The three deployment options for Microsoft Dynamics CRM are:

- **Microsoft Dynamics CRM Online** In this deployment, a business uses the Microsoft Dynamics CRM software over the Internet on servers hosted by Microsoft.

- **On-premise** With this option, a business purchases the Microsoft Dynamics CRM software and installs it on its local network. Depending on the configuration, employees might also be able to access the Microsoft Dynamics CRM system over the Internet.

- **Partner-hosted** For this option, a business deploys the software at a third-party hosting environment.

In early 2011, Microsoft released new versions of Microsoft Dynamics CRM across all three deployment models. This latest release is called Microsoft Dynamics CRM 2011 for on-premise and partner-hosted deployments, but it is simply named Microsoft Dynamics CRM Online for the Microsoft-hosted version. The system functionality across all three deployment options is nearly identical, but differences do exist. The examples in this book apply to all three deployment options. If necessary, we will highlight any areas of the software in which the book examples vary by deployment type.

Integrating with Other Microsoft Products

In addition to the integration with Microsoft Outlook discussed earlier in this chapter, Microsoft Dynamics CRM integrates with several other Microsoft software applications:

- **Excel** You can export your Microsoft Dynamics CRM data into Excel with the click of one button and create Excel files that dynamically update when data in the Microsoft Dynamics CRM system changes. After you export the data into Excel, you can also update the information within Excel and then re-import it back into Microsoft Dynamics CRM. Editing large data sets within Excel frequently provides a better user experience, because many users are very comfortable working with data in Excel.

- **Word** You can use Word to create mailings (such as letters and envelopes) to your customers by performing a mail merge in Microsoft Dynamics CRM. This integration also allows you to save copies of the mail merge documents.

- **Microsoft Lync (formerly known as Office Communications Server)** You can access features of Lync (such as instant messaging and presence information) directly within Microsoft Dynamics CRM to improve team collaboration.

- **Microsoft SharePoint Server** If your company uses SharePoint Server, you can connect it to Microsoft Dynamics CRM to take advantage of the document library functionality that SharePoint offers. This integration provides a streamlined user experience in which the user can perform common tasks such as checking documents in and out via the Microsoft Dynamics CRM interface (without needing to browse to a separate SharePoint website in a separate window).

Logging On to Microsoft Dynamics CRM Online

Before you can start using Microsoft Dynamics CRM, you will need to log on to the software. How you access Microsoft Dynamics CRM will depend on how your company chose to deploy the software. If you are unsure how to access your Microsoft Dynamics CRM system, contact your system administrator. In this exercise, you will practice logging on to Microsoft Dynamics CRM Online. In the next section, you will log on to the on-premise deployment of Microsoft Dynamics CRM through the web client. Select the exercise that matches your deployment model.

> **Tip** The steps for accessing the partner-hosted deployment model of Microsoft Dynamics CRM are similar to those for accessing an on-premise deployment. If your organization has deployed the partner-hosted model, follow the steps in the on-premise exercise to log on to Microsoft Dynamics CRM.

If your company uses the Microsoft-hosted version of the software through Microsoft Dynamics CRM Online, you will need to use your Windows Live ID to log on to the system. Many users find that Windows Live ID is a convenient authentication method, because they can use a single logon and password for a wide variety of websites on the Internet. In this exercise, you'll log on to Microsoft Dynamics CRM Online.

SET UP Open the Internet Explorer web browser.

1. In the Address bar, type the following web address (also known as the URL): ***http://crm.dynamics.com***.

2. Click the red **CRM Online Login** button.

3. Enter the email address and password of your Windows Live ID.

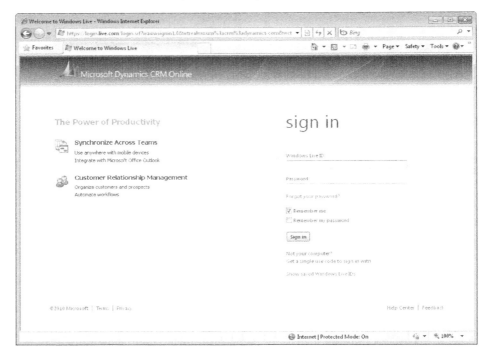

4. Click **Sign in**.

   The Dashboards page of Microsoft Dynamics CRM Online appears.

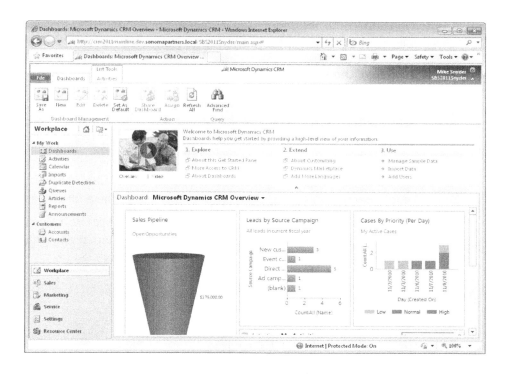

Logging On to Microsoft Dynamics CRM

If your company is not using Microsoft Dynamics CRM Online, you will use different steps to log on to Microsoft Dynamics CRM. The exact steps you follow will depend on how your system administrator set up the configuration, but the two most common logon methods are:

- Logging on from your corporate network
- Logging on at an external Internet-facing address (such as a .com or .net website address)

After you have contacted your system administrator and retrieved the website address of your Microsoft Dynamics CRM system, you can log on by following the steps in this exercise.

 SET UP Open the Internet Explorer web browser.

1. In the Internet Explorer Address bar, type the web address (also known as the URL) of your Microsoft Dynamics CRM site: ***http://<yourcrmserver/organization>***.

   The *<yourcrmserver/organization>* portion of the URL is the name and organization name of the Microsoft Dynamics CRM site you will be using for the exercises in this book. Depending on how your Microsoft Dynamics CRM server is configured, you might need to include the organization portion in the address bar.

2. If you are logging on from your corporate network, Microsoft Dynamics CRM should automatically log you on. However if you are prompted, simply enter your user name and password.

3. If you are logging on from an external Internet-facing address, enter your user name and password on this screen.

   It is possible that your login screen appears different than the following graphic, depending on your system configuration. If so, please contact your system administrator for login instructions specific to your organization.

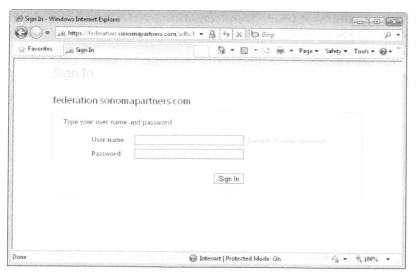

4. Click **OK**.

The start page of your Microsoft Dynamics CRM system appears. By default, the Dashboards page is the start page.

Accessing Microsoft Dynamics CRM by Using Microsoft Dynamics CRM for Outlook

In addition to the web client, Outlook can be used to access Microsoft Dynamics CRM. Many users find accessing Microsoft Dynamics CRM within Outlook particularly convenient because they already spend a lot of time working within Outlook. The Microsoft Dynamics CRM integration with Outlook provides a single application to manage all of your customer sales, marketing, and service information. Many competing CRM software applications require users to open a second application to access their customer data. The Outlook integration of Microsoft Dynamics CRM is a unique benefit of the software that enables users to work more efficiently in a familiar software application.

In this exercise, you will access Microsoft Dynamics CRM within Outlook.

> **See Also** For more information on the integration between Microsoft Dynamics CRM and Outlook, see Chapter 5, "Using Microsoft Dynamics CRM for Outlook."

SET UP Confirm that your system administrator has installed the Microsoft Dynamics CRM for Outlook software on your computer before beginning this exercise.

1. Launch Outlook. You will see that Microsoft Dynamics CRM added a **CRM** tab to the ribbon. In addition, you will see a **CRM** group with buttons such as **Track** and **Set Regarding** on the **Home** tab of the ribbon for the **Mail**, **Contacts**, **Calendar**, and **Tasks** modules.

2. In the Outlook navigation pane, you will see a button with the name of your Microsoft Dynamics CRM organization listed next to the **Mail**, **Calendar**, and **Contacts** buttons. Click the button with your organization's name on it.

3. In the folder list, expand the **Workplace** folder.

4. Expand the **My Work** folder, and then click the **Activities** folder. You will see a list of the Microsoft Dynamics CRM activities. These are the same activities that you see when you log on to Microsoft Dynamics CRM through the web client.

Logging On to Microsoft Dynamics CRM via Mobile Express

If you need to access your Microsoft Dynamics CRM system while you are out of the office and away from a computer, you can use the Mobile Express module to access the system with an Internet-enabled device such as a cell phone. Mobile Express displays webpages in a streamlined format specifically designed to work on small screens and with a wide variety of mobile web browsers so that you can access the system from most Internet-enabled cell phones (even devices that do not use Microsoft software).

 SET UP Confirm that your system administrator has enabled Mobile Express for your Microsoft Dynamics CRM system before beginning this exercise.

1. On your mobile device, open the web browser.

2. In your mobile web browser, type the web address of your Microsoft Dynamics CRM site and add an **/m** after the address. For example, if your Microsoft Dynamics CRM URL address is *http://sonoma3.crm.dynamics.com*, then you should type **http://sonoma3.crm.dynamics.com/m** in the address bar.

3. If you are using Microsoft Dynamics CRM Online, you will need to enter your Windows Live ID user name and password. Then click **Sign In**.

4. In an on-premise or partner-hosted deployment of Microsoft Dynamics CRM, you will see a logon screen on which you must enter your user name and password. Then click **Sign In**.

It is possible that your login screen appears different than the following graphic, depending on your system configuration. If so, please contact your system administrator for login instructions specific to your organization.

After you log on, you will see the Mobile Express interface of Microsoft Dynamics CRM.

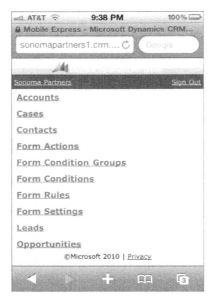

> **Tip** The list of records you see in Mobile Express will vary depending on how your system administrator configured your system; therefore, what you see will differ from what is shown in these images.

Key Points

- Microsoft Dynamics CRM is a web-based application that lets businesses easily track and manage their customer data.
- The three modules of Microsoft Dynamics CRM are Sales, Marketing, and Service.
- You can access Microsoft Dynamics CRM data through Internet Explorer, Microsoft Dynamics CRM for Outlook, or Mobile Express on a handheld device such as a cell phone.
- Microsoft Dynamics CRM integrates with other Microsoft products such as Word, Excel, Microsoft Lync, and SharePoint Server.

Chapter at a Glance

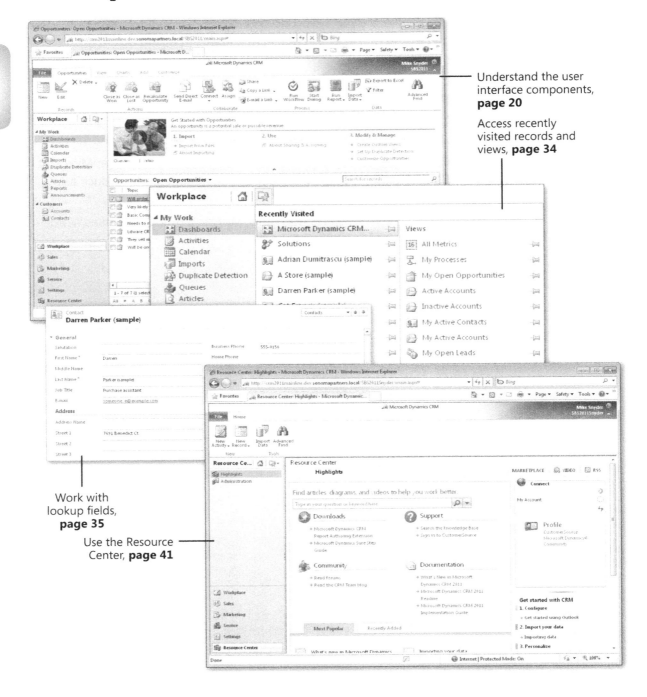

Understand the user interface components, **page 20**

Access recently visited records and views, **page 34**

Work with lookup fields, **page 35**

Use the Resource Center, **page 41**

2 Getting Around in Microsoft Dynamics CRM

In this chapter, you will learn how to

✔ Understand and work with the components of the user interface.

✔ Use Microsoft Dynamics CRM views to work with records.

✔ Use Quick Find to search for records in a view.

✔ Work with lookup fields and use the automatic resolution feature.

✔ Modify your personal options to suit your preferences.

✔ Use the Resource Center to learn more about Microsoft Dynamics CRM.

✔ Access software help within the system.

Before showing you how to track and manage customer data in Microsoft Dynamics CRM, we want to explain where to find the areas referenced in this book and show you how to navigate through the software. You'll also learn about the resources available for more information on how to work with the software.

> **Practice Files** There are no practice files for this chapter.

> **Important** The images used in this book reflect the default form and field names in Microsoft Dynamics CRM. Because the software offers extensive customization capabilities, it's possible that some of the record types or fields have been relabeled in your Microsoft Dynamics CRM environment. If you cannot find the forms or fields referred to in this book, contact your system administrator for assistance.

> **Important** You must know the location of your Microsoft Dynamics CRM website to work the exercises in this book. Check with your system administrator to verify the web address if you don't know it.

Understanding the Microsoft Dynamics CRM User Interface

Most of the time, you will access Microsoft Dynamics CRM through one of its two primary user interfaces: the web client or Microsoft Dynamics CRM for Outlook. The exercises and examples in this chapter use the web client, unless otherwise specified. Chapter 5, "Using Microsoft Dynamics CRM for Outlook," explains the system navigation specific to the Microsoft Outlook interface. To help you better understand how to navigate the software, the various components of the web interface are described here.

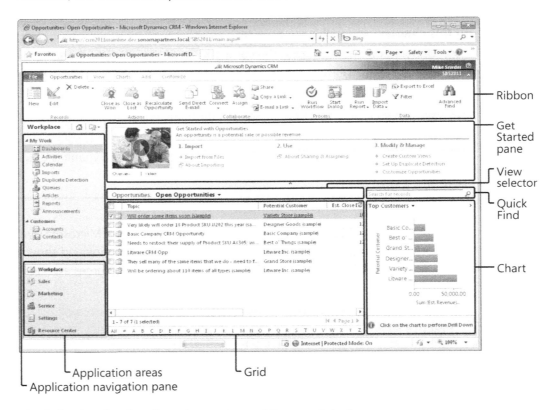

The following list describes the sections of the user interface:

- **Ribbon** The ribbon includes buttons and tabs that let you quickly access system actions. If you have used the 2007 Microsoft Office system or Office 2010, you will recognize the ribbon because it appears in most of the Office applications as well. The ribbon is unique because the buttons and tabs dynamically update based on what the user is doing within the system. For example, navigating to Contacts will display different ribbon buttons and tabs than when you navigate to Opportunities. The idea behind the ribbon is to display the most common activities to a user relative to where he or she is in the system, which will save clicks.

- **Grid** The grid displays a list of records. Each record set is known as a data view in Microsoft Dynamics CRM. The grid consists of rows and columns of data. At the bottom of the grid, you can find information about the number of records in the view. The grid also includes an index bar that allows you to quickly filter records in the grid based on the starting letter. Microsoft Dynamics CRM applies the ribbon actions against the records selected in the grid. For example, if you select three records in a grid and click a button on the ribbon, Microsoft Dynamics CRM will apply that button's action to the three records you selected.

- **Application navigation pane** This portion of the user interface provides access to the various types of Microsoft Dynamics CRM data. Simply click a hyperlink in the application navigation pane to view that set of records.

- **Application areas** Each application area provides a logical grouping of Microsoft Dynamics CRM records. The default application areas are Workplace, Sales, Marketing, Service, Settings, and Resource Center. If you click one of these buttons, Microsoft Dynamics CRM will update the application navigation pane to display the records grouped within that section.

- **Get Started pane** The Get Started pane displays help information about how to work with Microsoft Dynamics CRM. The help information consists of different types of content such as videos, hyperlinks to help pages, or links that launch system actions. The Get Started pane content dynamically updates with different help information depending on the type of records you are viewing.

> **Tip** You can collapse and expand the Get Started pane by clicking the arrow located directly beneath the pane. You can also turn off the Get Started pane for all records by updating your personal options. For more information, see "Setting Personal Options" later in this chapter.

- **View selector** The view selector allows you to select different views of data.

- **Quick Find** The Quick Find functionality allows you to enter text to quickly search for specific records.

- **Chart** This area of the user interface displays charts and graphs. The data that appears in the chart is specific to the currently selected view. For example, viewing a top-customers chart with the Open Opportunities view selected will show the chart with all of the open opportunities. Viewing a top-customers chart with the My Open Opportunities view selected will show the chart only with the opportunities that you own. The actual appearance of the chart might vary, depending on your data.

> **Tip** As with the Get Started pane, the chart can be collapsed and expanded by click-ing the arrow located in the upper-right corner of the Chart area.

When you open a record in Microsoft Dynamics CRM, you'll see additional parts of the user interface.

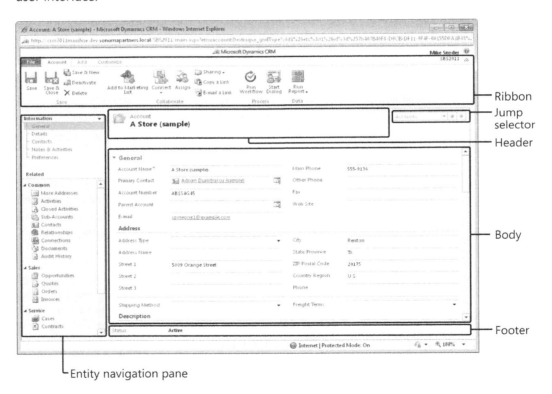

- **Ribbon** Just like the ribbon in the main user interface, the ribbon on each individual record includes buttons and tabs related to that record type.

- **Entity navigation pane** Similar to the application navigation pane, the entity navigation pane displays different types of Microsoft Dynamics CRM records. However, the entity navigation pane displays only those records that are linked to the open record. For example, clicking the Contacts link in the entity navigation pane of an account record will display only those contacts that have the open account record listed as their parent customer. In addition to showing related records, you can click the text links located under Information in the navigation pane to jump to specific sections of the form.

- **Body** The body displays the data related to the open record. The fields on the entity form are sometimes referred to as attributes.

- **Header** The record header includes data about the record, and it always remains visible when the record is open even if you click one of the related entities in the navigation pane.

- **Footer** Just like the header, the footer remains visible at all times when you have the record open. You might want to include certain data fields in the footer so that you can view them at any time when working with a record.

- **Jump selector** If you open a record from a view of data, the jump selector allows you to quickly jump to other records in the view. By clicking the picklist, you can see a list of contacts from the originating view and select one. In addition, you can click the Up or Down arrow to open the previous or next record from the view.

> **Tip** You can use the Ctrl+> (right angle bracket) keyboard shortcut to advance to the next record or Ctrl+< (left angle bracket) to move back to the previous record.

Using Views to Work with Data Records

Now that you understand the main components of the Microsoft Dynamics CRM user interface, you're ready to start working with data records. Microsoft Dynamics CRM uses a view to display a list of data records in a grid. You will spend a lot of time working with views, so it's important to understand the utilities that Microsoft Dynamics CRM offers to work with views of data.

Each view can contain an unlimited number of data records. Microsoft Dynamics CRM splits the view data into multiple pages of records, so you might need to click the page arrows located in the lower-right corner of the grid to access the additional records contained in your view. If the page arrows are disabled, your view does not contain multiple pages of records.

> **Tip** Even though Microsoft Dynamics CRM splits the view into multiple pages, you can view the total count of records in the view by looking in the lower-left corner of the grid. If your view contains more than 5,000 records, Microsoft Dynamics CRM will simply state that the record count is 5000+.

In this exercise, you will change the data records that appear in the grid by selecting a different view of the data. You might want to change views for various purposes, such as exporting the records from the view into Microsoft Excel for a report or editing multiple records at one time.

> **Tip** You can change the width of a view column by clicking the column divider and dragging it to the left or right. Resizing the column allows you to see more or less of the record's data.

 SET UP Use the Windows Internet Explorer web browser to navigate to your Microsoft Dynamics CRM website before beginning this exercise.

1. In the application areas, click the **Sales** button.

2. In the application navigation pane, click the **Accounts** link.

   By default, you will see a view of all of the active account records that you own in your system.

3. Click the arrow in the view selector.

   Microsoft Dynamics CRM displays a list of the views available for the account entity.

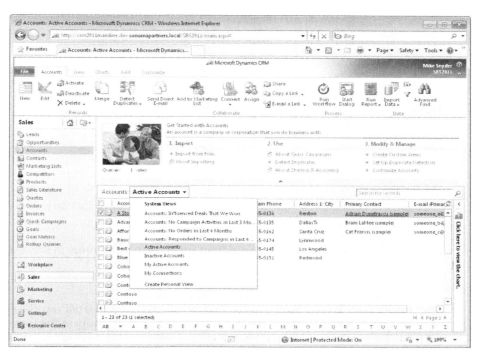

4. Select **Active Accounts**.

Microsoft Dynamics CRM changes the records displayed in the grid to show all of the active accounts in the database.

Sorting Records in a View

Within each view, you can sort the records to see them in a particular order. Each view contains a default sort order, but you can change the record order in any grid. When you're looking at a view, Microsoft Dynamics CRM includes visual indicators to show how it has sorted the records. In the column header, next to one of the column names, you will see a small triangle pointing up or down. This triangle indicates that this column's data is used to sort the view records. An upward-pointing triangle means that the records are displayed in ascending order (low to high or A to Z); a downward-pointing triangle means that the records are displayed in descending order (high to low or Z to A). In addition to the triangle in the column heading, Microsoft Dynamics CRM shades the column a light blue color in the background to visually indicate that the view is sorting on this column.

Changing the sort order of a column is very straightforward; all you need to do is click the column heading. Clicking the column heading toggles the sort order between ascending and descending.

You can also sort records by more than one column at a time. In this exercise, you will sort a view by using multiple columns.

> **Important** Even though you can display columns from related records in a view, you can sort only on columns that are attributes of the primary entity in the view. For example, if you have a contact view that contains columns from the related account records, you can sort the contact view only by clicking the columns that contain contact data; clicking the related account columns will not sort the records. You will not receive an error message when you click the related columns; instead, Microsoft Dynamics CRM will not react at all.

SET UP Use the Internet Explorer web browser to navigate to your Microsoft Dynamics CRM website, if necessary, before beginning this exercise. Open a webpage that contains multiple records in a view.

1. Click the heading of the column by which you want to sort the records.

   Microsoft Dynamics CRM adds the upward-pointing sort arrow and sorts the records in the view in ascending order.

2. Hold down the Shift key and click the second column heading by which you want to sort the records.

   Microsoft Dynamics CRM adds another upward-pointing sort arrow to this column and sorts in ascending sort order, while preserving the first sort column.

3. While keeping the Shift key down, click the second column heading again.

Microsoft Dynamics CRM toggles the sort order to display the records in descending order.

Selecting and Refreshing Records in a View

As you learned earlier in this chapter, you can use the buttons on the ribbon to perform actions on selected records in a view. Microsoft Dynamics CRM offers a few different ways to select records within a view. If you want to select one record, simply click the record row. Alternatively, you can also point to the row you want to select and then select the check box that appears on the far left. Taking either of these actions will cause Microsoft Dynamics CRM to highlight the record with a blue background to indicate which record you selected. If you want to select all of the records, select the check box that appears in the upper-left corner of the view. Microsoft Dynamics CRM will highlight all of the records that appear on the page. Deselecting the check box will deselect all of the records.

> **Important** When you select the check box to select all of the records, you are only selecting all of the records on the page. You are not selecting all of the records in the view. For example, if your view contains 500 records and your page contains 25 records, selecting the check box will select only the 25 records displayed on the page. Some of the features in the ribbon, such as Export To Excel and Send Direct E-Mail, allow you to select all of the records from the view, but many of the features in the ribbon (such as assigning records and editing records in bulk) apply only to a single page of records. Unfortunately, in these scenarios, you will need to repeat the action on each page of records if your view contains multiple pages of records. Later in this chapter, we will explain how to display up to 250 records per page in a view (instead of the default of 25 records per page). Displaying more records per page decreases the number of times you need to repeat an action on a set of records.

If you want to select more than one record in a view (but not all of them), you can do so by pressing the Ctrl and Shift keys. This technique should be familiar to users of Office, because other applications such as Excel and Outlook also allow users to select multiple items by holding down the Ctrl or Shift key while clicking the desired records.

As you work with the records in a view, you might find that the view does not refresh the data set as you expect. This might happen when you're working with different sets of records in multiple Internet Explorer windows or if a different user is editing the records in your view.

> **Tip** As a best practice, refresh the data in a view before performing any actions on the data set.

In this exercise, you will manually refresh the data that appears in a view, and then select multiple records in the view.

SET UP Use the Internet Explorer web browser to navigate to your Microsoft Dynamics CRM website, if necessary, before beginning this exercise. Open a webpage that contains multiple records in a view.

1. In the upper-right corner of the view, click the **Refresh** button. Microsoft Dynamics CRM refreshes the data in the view.

2. Click a record in the view. Microsoft Dynamics CRM highlights the row, indicating that the record is selected.

3. To add one record to your selection, hold down the Ctrl key and select another record.

   Microsoft Dynamics CRM highlights this new record as well, indicating that you've selected it.

4. To include multiple records in a selection, click one record, and then hold down the Shift key and select another record.

   Microsoft Dynamics CRM selects and highlights the two records you clicked and all of the records in between.

   With the appropriate records selected, you can apply the desired action to the records.

Editing Multiple Records in a View

As you work with various records in a view, you might want to update the data in multiple records at one time. Microsoft Dynamics CRM allows you to select multiple records in a view and edit them with one form so that you don't have to modify each record individually. This feature can provide a significant time savings if you need to modify a large number of records. Although the edit multiple records feature is very convenient, it does contain a few notable restrictions:

- If a particular field contains programming script behind the scenes (as configured by your system administrator), you cannot edit the data in that field while editing multiple records.

- You cannot use the edit multiple records feature to remove values from a field. You can only modify or add data to a field.

- You cannot use the edit multiple records feature to edit certain fields in Microsoft Dynamics CRM, such as the Parent Account field of the account record or the Parent Customer field of a contact record.

- The edit multiple records feature updates only the selected records on the page; you cannot use it to update all of the records in the view if the records span multiple pages.

- If a data field is read-only on the form, you cannot edit it with the multiple record edit tool.

> **Tip** Even though you cannot edit the owner of a record by using the edit multiple records feature, you can easily change the owner of multiple records at one time by using the Assign feature located on the ribbon.

In this exercise, you will update the State/Province field for multiple contacts.

 SET UP Use the Internet Explorer web browser to navigate to your Microsoft Dynamics CRM website, if necessary, before beginning this exercise. Open a view of Contacts that contains more than one record.

1. While holding down the Ctrl key, click two or more of the contact records.

   Microsoft Dynamics CRM highlights the records you click to indicate that they are selected.

2. On the ribbon, click **Edit**.

Edit

The Edit Multiple Records dialog box appears. This dialog box is very similar to the contact form, with the same layout and fields.

3. Locate the **State/Province** field, and type *Illinois* in the field.

4. Click the **Save** button.

Microsoft Dynamics CRM updates the State/Province field of the selected records and closes the Edit Multiple Records dialog box.

Using Quick Find to Search for Records in a View

Even with the sorting features in views, sometimes it can be time consuming to manually look for a particular record, especially if the view contains a large number of records. To help address this concern, Microsoft Dynamics CRM includes a Quick Find feature that allows you to search for records by using keywords or wildcard characters. You can find the Quick Find search box above the grid and to the right of the view selector. To use it, enter a search phrase and press Enter on the keyboard or click the button with the magnifying glass to start the search. Even though Quick Find is simple to use, there are a few tips and tricks that will help you find records more efficiently.

- Your system administrator can configure Microsoft Dynamics CRM to search for matching records across multiple columns. For example, you could search for particular contacts by name, phone number, or email address. You can even include custom data fields as part of the search criteria.

- When you enter search text, Microsoft Dynamics CRM will search for the value as it is entered. By default, it will not search for partial records. For example, if you search for a phone number by entering 555-1212 and the contact's phone number is (312) 555-1212, Microsoft Dynamics CRM will not consider that a match. It will return only those records that have 555-1212 as the start of their phone number.

- Of course, there will be times when you don't know the exact value you're searching for. In these cases, you can enter an asterisk (*) as a wildcard character in your Quick Find search. In the previous example, if you did not know the exact phone number, you could search for *555-1212 and Microsoft Dynamics CRM would find the (312) 555-1212 matching record, plus any other records that ended with 555-1212.

> **Tip** You can enter the wildcard character anywhere in your search criteria: at the beginning, in the middle, or at the end. If you can't find the record you're looking for, be sure to try different combinations with the asterisk wildcard. Note that the Quick Find feature is not case sensitive in its searches.

- If you start a Quick Find search when you're working with a specific view, such as My Active Contacts, you might expect that Microsoft Dynamics CRM would search for matching records only within the My Active Contacts view. However, Quick Find always searches for matching records across all active records for that entity. Quick Find ignores inactive records.

> **Tip** To filter records within a specific view, you can click the letters that appear at the bottom of the view (also referred to as the index bar). Clicking a letter will update the view to show only those records whose entry in the current sort column starts with the selected letter. For example, if you're looking at the My Active Contacts view with the records sorted by City and you click B in the index bar, Microsoft Dynamics CRM will show you only those records in which the city starts with the letter *B*. If you then click the Full Name column to sort by that field and click the letter *C* in the index bar, Microsoft Dynamics CRM will update the My Active Contacts view to show only those records in which the Full Name entry starts with the letter *C*.

In this exercise, you will use the Quick Find feature to search for records in Microsoft Dynamics CRM.

SET UP Use the Internet Explorer web browser to navigate to your Microsoft Dynamics CRM website, if necessary, before beginning this exercise. Open a view of Contacts that contains more than one record.

1. In the **Quick Find** box, type *ca** and press Enter.

Microsoft Dynamics CRM will search for and return all active contacts with matching records.

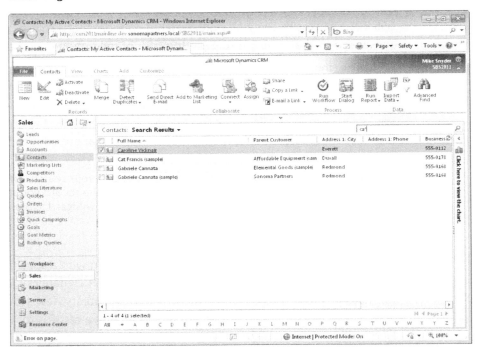

2. To cancel the search, click the X button to the right of the **Quick Find** box, or simply select a new view in the view selector.

Setting a Default Personal View

For each type of record, your system administrator can specify the default view that you see when you navigate to a list of those records. However, Microsoft Dynamics CRM also allows each user to specify his or her own personal default view independent of the system administrator's settings. You might find that using this feature saves you dozens of mouse clicks per day.

> **Important** The default view loads first for each web browsing session; however, Microsoft Dynamics CRM also keeps track of your most recently visited view within a web session and displays that first for convenience.

In this exercise, you will set a new default personal view.

 SET UP Use the Internet Explorer web browser to navigate to your Microsoft Dynamics CRM website, if necessary, before beginning this exercise.

1. Navigate to the **Accounts** view. The default view for **Accounts** is **My Active Accounts**, so you will see that first. Let's assume that you want to change the default view (just for you) to **Active Accounts**.

2. Click the view selector and select **Active Accounts**.

3. On the ribbon, click the **View** tab.

 4. Click the **Set as Default View** button.

   You have now set this view as your personal default for Accounts. The next time you log on to Microsoft Dynamics CRM and navigate to Accounts, you will see the Active Accounts first.

5. Let's see how the default view works within a single web browsing session. Click the view selector and select **Inactive Accounts**.

6. In the application navigation pane, click **Contacts**. Now let's navigate back to **Accounts** to see which view appears first.

7. In the application navigation pane, click **Accounts**.

   You will see the Inactive Accounts view first, even though the Active Accounts view is your personal default. This is because Microsoft Dynamics CRM displays the last view you accessed within the web browsing session by default.

8. Now close the Internet Explorer window, open a new window, and access Microsoft Dynamics CRM again.

9. Navigate to the **Accounts** views, and you will see the **Active Accounts** view first (your default personal view).

Accessing Recently Visited Records and Views

As you spend the day working in Microsoft Dynamics CRM, you will probably find that you frequently use the same records or views again and again. Fortunately, Microsoft Dynamics CRM includes a recently visited feature that allows you to quickly access records and views. This will save you time and clicks.

As you would expect, the recently visited section keeps track of the various records and views you have worked with recently. In addition, as with the other Office applications that include this type of recently used functionality, you can pin specific views or records so that they always remain in your recently visited list.

In this exercise, you will access the recently visited list and pin a view for future quick access.

 SET UP Use the Internet Explorer web browser to navigate to your Microsoft Dynamics CRM website, if necessary, before beginning this exercise.

 1. Click the recently visited button, which always appears in the upper-left corner of the application window, directly under the ribbon.

A new menu appears, and you will see two lists of records and views. The left column lists your recently visited records, and the right column lists your recently visited views. Both columns also include an icon of the record or view type so that you can visually determine which type of entity the record or view corresponds to.

2. Click one of the gray pin icons to permanently pin that record or view. After you click the pin, the pin icon will update by turning green and changing to look like it is standing upright. That pinned record or view will always remain in your recently visited list.

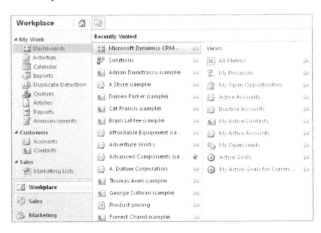

3. To load the record or view from the recently visited list, simply click its name. To unpin a record or view, follow the same steps and click the green pin icon to unpin the record or view from your recently visited list.

> **Tip** You can click the Home button located to the left of the recently visited button at any time to return to your default home page.

Using Lookups and Automatic Resolution

One of the main benefits of any customer relationship management system is that the software allows you to create relationships between records in your database. These relationships allow you to understand the different types of data about your customers, vendors, and partners, and how they interact with one another. The Microsoft Dynamics CRM user interface displays the link between two records by using a lookup. The default contact form includes two lookups: one for the Parent Customer and one for the default currency.

You can visually determine that a field is a lookup because:

- The text in the field is hyperlinked (blue and underlined).
- There is an icon to the left of the text that indicates the entity of the linked record.

- The field includes an icon with a window and a magnifying glass.

Clicking the hyperlinked text in the field will launch a new window displaying the linked record. Unlike the other fields on the form, in which you simply enter data into the field, lookup fields require you to select a record to link to. You can link records in the lookup field by using one of three techniques:

- **Use the Look Up Records dialog box** To use this technique, click the lookup icon. Microsoft Dynamics CRM will then launch the Look Up Records dialog box, which you can use to search for and select a specific record.

- **Use automatic resolution** To use this technique, simply start typing the name of the linked record in the lookup field. After you enter all (or a portion) of the linked record's name, click a different form field or press the Tab key. Microsoft Dynamics CRM will then try to automatically resolve your entry to an existing record.

- **Select recently used** As you start typing in a lookup field, you might notice that a list of records automatically appears under the lookup field. This list of records is known as the most recently used list. To choose one of these records, simply click the one you want.

> **Tip** The automatic resolution feature in lookups can provide a significant time savings when you work with many different records.

Microsoft Dynamics CRM will try to match records in the lookup by using the find fields of the entity. The record name is typically included as a find field, but your administrator might configure additional find fields that you can use with automatic resolution. If Microsoft Dynamics CRM finds just one matching record during the automatic resolution, it will populate the lookup field with a link to that record. If more than one match is found, the lookup field will display a yellow match icon and color the text you entered as red. Click the yellow match icon to view the potential matches, and then select the record you want. Microsoft Dynamics CRM will then use that value for the lookup field.

If Microsoft Dynamics CRM does not find any potential matches, it will color the text red and display a red circle with a white X.

If you want to remove a value from a lookup field, you can select the white portion of the field (without clicking the hyperlinked text) and then press the Backspace key or Delete key.

In this exercise, you will use the most recently used list to populate a lookup value.

SET UP Log on to the Microsoft Dynamics CRM website through the web client before beginning this exercise. Make sure that you have the Microsoft Dynamics CRM sample data loaded.

1. Navigate to a contact view and open any contact record.

2. In the **Parent Customer** field, click the white space and start typing an account name. For this exercise, type *good* and press the Tab key. You will see that Microsoft Dynamics CRM did not find any matching records, and therefore it displays the red circle with the white X.

3. In the same **Parent Customer** field, click the white space and type *good*. This time you added the asterisk wildcard in front of your entry. As you learned in the Quick Find section earlier in this chapter, the asterisk wildcard expands the search to include anything that has the text *good* in it. In our first example (without the wildcard), Microsoft Dynamics CRM only searches for matching records that *begin* with the text *good,* and it didn't find any matches.

4. With the wildcard included in the search, Microsoft Dynamics CRM will display the yellow match icon. Click this icon to see the list of records that matched your ***good** entry. You will see that four possible matches are listed: two accounts and two contacts. Even though the contact records don't appear to have the text *good* in their name, they appear as a possible match because these contacts are linked to the accounts that do have the text **good* in their name.

5. Select **Elemental Goods (sample)**. When you do so, Microsoft Dynamics CRM automatically adds this record to your most recently used list. Now you will access that list from a lookup field, but first you will need to clear out the existing value.

6. In the **Parent Customer** field, click the white space and press the Delete key. This will blank out the **Parent Customer** field.

7. Now click in the **Parent Customer** field and type *e*. Microsoft Dynamics CRM will display the most recently used list directly beneath the lookup field.

8. To select a record from this list, click it with your mouse. Alternatively, you can use the down arrow on your keyboard to select the record you want and then press Tab.

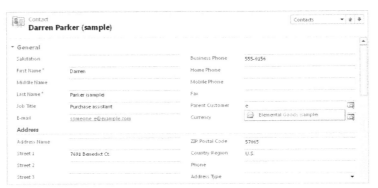

> **Tip** If you want to manually remove a record from the most recently used list, point to it with your mouse and click the Delete button.

Setting Personal Options

Microsoft Dynamics CRM allows you to set personal options to modify the user interface. You can access your personal options by clicking the File tab in the ribbon and then clicking Options to open the Set Personal Options dialog box. Although we won't review all of the personal options available, we do want to review a few common configuration options.

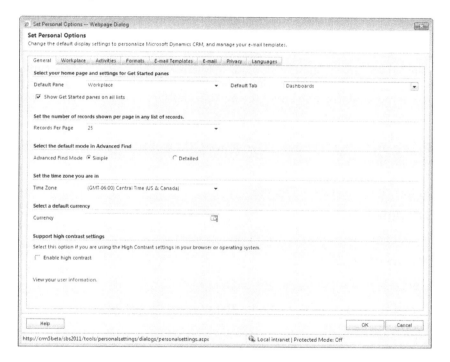

On the General tab, you can specify the following:

- **Default home page** By changing this selection, you can determine which page Microsoft Dynamics CRM will start on after you log on with the web client. Select the pane and tab you use most frequently.

- **Show Get Started panes on all lists** If you want to turn off the Get Started panes throughout the entire system, deselect this check box.

- **Records per page** As we mentioned earlier, you might want to change the number of records that appear on a page. By displaying more records on a page, you can apply actions to a larger data set. However, you should be aware that users with a large number of records per page might experience slower performance as the page loads, so use caution with this setting.

- **Time zone** Be sure to select the correct time zone to match the time zone of your computer. If this time zone setting does not match the time zone on your computer, you might find that appointments synchronized to Outlook are shifted by a few hours.

On the Workplace tab, you can select which application areas to display in the navigation pane. This setting will appear only to you as an individual user; it will not apply to all users in the system. Therefore, feel free to set up the Workplace area in whatever manner is most comfortable for you. In this exercise, you will modify your Workplace pane to include new areas of the user interface.

> **Tip** The Set Personal Options dialog box in Microsoft Dynamics CRM for Outlook provides additional configuration options when compared with the dialog box in the web client. For more information about the personal options in Outlook, see Chapter 5.

 SET UP Log on to the Microsoft Dynamics CRM website through the web client before beginning this exercise.

1. On the ribbon, click the **File** tab.

2. Click **Options**.

   The Set Personal Options dialog box appears.

3. Click the **Workplace** tab.

4. Select the check box to the left of **Sales**.

   Microsoft Dynamics CRM updates the preview on the left side of the dialog box to include the Sales area.

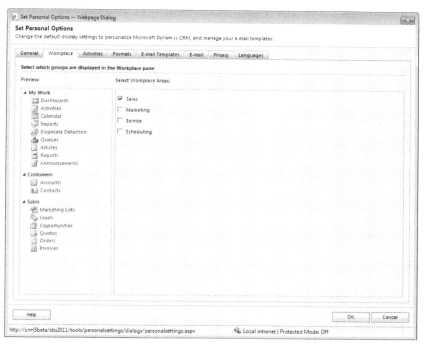

5. Click **OK**.

6. Click **Workplace** in the application areas.

   Microsoft Dynamics CRM now includes the Sales area that you just added in the application navigation pane.

Using the Resource Center

Microsoft Dynamics CRM includes a Resource Center that provides additional information about the software. To access the Resource Center, simply click Resource Center in the application navigation pane. The Resource Center contains dynamic content hosted on the Microsoft servers, and Microsoft provides continual updates to this content. You will need an Internet connection to access content from the Resource Center.

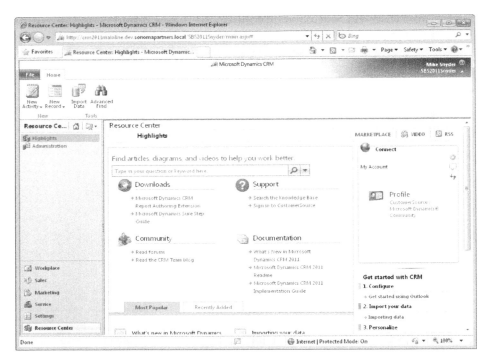

In addition to articles about using the software, the Resource Center contains links to other Microsoft Dynamics CRM resources such as downloads, support information, online communities, and documentation.

Accessing Help in Microsoft Dynamics CRM

Even though most users indicate that Microsoft Dynamics CRM is intuitive and easy to learn, you might have questions about the software. Fortunately, Microsoft Dynamics CRM includes help guides for end users as well as for administrators. To access help, you can click the Help button that is always located in the upper-right corner of the screen.

Alternatively, you can access the help information by clicking the File tab on the ribbon and then clicking Help on the submenu.

Microsoft Dynamics CRM Help is context sensitive, so the software can show you the portion of the help content most relevant to the page you're currently viewing. For example, if you're viewing a lead record and you click the Help On This Page option, Microsoft Dynamics CRM will automatically direct you to the Help topic titled "Work with Leads."

> **Tip** Your system administrator can customize the help content that appears in Microsoft Dynamics CRM to include specific instructions about your unique Microsoft Dynamics CRM deployment.

Key Points

- To sort records in a view, click the column heading to toggle the records in ascending or descending order. To sort by more than one column, hold down the Shift key and click a second column header.

- To select records in a view, use the Ctrl or Shift key to select multiple records. Selecting the check box will select all of the records on the page, but not all of the records in the view.

- You can modify multiple records at once, but you can only edit records one page at a time.

- The Quick Find feature allows you to search for records in a view. You can use the asterisk (*) as a wildcard character in your searches. You can also use the wildcard character in lookup fields.

- You can access recently viewed records and views through the recently visited menu, and you can pin views and records that you want to keep on the recently visited list.

- Lookups link records in the user interface. You can use the automatic resolution feature by typing text directly into the lookup field. You can also select records from the most recently used list with lookup fields.

- You can modify your personal options to specify your preferences, including the start page that will be displayed when Microsoft Dynamics CRM first loads or the number of records displayed on each page.

- The Resource Center and the Help section include additional information about using the Microsoft Dynamics CRM software.

Chapter at a Glance

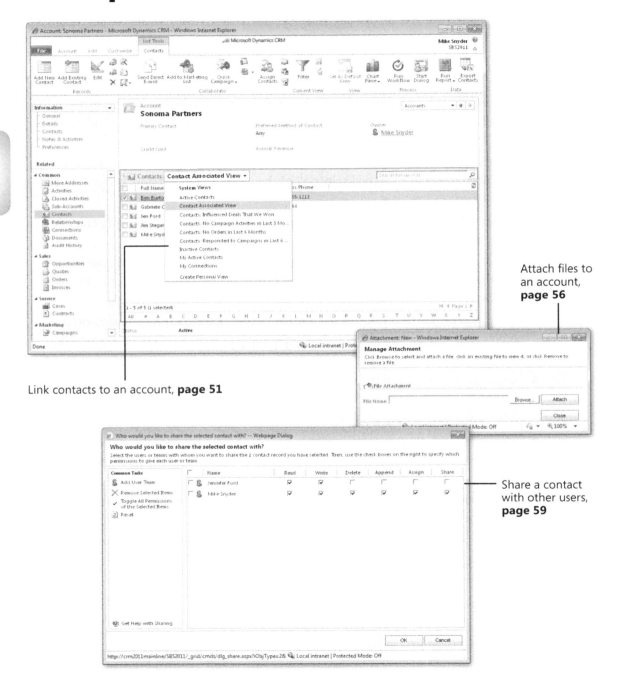

Attach files to
an account,
page 56

Link contacts to an account, **page 51**

Share a contact
with other users,
page 59

3 Working with Accounts and Contacts

In this chapter, you will learn how to

- ✔ Create an account.
- ✔ Use parent accounts and sub-accounts.
- ✔ Create a contact.
- ✔ Attach files to accounts and contacts.
- ✔ Deactivate and activate records.
- ✔ Share accounts and contacts with other users.
- ✔ Assign accounts and contacts to other users.
- ✔ Merge account or contact records.

The previous chapters covered a lot of the background information about Microsoft Dynamics CRM. In this chapter, you'll start working with customer records. Accounts and contacts are two of the most important and frequently used types of records in the system. As you learned in Chapter 1, "Introduction to Microsoft Dynamics CRM," CRM stands for *Customer Relationship Management*, and capturing the relationships between the accounts and contacts that work with your organization is one of the most valuable benefits of the Microsoft Dynamics CRM software.

In Microsoft Dynamics CRM, an account is a company or other business entity that interacts with your organization. If your business sells products and services to other businesses, accounts might represent your customers. Contacts in Microsoft Dynamics CRM represent specific individuals, who might or might not have a relationship with an account record. Contacts records can be managed within the system without any association to specific account records, which you might find useful if your organization's target customers include consumers. In addition to tracking customers, you might also want to track the other organizations and people that interact with your company, such as competitors, consultants, partners, suppliers, and vendors. This chapter will teach you how to distinguish between these different types of records. You'll also learn how to link contacts to accounts so that you can track how each person relates to a different business. By capturing as much data as possible about accounts and contacts, you can begin to develop a 360-degree view of each person and business related to your organization. When you understand all of the interactions with each account and contact, you will be able to work more efficiently, make better decisions, and provide improved customer service.

For example, assume that you're a sales representative who is using Microsoft Dynamics CRM, and you want to approach an existing customer about purchasing an additional product from your company. Before you pick up the phone to call the customer, it would be ideal for you to know whether the customer is experiencing any problems or issues with the product he or she purchased from you last year. A happy customer without any service issues will be more likely to purchase from you than a customer who is experiencing a lot of problems. Now let's assume that your customer service department is also using Microsoft Dynamics CRM and tracking all of the service requests in the same system you're using to track sales and marketing activities. When you view the customer record in Microsoft Dynamics CRM, you will be able to easily view all of your sales information *and* all of the customer service requests. If sales and service were using two different systems, you might have to make multiple phone calls or check in two different places to get the full picture of a customer's dealings with your organization. Microsoft Dynamics CRM allows you to quickly review a customer record to understand the whole picture before you approach the customer about purchasing additional products or services.

In this chapter, you will create accounts and contacts within Microsoft Dynamics CRM, then work with them to track business relationships, attach related files, and share permissions to the customer data with another member of your team.

> **Practice Files** Before you can complete the exercises in this chapter, you need to copy the book's practice files to your computer. The practice files you'll use to complete the exercises in this chapter are in the Chapter03 practice file folder. A complete list of practice files is provided in "Using the Practice Files" at the beginning of this book.

> **Important** In this chapter, you will work with accounts and contacts by using the web client, not the Microsoft Dynamics CRM for Outlook client. Both clients share almost all of the concepts and steps for working with accounts and contacts. However, Microsoft Dynamics CRM for Outlook includes some additional account and contact functionality. One of the most important benefits of Microsoft Dynamics CRM for Outlook is the ability to synchronize contacts from Microsoft Dynamics CRM with your Microsoft Outlook contact list. You can then synchronize your Microsoft Dynamics CRM contacts in Outlook to a mobile or handheld device. Chapter 5, "Using Microsoft Dynamics CRM for Outlook," discusses the Outlook synchronization process in detail.

> **Important** The images used in this book reflect the default form and field names in Microsoft Dynamics CRM. Because the software offers extensive customization capabilities, it's possible that some of the record types or fields have been relabeled in your Microsoft Dynamics CRM environment. If you cannot find the forms, fields, or security roles referred to in this book, contact your system administrator for assistance.

> **Important** You must know the location of your Microsoft Dynamics CRM website to work the exercises in this book. Check with your system administrator to verify the web address if you don't know it.

Creating an Account

Accounts represent businesses or organizations in Microsoft Dynamics CRM. You can access account information from the Sales, Marketing, and Service areas. The Account form consists of multiple sections, each of which contains data fields.

In accounts, contacts, or any other type of record in Microsoft Dynamics CRM, required attributes are marked with a red asterisk (*) to the right of the field name. The red asterisk indicates that you must enter a value in that field before you can create or save the record. If you try to create or save a record in which a required field does not contain data, Microsoft Dynamics CRM will prompt you to enter data in the field, and it will not save your changes.

A blue plus (+) symbol to the right of a field's name indicates that the field is recommended. You can still create or edit records without entering data in a recommended field.

In this exercise, you will create a new account record.

SET UP Use the Windows Internet Explorer web browser to navigate to your Microsoft Dynamics CRM website before beginning this exercise.

1. In the **Sales** area, click **Accounts**.

2. In the ribbon, click the **New** button to launch the **New Account** form.

3. In the **Account Name** field, enter **Sonoma Partners**. If your system includes additional required fields (as indicated by a red asterisk), you will need to enter values into those fields as well.

4. In the **Street 1** field, enter **525 W. Monroe St**.

5. In the **City** field, enter **Chicago**.

6. In the **State/Province** field, enter **IL**.

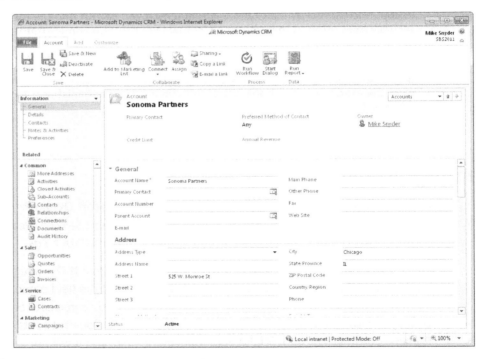

7. Click the **Save** button to create the account.

Tip You can also create an account by clicking the File tab on the ribbon and then clicking the New Record menu and clicking Account.

Using Parent Accounts and Sub-Accounts

In the previous example, you created a new account named Sonoma Partners. Now let's assume that Sonoma Partners is a division of a much larger organization named Contoso. Knowing that a relationship exists between Sonoma Partners and Contoso might be beneficial when you're working with either company. Microsoft Dynamics CRM allows you to capture and record this type of relationship by using parent accounts and sub-accounts. In this example, you would specify Contoso as the parent account of Sonoma Partners. When you do so, Microsoft Dynamics CRM automatically denotes that Sonoma Partners is a sub-account of Contoso.

> **Important** You can use parent accounts and sub-accounts to record a link between two organizations. Specifying one account as the parent account automatically makes the other a sub-account. Each account can have only one parent account, but you can specify as many sub-accounts as necessary.

Most companies that use Microsoft Dynamics CRM use parent accounts and sub-accounts to denote a legal or ownership relationship between two accounts. When one or more sub-accounts are related to a parent account, all activities and history for the sub-accounts are rolled up to the parent account. Therefore, when you're looking at the history of the Contoso account, Microsoft Dynamics CRM also displays the history of records attached to the Sonoma Partners account. This provides a complete picture of the interactions between the various records in your system, allowing your organization to understand your customers and tailor your sales, marketing, and customer service efforts accordingly.

> **See Also** For more information about how to track activities, see Chapter 4, "Working with Activities and Notes."

In this exercise, you will create a new Contoso account and link it to the Sonoma Partners account created in the previous example.

 SET UP Use the Internet Explorer web browser to navigate to your Microsoft Dynamics CRM website, if necessary, before beginning this exercise. You need the Sonoma Partners account record you created in the previous exercise.

1. On the ribbon, click the **File** tab, and then select the **New Record** menu and click **Account**. A new, blank account form opens.

2. In the **Account Name** field, enter **Contoso**.

3. Enter values in any other required fields marked by a red asterisk, and then click the **Save & Close** button.

4. In the application navigation pane, click **Accounts**, and then double-click the **Sonoma Partners** record.

5. In the **Parent Account** text field, enter ***Contoso***, and then press the Tab key.

   Microsoft Dynamics CRM automatically resolves the text you entered to the Contoso record, indicated by the underline and blue text color of the parent account name.

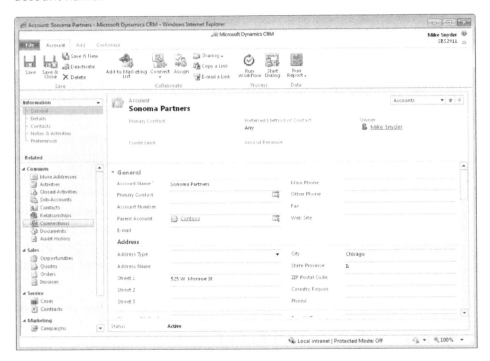

6. Click the **Save** button.

Tip Alternatively, you also could have selected Contoso as the parent account by using the Lookup button located on the right side of the Parent Account text box. For a quick refresher on using lookups, see Chapter 2, "Getting Around in Microsoft Dynamics CRM."

Creating a Contact

Contacts represent the various people with whom you do business. For each contact record, you can specify one (and only one) account as its parent customer. Most companies use the Parent Customer field to record the contact's employer, but you are not obligated to do so.

By specifying a parent customer for a contact, you create a relationship between those two records. When you create relationships between accounts and contacts, you can view all of an account's contacts by clicking the Contacts link in the Account's entity navigation pane. This list of contacts related to the account is known as the *contact associated view*.

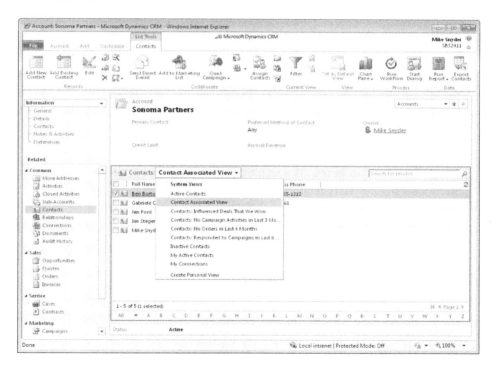

Why Is It Called "Parent Customer"?

In the examples in this chapter, an account is being set as the parent customer of a contact. However, most companies running Microsoft Dynamics CRM use this field to track the *employer* of the contact. Why does Microsoft Dynamics CRM call this field the parent customer?

The customer field is special in Microsoft Dynamics CRM, because you can use it to select either an account or a contact record. The customer field appears in multiple places throughout the system (in cases and opportunities, for instance) in which you might want to select an account *or* a contact, depending on how your organization tracks customers in Microsoft Dynamics CRM. Your system administrator can rename this field to Parent Account if necessary.

In addition to viewing all of the contacts associated with the account, you can click the view selector to choose different contact filters. Each of the different views can have its own unique filter criteria and display different columns of data. Note that the filter will only display contacts associated with the account you're viewing. For example, if you select the Inactive Contacts view, Microsoft Dynamics CRM will show you all of the inactive accounts associated with the account record you're viewing.

Similar to linking sub-accounts and parent accounts, linking contacts to an account allows you to view the contacts related to an account, including a roll-up of the activities from the related contacts to the parent account. Therefore, if you log a phone call activity with the Mike Snyder contact record, whose parent account is Sonoma Partners, you will be able to view that phone call record when you're looking at the Sonoma Partners record.

> **Tip** By default, Microsoft Dynamics CRM lists the contact's full name and business phone number when you're looking at the contact associated view related to an account. Your system administrator can customize this contact associated view to include additional columns, such as title, city, or email address.

As with accounts, there are several methods for creating a contact:

- Create a contact from the ribbon by clicking the File tab, and then selecting the New Record menu and clicking Contact.
- Create a contact by navigating to a contact view and then clicking the New button on the ribbon.

- Create a contact by clicking the Add New Contact button in the grid toolbar of the contact associated view of an account.

- Create a contact by clicking the New button in the contact Look Up Record webpage dialog box.

One benefit of creating a contact from the associated view is that Microsoft Dynamics CRM will automatically populate several fields on the contact record based on the account record you're currently viewing. For example, if you have the Sonoma Partners account record open and you then click the New Contact button in the associated view, Microsoft Dynamics CRM will fill out many of the fields on the new contact record—Street 1, City, State/Province, and others—with data from the Sonoma Partners account record. Microsoft Dynamics CRM will also automatically fill out the Parent Customer field of the new contact as Sonoma Partners. This concept of pre-populating data fields is known as field mapping. Your system administrator can determine how fields are mapped between two types of records.

> **Tip** Creating a new contact from the associated view will automatically fill out the mapped fields, such as the Parent Customer field and the address fields. Using this technique will save you time if the contact shares the same address information with the account.

> **Tip** If you create a new contact record by using one of the first two methods described above, Microsoft Dynamics CRM will not automatically fill out the mapped fields for you. This can be useful when the contact has different address information than the account (as could be the case when an employee works from home).

Although field mapping will pre-populate the contact record with data from the parent account, it will not maintain an ongoing link between the two records. If the account address changes because the business moves to a new office, you will need to explicitly update the address of the contacts related to that account. The edit feature located on the ribbon of the associated view allows you to update the address of multiple contacts at the same time.

For each account record, you can specify a primary contact. As you would expect, the primary contact denotes the individual that your organization should initiate interactions with. Although most of the time the primary contact works for the account organization as an employee, this is not a requirement. You can select any contact in the database as the primary contact for an account. Consequently, assigning a primary contact to an account does not automatically map the data fields and pre-populate the mapped values.

In this exercise, you will create two new contacts for the Sonoma Partners account. First, you will create a contact from the associated view, which will pre-populate certain values for the contact. Then you will use a different method, in which Microsoft Dynamics CRM does not pre-populate the mapped fields.

SET UP Use the Internet Explorer web browser to navigate to your Microsoft Dynamics CRM website, if necessary, before beginning this exercise. You need the Sonoma Partners record you created earlier in this chapter.

1. Navigate to **Accounts** and open the **Sonoma Partners** record.

2. In the entity navigation pane, click the **Contacts** link.

3. On the ribbon, click the **Add New Contact** button.

   Microsoft Dynamics CRM opens a new window. Note that the following fields already contain data: Parent Customer, Street 1, City, and State/Province.

4. In the **First Name** field, enter **Ben**, and in the **Last Name** field, enter **Burton**.

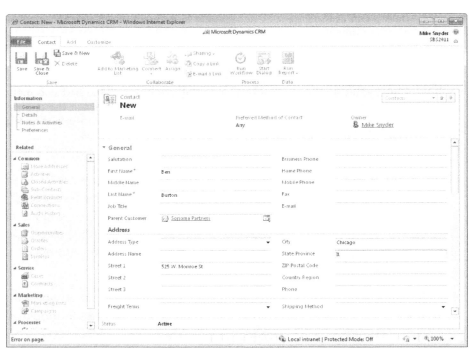

   5. Click **Save and Close**.

   You'll see that the Ben Burton contact now appears in the contact associated view of the Sonoma Partners account record.

   6. In the main application window, click the **File** tab, and then click **New Record** and click **Contact** to launch the **New Contact** form.

   7. In the **First Name** field, enter *Alan*, and in the **Last Name** field, enter *Jackson*.

   8. In the **Parent Customer** text box, click the **Lookup** button to launch the **Look Up Record** webpage dialog box.

   9. In the **Search** box, type *Sonoma Partners*, and then press Enter.

   10. In the results, click the **Sonoma Partners** record.

   11. Click the **OK** button to close the webpage dialog box.

   12. Click **Save and Close**.

   You will see that now both Ben Burton and Alan Jackson are linked to the Sonoma Partners account record, but Microsoft Dynamics CRM only pre-populated the mapped fields on the Ben Burton record because you created it from the associated view.

Attaching Files to Accounts and Contacts

In addition to entering information about accounts and contacts in the forms, you also can attach files (such as a Microsoft Excel spreadsheet or an Adobe Acrobat PDF file) with the record. Microsoft Dynamics CRM allows you to easily upload and save files related to accounts and contacts so that you can refer to them later.

In this exercise, you will save a file as an attachment to an account and download it for viewing. You can follow a similar sequence of steps to attach a file to a contact record.

SET UP Use the Internet Explorer web browser to navigate to your Microsoft Dynamics CRM website, if necessary, before beginning this exercise. You need the Sonoma Partners account record you created earlier in this chapter and the Orders1.xlsx practice file.

1. Navigate to the accounts view and open the **Sonoma Partners** record.

2. On the ribbon, click the **Add** tab, and then click the **Attach File** button to launch the **Manage Attachment** dialog box.

3. Click **Browse** and navigate to the **Chapter03** folder.

4. Select **Orders1.xlsx** and click **Open**.

   The navigation window closes.

5. Click the **Attach** button to upload the file to the account.

6. Click the **Close** button.

7. On the **Sonoma Partners** record, click the **Notes & Activities** link in the entity navigation pane. If necessary, scroll down to the Notes section.

   You can now see that Microsoft Dynamics CRM has attached the Orders1.xlsx file to the account record. Microsoft Dynamics CRM has automatically recorded the name of the user who uploaded the attached file, in addition to the date and time.

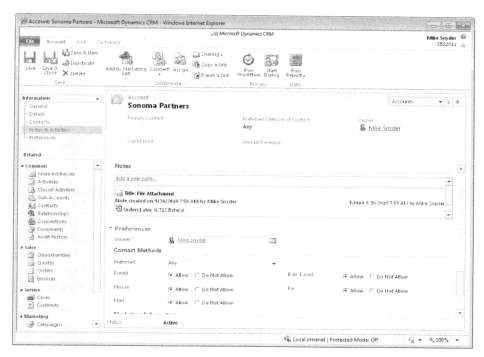

8. To open the attachment, click the file name and select either **Open** or **Save**.

Deactivating and Activating Records

Most of the records in Microsoft Dynamics CRM include values for status and status reason. A record's status defines the state of the record, and the most common status values are *Active* and *Inactive*. However, some types of records include additional status values. For example, case records can have a status value of *Active*, *Resolved*, or *Canceled*. Records that do not have a status value of *Open* or *Active* are considered to be deactivated (also referred to as Inactive). Microsoft Dynamics CRM retains deactivated records in the database; it does not delete them. However, inactive records will not appear in several areas throughout the user interface, such as in Quick Find searches or in lookup windows.

> **Important** Microsoft Dynamics CRM removes inactive records from parts of the user interface. In addition, you cannot edit an inactive record by using its form.

A record's status reason provides a description of the record's status. The status reasons vary depending on the type of record and the status value. In the case example, a record with an Active status could have one of multiple status reasons: In Progress, On Hold, Waiting For Details, or Researching. The following table illustrates how status and status reason values can vary by record.

Record type	Status value	Status reason value
Account	Active	Active
	Inactive	Inactive
Contact	Active	Active
	Inactive	Inactive
Case	Active	In Progress On Hold Waiting For Details Researching
	Resolved	Problem Solved
	Canceled	Canceled
Phone Call	Open	Open
	Completed	Made Received
	Canceled	Canceled

When working with accounts and contacts, you might want to deactivate records for multiple reasons. For example, you might want to deactivate a record if:

- A contact has changed companies or does not work for the account anymore.
- An account has gone out of business.
- A duplicate of the account or contact record already exists in the system.
- You do not want to continue tracking interactions with the account or contact.

In this exercise, you will deactivate a contact record and then reactivate it.

 SET UP Use the Internet Explorer web browser to navigate to your Microsoft Dynamics CRM website, if necessary, before beginning this exercise.

1. In the **Sales** area, click **Contacts**.
2. In the **Quick Find** box, type **Burton** and then press Enter.

3. You will see the Ben Burton record in your results. Click the record to select it. On the ribbon, click the **Deactivate** button. When a dialog box opens, asking you to confirm the deactivation, click **OK**. Microsoft Dynamics CRM deactivates the record.

4. In the **Quick Find** box, type ***Burton*** and then press Enter.

   You will not see the Ben Burton record in your results because you deactivated the record. Microsoft Dynamics CRM does not include inactive records in the Quick Find results.

5. Now that you have deactivated the contact, you will reactivate it. In the view selector, select **Inactive Contacts**. You will see a list of deactivated contacts, including the Ben Burton record.

6. Double-click the Ben Burton contact record to open it. Note that Microsoft Dynamics CRM has made the fields on the form unavailable so that you cannot edit the inactive record.

7. On the ribbon, click the **Activate** button. When a dialog box opens, asking you to confirm the activation, click **OK**.

8. Microsoft Dynamics CRM activates the contact and enables the form fields so that you can edit the record.

Sharing Accounts and Contacts with Other Users

Microsoft Dynamics CRM includes a robust security model that allows administrators to set up and configure which users can view or perform actions on the different types of records in a system. For those times when you want to share a particular account or contact record with a user because he or she cannot access it, Microsoft Dynamics CRM allows you to easily share records, assuming that your system administrator has given you permission to do so. Microsoft Dynamics CRM allows your organization to create teams of users, which can be beneficial when your organization wants to share records, because team members can belong to any business unit within your organization.

> **Important** Microsoft Dynamics CRM allows you to share records on an ad-hoc basis with a specific user or a team of users. When you share records, you can also determine which types of security privileges to grant for the shared record or records. You can grant privileges to other users only if you yourself already have those permissions for the shared record.

In this example, you will share a contact record with two users so that they can view and edit the record. You can follow a similar process to share account records.

 SET UP Use the Internet Explorer web browser to navigate to your Microsoft Dynamics CRM website, if necessary, before beginning this exercise. You need the Ben Burton contact record you created earlier in this chapter.

1. Navigate to a contact view and open the **Ben Burton** contact.

 2. On the ribbon, click the **Sharing** button, and then click **Share**.

   A new window opens.

3. In the **Common Tasks** pane, click **Add User/Team**.

   A Look Up Records webpage dialog box opens.

4. Because you are sharing this contact record with a user, leave the **Look for** list value set to **User**. Select any two active users in your system, and then click the **Add** button.

5. Click **OK**.

   Microsoft Dynamics CRM lists the selected users in the sharing window.

6. Within this window, you can decide what types of privileges to grant to each user for the **Ben Burton** contact record. Because you want these users to have permission to edit the contact record, select the **Write** check boxes for both of the users you selected.

7. Click **OK**.

   Microsoft Dynamics CRM updates the security permissions and closes the sharing window.

8. To view the current share permissions for a record, click the **Sharing** button on the ribbon, and then click **Share**.

A new window appears that displays the share information that you just configured.

> **Tip** When working collaboratively with other users on a record, you might want to send someone a specific record to review. To simplify this process of referencing a specific record, Microsoft Dynamics CRM offers a web address shortcut (URL) for each record. Users who click the record shortcut address will automatically open that record in the system without being required to look for it in the user interface. To copy the shortcut address to your Microsoft Office Clipboard, click the Copy A Link button on the ribbon. Now you can paste the record's address into another application, such as an email message or document, by pressing Ctrl+V. Microsoft Dynamics CRM includes shortcuts for almost every type of record in the system, including accounts, contacts, cases, and activities. If you click the Email A Link button, Microsoft Dynamics CRM will launch your default email program with the record shortcut already inside the message.

Assigning Accounts and Contacts to Other Users

In addition to sharing records with other users, you can change the ownership of a record. Most of the records in Microsoft Dynamics CRM (such as accounts, contacts, leads, cases, and opportunities) are "owned" by a user or a team, and the record owner is a key component of the security model within the system. Microsoft Dynamics CRM allows you to change the record owner (or assign the record) by using multiple techniques in the user interface. For example, you can:

- Open the record and change the value in the Owner field.
- Open the record and click the Assign button on the ribbon.
- In views that contain lists of records, select one or more records and then click the Assign button.

Regardless of the technique you use, you will follow the same steps to assign account, contact, and most other records in Microsoft Dynamics CRM.

In this exercise, you will change the ownership of a contact record by using the second technique just mentioned to assign it to a different user.

 SET UP Use the Internet Explorer web browser to navigate to your Microsoft Dynamics CRM website, if necessary, before beginning this exercise. You need the Ben Burton contact record you created earlier in this chapter.

1. Open the **Ben Burton** contact record.

2. On the ribbon, click the **Assign** button.

   A new window opens.

3. Click **Assign to another user or team**.

4. Select a different user by typing the user name directly in the box or by clicking the **Lookup** button.

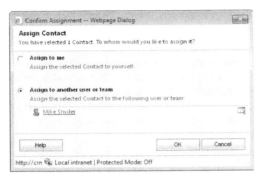

5. Click **OK**.

   The window closes, and Microsoft Dynamics CRM updates the record owner to the value you selected.

> **Tip** Inactive users can own records, but you can assign records only to active users. If a user record is deactivated, records already assigned to that user will remain assigned, but no other records can be assigned to the user as long as he or she is inactive in Microsoft Dynamics CRM.

Merging Account or Contact Records

When working with account and contact records in Microsoft Dynamics CRM, you might notice that two or more records appear very similar. For example, your database might contain multiple contact records for the same person in your system. Although you obviously wouldn't knowingly enter two records for the same person, it is possible that your system might contain duplicate records.

> **See Also** Microsoft Dynamics CRM includes multiple tools to help your organization avoid creating duplicate records in your database. For more information on configuring the duplicate check features, contact your system administrator to enable and configure Microsoft Dynamics CRM's duplicate checking functionality.

Even though Microsoft Dynamics CRM contains powerful tools to help you avoid duplication, you will undoubtedly find a few duplicate records within your database. Fortunately, Microsoft Dynamics CRM includes a merge tool that allows you to consolidate two different records into a single merged record.

When merging two records, you specify one record as the master record, and Microsoft Dynamics CRM treats the other record as the child record. The software will deactivate the child record and copy all of the related records (such as activities, notes, and opportunities) to the master record. During the merge process, Microsoft Dynamics CRM presents you with a dialog box that allows you to select data from individual fields in the child record so that you keep data from specific fields with the surviving master record.

> **Tip** You can merge lead records, in addition to merging accounts or contacts. However, you cannot merge two different types of records together. You can only merge leads with other leads, accounts with other accounts, and contacts with other contacts..

By merging duplicate records, you will maintain a clean customer database, which will help with sales, marketing, and service productivity.

In this exercise, you will create a new contact record and merge it with an existing contact record. You would follow this same process for merging account and lead records.

 SET UP Use the Internet Explorer web browser to navigate to your Microsoft Dynamics CRM website, if necessary, before beginning this exercise.

1. On the ribbon, click the **File** tab, and then select the **New Record** menu and click **Contact**.

2. In the **First Name** field, enter *Ben*, and in the **Last Name** field, enter *Burton*. In the Fax field, enter *(312) 555-1212*.

3. In the **Parent Customer** field, click the **Lookup** button to launch the **Look Up Record** webpage dialog box.

4. In the **Search** field, enter *Sonoma Partners*, and then press Enter.

5. In the results, click the **Sonoma Partners** record.

6. Click the **OK** button to close the webpage dialog box.

7. On the ribbon, click **Save and Close**.

8. In the **Sales** area, click **Contacts**.

9. In the **Quick Find** text box, enter *Burton*, and then press Enter.

Microsoft Dynamics CRM lists the contact you just created and the Ben Burton contact record you created previously in this chapter.

10. Holding the **Shift** key down, click both **Ben Burton** records in the grid so that they are highlighted. On the ribbon, click the **Merge** button. The Merge Records dialog box appears.

11. In this dialog box, you choose the master record by clicking the button next to the appropriate contact record. You can also select which data fields you want to keep from the child record and transfer onto the surviving master record. Click **(312) 555-1212** in the **Fax** field. When you do so, Microsoft Dynamics CRM will keep this fax data on the final record.

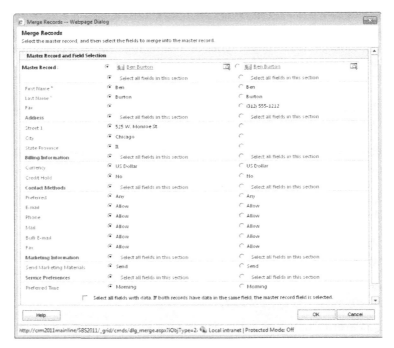

12. Click the **OK** button.

Microsoft Dynamics CRM will merge the two records together by updating the master record and deactivating the child record. When the process is complete, Microsoft Dynamics CRM will display an alert window telling you that the selected records are merged and the subordinate record is deactivated.

13. Click **OK** to close the **Merge Records** dialog box.

Key Points

- You can create accounts and contacts by clicking the New button on the ribbon or by using the New Record option located by clicking the File tab on the ribbon on the main screen.

- You can link multiple accounts together by specifying one account as the parent account, which automatically makes the other a sub-account.

- Each account can have only one parent account, but accounts can have as many sub-accounts as you need.

- Microsoft Dynamics CRM allows you to upload file attachments to many records, such as accounts and contacts.

- Sharing accounts with other users or teams allows you to grant security privileges to groups that might not otherwise have access.

- Most records in Microsoft Dynamics CRM, such as accounts and contacts, have a single user as the record owner. Record ownership helps determine security settings. You can change record owners by assigning a record to a different user or team.

- You can use the merge tool to consolidate duplicate records into a single record while preserving the history of both records.

Chapter at a Glance

Create a follow-up activity, **page 76**

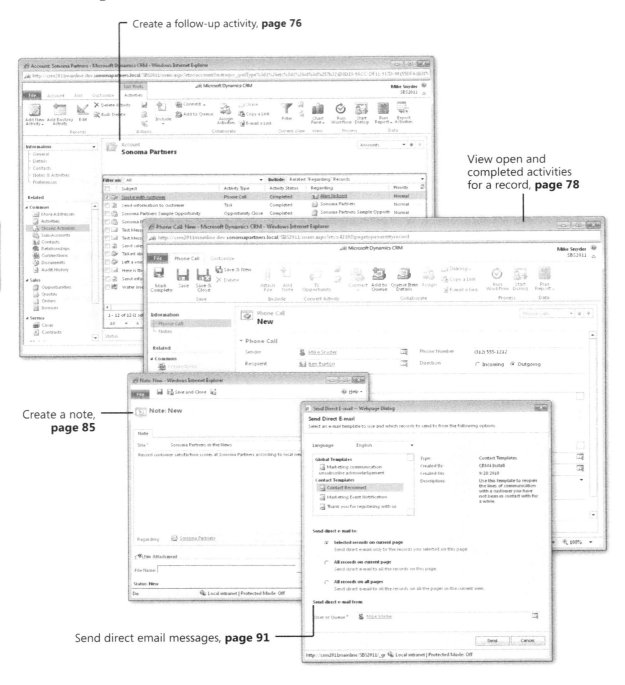

View open and completed activities for a record, **page 78**

Create a note, **page 85**

Send direct email messages, **page 91**

4 Working with Activities and Notes

In this chapter, you will learn how to

- ✔ Understand different activity types.
- ✔ Understand the Regarding field.
- ✔ Create follow-up activities.
- ✔ View open and completed activities.
- ✔ Create a note.
- ✔ Manage your activities.
- ✔ Send direct email messages.

In the previous chapter, you learned how to create and manage accounts and contacts in Microsoft Dynamics CRM. In this chapter, you will learn how to record, manage, and report on the *activities* and *notes* related to those records. The word *activity* is a generic term that Microsoft Dynamics CRM uses to describe business interactions, such as phone calls, tasks, and email messages. Notes are comments or other descriptive text related to a record.

Tracking activities and notes allows you and your company to:

- Record the phone calls to and from a particular person or account.
- Track customer service calls regarding a product or service.
- Assign tasks to ensure that a sales representative follows up with new leads in a timely fashion.
- Save copies of the email correspondence on a particular topic.
- Understand the marketing activities a prospect or customer participated in during his or her history with your firm.

Think back to a time when you called a company with a question, and each time you called about the same topic the representative acted as though you had never spoken with the company before. This type of situation causes frustration for the customer and for the company. If that company had recorded calls and notes related to your request in a customer relationship management system, the representatives could resolve your subsequent calls more quickly because they could access the complete history of your interactions with the company.

Capturing all of the interactions with your customers and prospects as activities allows you to provide a higher level of customer service, improve sales efficiency, make better business decisions, and market more effectively.

Creating Activities by Using Microsoft Dynamics CRM Workflow

Although you can create activities one at a time, Microsoft Dynamics CRM also allows you to create and assign activity records automatically by using workflow rules. Conceptually, you can think of Microsoft Dynamics CRM workflow as an application or service that runs in the background, 24 hours a day, 7 days a week, constantly evaluating your Microsoft Dynamics CRM data and the multiple workflow rules in your deployment. When the workflow service encounters a trigger event, it fires the appropriate workflow rules to run the workflow actions. Typical workflow actions include sending an email message, creating a task, and updating a data field on a record. Workflow rules are typically set up by system administrators to automate follow-up tasks or other actions in Microsoft Dynamics CRM at key milestones during sales or other business processes.

Creating activities with workflow helps your business ensure that everyone follows a consistent process when dealing with customers. Contact your system administrator about creating workflow rules to ensure that important follow-up activities are created as key events occur in Microsoft Dynamics CRM, such as assigning a follow-up task when a new lead is created or sending a birthday email message to a preferred customer.

> **See Also** Creating and designing workflow rules is beyond the scope of this book, but you can learn more about creating workflow in Working with Microsoft Dynamics CRM 2011 by Mike Snyder and Jim Steger (Microsoft Press, 2011).

In this chapter, you will learn how to capture the tasks, email messages, faxes, appointments, and other customer interactions in Microsoft Dynamics CRM, and relate them to customer and other records to gain a full picture of how your organization communicates with its customers.

> **Practice Files** The exercises in this chapter require only records created in earlier chapters; none are supplied with the book's practice files. For more information about practice files, see "Using the Practice Files" at the beginning of this book.

> **Important** The images used in this book reflect the default form and field names in Microsoft Dynamics CRM. Because the software offers extensive customization capabilities, it's possible that some of the record types or fields have been relabeled in your Microsoft Dynamics CRM environment. If you cannot find the forms, fields, or security roles referenced in this book, contact your system administrator for assistance.

> **Important** You must know the location of your Microsoft Dynamics CRM website to work the exercises in this book. Check with your system administrator to verify the web address if you don't know it.

Understanding Activity Types

Microsoft Dynamics CRM uses the term *activity* to describe several types of interactions. The types of activities are:

- **Phone Call** Use this to record a received or initiated telephone call.

- **Task** Use this to record a to-do or follow-up item.

- **E-mail** Use this to record a received or sent email message.

- **Letter** Use this to record the mailing of a physical letter or document.

- **Fax** Use this to record a received or sent facsimile.

- **Appointment** Use this to record a meeting or appointment. Many companies use appointments to track conference calls or online meetings, in addition to face-to-face meetings.

- **Recurring Appointment** Use this to record meetings or appointments that occur on a regular, scheduled basis, such as the 15th of each month or every other Tuesday. Recurring appointment activities function the same as appointments except that you can set them up on a recurring schedule.

- **Service Activity** Use this to record a service that you performed for a customer.

> **Tip** To create and use service activities, you must first make sure that your administrator has set up and configured the services, sites, and resources that your company offers. Service activities do not apply to every type of business; they are best suited to businesses that need to schedule customer services in specific time slots. Your business might not use service activities at all.

- **Campaign Response** Use this to record a customer or prospect response to a marketing campaign. For example, you might create a campaign response to record that a customer registered for a seminar.

> **See Also** Campaign responses offer unique marketing functionality that differs from that of the other activities. See Chapter 9, "Working with Campaign Activities and Responses," to learn more about this activity type.

Custom Activity Types

Microsoft Dynamics CRM 2011 includes new functionality that allows your system administrator to set up and configure custom activity types that match your company's specific business needs. Some potential custom activity types might include a sales demonstration or a visit to your website. How you use custom activity types is up to your organization to decide.

Tracking activities and notes on customer records helps you and others in your organization understand all of the communication your organization has had with each customer. You can also create search queries, views, and reports to track activities by customer or activity type. For example, a sales manager can view information about her team's phone calls for review during a weekly sales meeting, or a customer service manager can view the open service activities scheduled for an upcoming week to ensure that his team is available.

> **See Also** For more information about analyzing data and creating reports in Microsoft Dynamics CRM, see Chapter 15, "Using the Report Wizard."

The most commonly used data fields in activity records include those listed in the following table.

Data Field	Description
Subject	A brief description of the activity
Regarding	The customer or other record to which the activity is related
Description	Additional notes or information about the activity
Status	The status of the activity, such as Active, Completed, or Canceled
Duration	The estimated time it will take for the activity to be completed
Actual Duration	The actual time it takes for the activity to be completed
Scheduled Start	The estimated start date of the activity
Due Date	The estimated completion date of the activity
Actual Start	The date the activity was started
Actual End	The date the activity was completed

Each activity record also includes data fields specific to the activity type. For example, only phone calls will contain information about the phone number or the call direction.

> **Tip** Even though the activity forms include category and subcategory fields, Microsoft Dynamics CRM categories are not related to the categories configured in Microsoft Outlook. Consequently, updating an activity's category in Microsoft Dynamics CRM will not update the activity's Outlook category. Even though they share the same name, Microsoft Dynamics CRM categories are unrelated to Outlook categories.

Understanding the Regarding Field

You can track to-dos and other follow-up activities as tasks in Microsoft Dynamics CRM, much as you can in Outlook. When you create an activity in Microsoft Dynamics CRM, you can use the Regarding field to specify a customer or other record to which the activity is associated. By entering a value in the Regarding field, you can create a link between the activity and the selected record, so that the activity is displayed from the specified record. Without the Regarding field, you'd be able to tell how many phone calls you made in a week—but by specifying the customer in the Regarding field of each phone call activity, you can also tell *what* you contacted them about.

By default, you can set an activity to be regarding any of the following records:

- Account
- Campaign
- Campaign Activity
- Case
- Contact
- Contract
- Invoice
- Lead
- Opportunity
- Order
- Quote

> **Tip** You might be able to track activities and notes to additional record types if your system administrator has configured additional, custom entities in your Microsoft Dynamics CRM environment.

By properly setting the Regarding field for activity records, you can more easily look up and reference customer information later. For example, if you set all of your tasks so that they are regarding an account record, it might become cumbersome to find a particular task if you have several hundred activities for that account record. However, if you set activities so that they are regarding certain records related to the account (such as quotes or cases), you can find all of the activities related to those entities without having to sort through hundreds of activities.

> **Tip** It is a best practice to use the Regarding field to link activities to records in Microsoft Dynamics CRM.

In this exercise, you will create a task regarding the Sonoma Partners account created in the previous chapter, and then mark it as completed.

SET UP Use the Windows Internet Explorer web browser to navigate to your Microsoft Dynamics CRM website before beginning this exercise. You need the Sonoma Partners account record you created in Chapter 3, "Working with Accounts and Contacts." If you cannot locate the Sonoma Partners record in your system, select a different account record for this exercise.

1. On the ribbon, click the **File** tab, and then select **New Activity**.

2. Click **Task** to launch the **New Task** form.

3. In the **Subject** field, enter *Send information to customer*.

   By default, the Subject and Owner fields are the only data fields in which you must enter values before you can create a task.

4. In the **Description** field, enter *Sample description of the task*.

5. In the **Regarding** field, click the **Look Up** button. A **Look Up Record** dialog box appears. Leave **Account** selected in the **Look for** field, and enter *Sonoma Partners* in the **Search** field. Press the Enter key to submit your search.

> **Tip** Although only one record can be entered in the Regarding field for each activity, the selected record can be one of many different types, such as Lead, Account, Opportunity, or Case. You can also type in the name of the record you're looking for in the Regarding field and Microsoft Dynamics CRM will try to automatically find the matching record.

The Look Up dialog box filters the records to show the accounts that match your search phrase.

6. Click the **Sonoma Partners** record, and then click **OK**.

7. In the **Due** field, click the **Calendar** button and select the date by which you want this task to be completed.

8. After you have selected a date, a list of times is activated on the form so that you can select the specific time of day by which you want the task to be completed. Select **1:00 PM**.

9. Click the **Save** button to create the task.

10. Now that you have created the task, let's mark the task as completed. There are two different ways to mark the task as completed. First, in the ribbon, click the **Close Task** button.

The Close Task dialog box launches.

11. In the **Close Task** dialog box, click the arrow in the **Status** list to show the possible values.

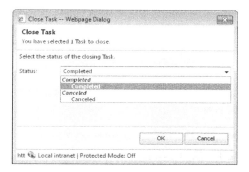

With this technique, you can mark the task as Completed or Canceled. You would cancel the task if you did not complete the task but want to remove it from your list of open tasks. After you select the value you want, you would click the OK button to close the task.

12. For this exercise, click the **Cancel** button to keep the task active. You will use an alternate method to close the task.

13. On the ribbon, click the **Mark Complete** button.

Microsoft Dynamics CRM marks the task as Completed and closes the task window. Using this technique will save you a few clicks, but you can't use it to mark a task as Canceled.

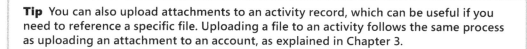

Tip You can also upload attachments to an activity record, which can be useful if you need to reference a specific file. Uploading a file to an activity follows the same process as uploading an attachment to an account, as explained in Chapter 3.

Creating Follow-Up Activities

In addition to creating activities from the ribbon, you can create them from customer or other records in Microsoft Dynamics CRM. Because activities are critical to developing a complete view of each customer's interactions with your company, you'll find several locations from which you can quickly create new activities—you can even schedule follow-up activities from an existing activity! For instance, you can enter notes from a phone call with a client contact, and then schedule a follow-up appointment activity based on a time and date discussed with the customer during your call. By doing so, you can save the phone call activity as completed while also ensuring that the dialogue with your customer continues by scheduling the future appointment.

In all record types for which you can create activities, Microsoft Dynamics CRM provides the following ways to create a new activity:

- You can click one of the activity buttons that appear on the Add tab of the ribbon.
- You can use the Activities option that appears in the entity navigation pane of the form. From this view, you can click the Add New Activity button on the ribbon to create an activity.

Any time an activity is created from a specific record, that record is automatically populated in the new activity's Regarding field. When you create a new activity from an existing lead, account, or contact, Microsoft Dynamics CRM can also pre-populate other activity fields for a record, such as the phone number for a phone call or the To: recipient for an email message.

In this exercise, you will create a phone call activity from a contact record. When you create a phone call record by using this technique, Microsoft Dynamics CRM automatically populates the mapped fields, such as the call recipient, the phone number, and the phone call's Regarding value.

 SET UP Use the Internet Explorer web browser to navigate to your Microsoft Dynamics CRM website before beginning this exercise.

1. Navigate to the **Contacts** view and open any contact record in your system. Ensure that the contact record includes a phone number in the **Business Phone** field.

 2. On the ribbon, click the **Add** tab, and then click the **Phone Call** button. A phone call record opens and is populated with data from the contact record.

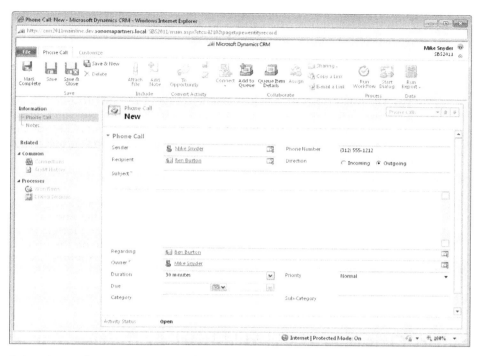

3. Select **Incoming** near the top of the form.

Microsoft Dynamics CRM automatically switches the values in the Sender and Recipient fields. This direction field indicates whether you placed the call or the contact called you.

4. In the **Subject** field, type *Spoke with customer*.

5. On the ribbon, click **Save**.

6. On the ribbon, click the **Close Phone Call** button. A new dialog box appears.

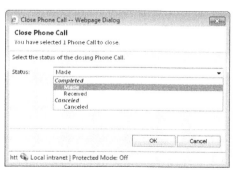

7. In this dialog box, you can select a value to record how you closed out the phone call. Select **Made**, and then click **OK**.

Microsoft Dynamics CRM closes the phone call as a completed activity.

> **Tip** The other types of activities can be created by using processes similar to those you just learned for creating tasks and phone calls; therefore, we won't repeat the exercises for each activity type. Chapter 5, "Using Microsoft Dynamics CRM for Outlook," shows how to create appointments, tasks, and email messages in Outlook that can be saved into Microsoft Dynamics CRM.

> **Tip** Certain activity types can be converted to opportunities and cases. You can convert phone calls, tasks, faxes, email messages, appointments, and letters to sales opportunities or service requests by clicking the Convert Activity button on the ribbon. Opportunities are detailed in Chapter 6, "Working with Leads and Opportunities," and cases are covered in Chapter 10, "Tracking Service Requests."

Viewing Open and Completed Activities for a Record

When you track activities related to your customers, you and other members of your organization can reference that information to understand the complete history of interactions with those customers. Imagine a scenario in which a customer has been working with one person from your office, but that employee leaves for a week's vacation. If the customer calls your office when that person is out, you could look up the customer's record in Microsoft Dynamics CRM and read the activity history to get up to speed on the customer.

As you learned earlier in this chapter, all of the activity types share some common data fields. One of the shared data fields across all activity types is the status field. The default status values for activity records are:

- Open
- Scheduled
- Completed
- Canceled

When you look up activities related to a customer, you will notice that Microsoft Dynamics CRM splits the activities into two categories: *Activities* and *Closed Activities*. The Activities section displays all of the activities related to the record that need to be completed. Only activities with a status of Open or Scheduled appear in the Activities display. The Closed Activities section lists all of the Completed or Canceled activities related to the record.

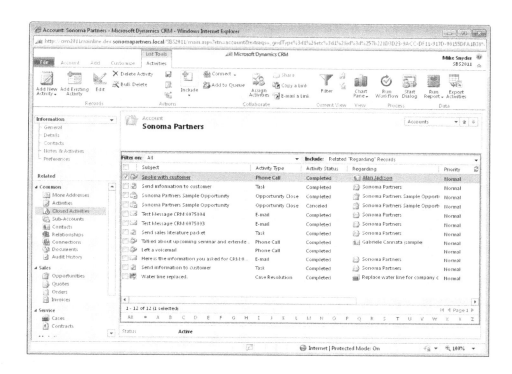

> **Tip** If your view contains a large number of records, you can use the Filter On list to show only those activities within a specific date range. You can also sort the columns in the record list just like you can sort the other grids.

In addition to displaying a view of all activities related to the record, Microsoft Dynamics CRM performs an *activity rollup* so that you can see the activities of records related to the record you're viewing. For example, in the images shown in this section, the Sonoma Partners account lists 12 different closed activities, but only 6 of those activities are regarding the Sonoma Partners account. The other completed activities are regarding records that are related to the Sonoma Partners account. For example, there is a phone call activity regarding the Gabriele Cannata contact. It appears in this view because Gabriele Cannata's parent account is Sonoma Partners. In addition, this view lists a completed activity regarding a case opened by Sonoma Partners. If you want to see only the activities regarding the Sonoma Partners account, you can use the Include list to select the This Record Only value. The Microsoft Dynamics CRM activity rollup works on both open and closed activities.

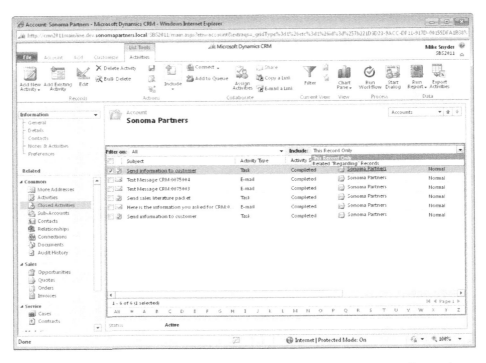

In this exercise, you will create two activities with different Regarding values to see how Microsoft Dynamics CRM displays those records in the Activities and Closed Activities sections.

SET UP Use the Internet Explorer web browser to navigate to your Microsoft Dynamics CRM website before beginning this exercise. You need the Sonoma Partners and Contoso account records you created in Chapter 3. If you cannot locate the Sonoma Partners and Contoso records in your system, select two different account records for this exercise.

1. Navigate to the **Accounts** view and open the **Sonoma Partners** account record.

2. On the ribbon, click the **Add** tab and then click the **Phone Call** button. A new window opens.

3. In the **Subject** field, enter *Open Phone Call Due 2 Months from Now*.

   Note that because you created this phone call from the Sonoma Partners record, Microsoft Dynamics CRM automatically populates the Regarding field with the Sonoma Partners account.

4. In the **Due** field, select a date two months from today.

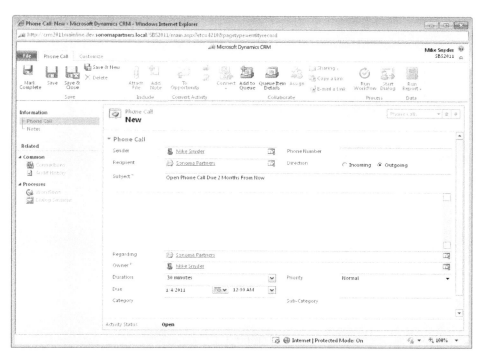

5. Click the **Save and Close** button.

The window closes and you are returned to the Sonoma Partners account record.

6. In the **Parent Account** field, select the **Contoso** account record that you created in the Chapter 3 exercises, and then save the **Sonoma Partners** account. You can also select any other account record if the Contoso account does not exist in your system.

7. You just created a phone call activity regarding the Sonoma Partners account, and now you will create a task activity on the parent account of Sonoma Partners. Click the account you selected in the **Parent Account** field to view the details of the parent account record.

8. On the ribbon, click the **Add** tab, and then click the **Task** button. A new window opens. Note that, because you created this task from the parent account record, Microsoft Dynamics CRM automatically populates the **Regarding** field with the parent account.

9. In the **Subject** field, enter *Task Regarding Contoso Due Today*.

10. In the **Due** field, select today's date.

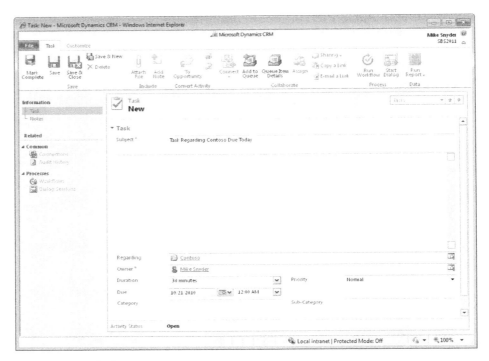

11. Click **Save and Close**.

    The window closes, and you are returned to the parent account record.

12. In the entity navigation pane, click **Activities**.

    The activity list displays the task that you just created, but the phone call record does not appear. By default, Microsoft Dynamics CRM shows activities within the next 30 days for open activities, or the previous 30 days for closed activities. Because you entered a due date two months from today for the phone call, that record doesn't fit the filter criteria.

13. To view the phone call, click the arrow in the **Filter On** list and select **All**.

The view updates to show the phone call too.

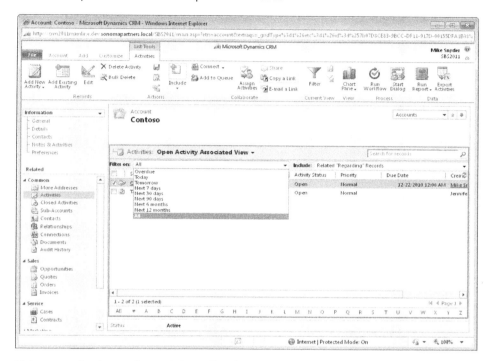

This example shows the activity rollup in action. You created two activities regarding two different records, but you can see them in a single view because the Sonoma Partners record lists Contoso as its parent.

14. To view only those activities regarding the parent account, click the arrow in the **Include** list and select **This Record Only**.

The view updates again to display only the task regarding Contoso.

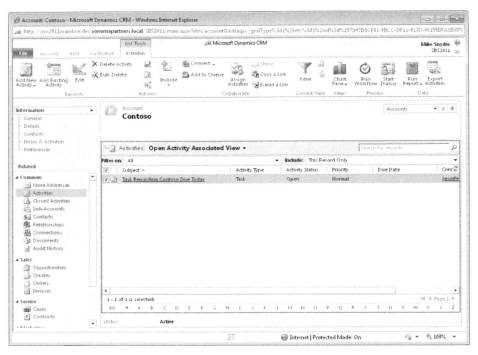

15. Double-click the task regarding the parent account to open that record. Click **Mark Complete** to mark the task as completed.

16. Click **Activities** in the entity navigation pane of the parent account record.

The task record does not appear anymore because you just closed it.

17. To view the closed task, click **Closed Activities** in the entity navigation pane.

The view shows the task you just completed.

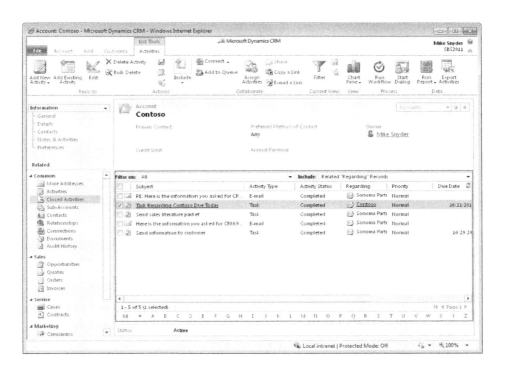

Creating a Note

In addition to using activities to capture the interactions with your customers and prospects, you might find that you want to jot down some notes about a record. For example, suppose that you read an article in the newspaper about one of your accounts, and the article includes some important information about the account's growth plans. You'd like to capture that information in Microsoft Dynamics CRM. Because you didn't interact with the customer or anyone else, the action of recording this data doesn't fit the "activity" concept. Fortunately, Microsoft Dynamics CRM allows you to create *notes* and link those notes to the various records in your system.

> **Tip** In addition to notes that you add to a record, Microsoft Dynamics CRM also displays file attachments that you upload in the Notes section of the user interface. For more information about attaching files to Microsoft Dynamics CRM records, see Chapter 3.

In this exercise, you will create a note about an account.

 SET UP Use the Internet Explorer web browser to navigate to your Microsoft Dynamics CRM website before beginning this exercise. You need the Sonoma Partners account record you created in Chapter 3. If you cannot locate the Sonoma Partners record in your system, select a different account record for this exercise.

1. Navigate to the **Accounts** view and open the **Sonoma Partners** record.

> **Important** If you cannot locate the Sonoma Partners account in your system, you can use any account for this exercise.

 2. On the ribbon, click the **Add** tab and then click the **Add Note** button. A new window will launch.

3. In the **Title** field, enter *Sonoma Partners in the News*.

4. In the text area under the title, enter *Record customer satisfaction scores at Sonoma Partners according to local newspaper article*.

5. On the toolbar, click the **Save and Close** button.

6. To view the note that you just created, along with other notes attached to the record, click the **Notes & Activities** link in the entity navigation pane of the **Sonoma Partners** account record.

7. To delete the note, right-click the **Note** title.

> **Important** To delete a note, you need to have a security role that has delete privileges. If you are unable to perform this step, contact your system administrator about deleting the note.

A new menu appears.

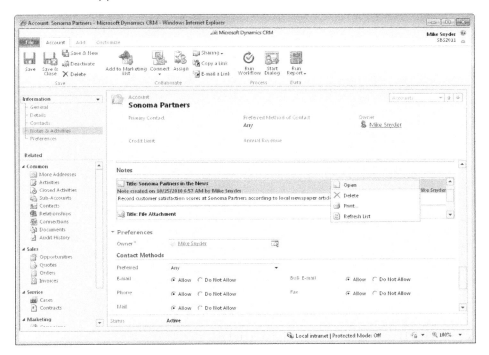

8. Click **Delete** to delete the note.

> **Tip** Unlike activities, notes do not roll up from related records. You will see only those notes regarding the record you're viewing.

Managing Your Activities

Now that you understand how to create and work with activities for a particular record, we'll review how you can manage your activities on a daily basis. For example, after you arrive at the office and log on to Microsoft Dynamics CRM, where should you start your day? What calls do you need to make? Which tasks do you need to complete? What does your schedule look like? Microsoft Dynamics CRM includes a *Workplace* that you can use to manage all of your activities.

The Workplace contains many different sub-areas, but the two related to managing activities are the links named Calendar and Activities. The Calendar displays a list of appointments that you can view by day, week, or month.

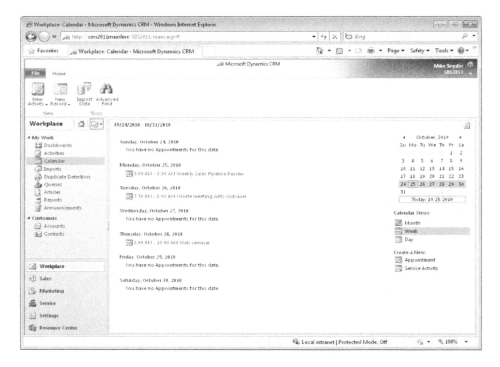

> **Important** The Calendar shows only those appointments from Microsoft Dynamics CRM; it does not show activities from your personal Outlook calendar. The Calendar also does not display other activity record types, such as tasks or phone calls. For more information about working with your calendar in Outlook, see Chapter 5.

The Activities area provides a list of all of the activity records you have privileges to view within Microsoft Dynamics CRM. You can access different views of the activity data in addition to filtering the records by activity type and due date. You can also use Quick Find to search for specific terms or keywords within the activities.

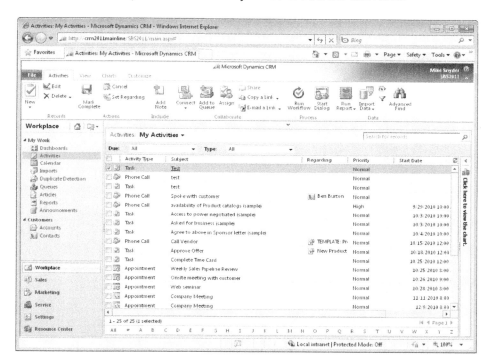

By using a combination of the Calendar and Activities views, you can quickly prioritize your open activities.

In this exercise, you will toggle the filters on the Activities view to see how they dynamically update.

SET UP Use the Internet Explorer web browser to navigate to your Microsoft Dynamics CRM website before beginning this exercise.

1. In the application navigation pane, click **Activities**.

2. Click the arrow in the view selector to display the list of activity views that apply to all of the activity types.

3. On the menu, click **Phone Call**. A submenu with additional phone call views appears. Note that these views are specific to the Phone Call entity. You do not need to click anything.

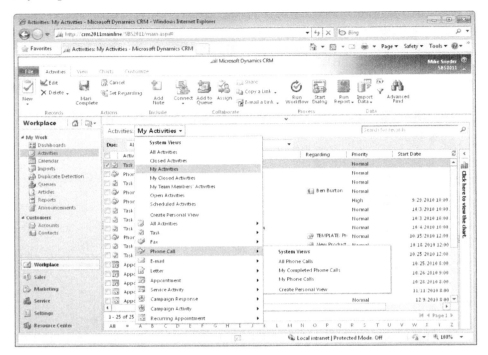

4. Now, in the menu, click **Task**. A new submenu with additional task views appears. These views are specific to the Task entity. Click the **My Tasks** view.

5. Now you see a list of all the Tasks you own. To see which tasks are due soon, click the **Due** filter to see a list of filter options such as Overdue, Today, Tomorrow, and Next 7 Days.

6. Click **Next 7 Days**. Microsoft Dynamics CRM updates your task list to show only those tasks with a due date that matches the filter criteria.

Sending Direct Email Messages

Another very important activity type is email. Because Microsoft Dynamics CRM integrates with Outlook, most users write and read email messages within Outlook. However, one feature that many users want to take advantage of is the ability to send an email message to a large list of recipients so that each message is individually addressed (in other words, sending an email message to 500 people generates 500 different email messages). Microsoft Dynamics CRM refers to this mass email generation as *direct email*, and you can access this features only within the web client.

Sending a direct email message requires you to select an *email template*. Microsoft Dynamics CRM includes several email templates, so you can use one of those for the exercise in this section. However, you will probably want to create new email templates specific to your business and use those for your email communications.

To send a direct email message, navigate to a view that supports direct email (such as accounts, contacts, leads, and so on), select one or more records in a view and click the Send Direct E-Mail button on the ribbon. Microsoft Dynamics CRM will open a dialog box that allows you to select an email template. If you selected a view with several pages of records, you can choose to send the direct email message to just the selected records, all the records on the page, or all the records on all of the pages. Finally, you can send the email message from someone other than yourself. You might want to do this if you want the email to come from a generic address, such as *info@sonomapartners.com*, instead of a person.

> **Tip** The Direct E-Mail feature will not send messages to records if your recipients' Bulk E-Mail preference is set to Do Not Allow. Direct E-Mail will simply exclude those records from the mailing list.

In this exercise, you will send a direct email message to contacts by using one of the out-of-the-box email templates.

SET UP Use the Internet Explorer web browser to navigate to your Microsoft Dynamics CRM website before beginning this exercise.

1. Navigate to the **Contacts** view.

2. Select one or more records in the view, making sure to select records with sample or test email addresses instead of real addresses.

3. On the ribbon, click the **Send Direct E-mail** button.

   A new window opens.

4. Select the **Contact Reconnect** template. Leave the other options set to the defaults.

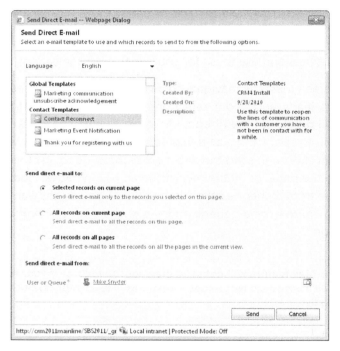

5. Click **Send**.

   Microsoft Dynamics CRM submits the email message for immediate delivery. If you view the closed activities of the contact records you selected, you will see the email message you just sent.

Key Points

- Activities are used to track interactions with customers, prospects, vendors, and other record types.

- Microsoft Dynamics CRM allows you to track many different kinds of activities, including tasks, phone calls, faxes, letters, email messages, appointments, service activities, and campaign responses. In addition to the default activity types, your system administrator can create custom activity types.

- You can create an activity from the ribbon or from an individual record. Creating the activity from the individual record maps the Regarding field to the corresponding record.

- You can view the activities associated with a record by clicking Activities or Completed Activities in the navigation pane. The Activities link displays open or scheduled activity records, and the Closed Activities link shows completed or canceled records.

- Microsoft Dynamics CRM automatically rolls up activities between related records so that you can view related activities in a single view. You can toggle the activity rollup while you are working with an activity view.

- In addition to activities, you can view notes about the records in your system. Microsoft Dynamics CRM displays notes attached to a record in the same place that it displays files attached to that record.

- Microsoft Dynamics CRM includes a Calendar view and an Activity view to allow you to manage a large list of activities.

- You can use the web client and the direct email feature to send mass email messages to leads, contacts, and accounts in your system.

Chapter at a Glance

Access Microsoft Dynamics CRM data within Outlook, **page 97**

Track email messages sent from Outlook in Microsoft Dynamics CRM, **page 113**

Access Microsoft Dynamics CRM data while offline, **page 121**

Modify your offline synchronization filters, **page 123**

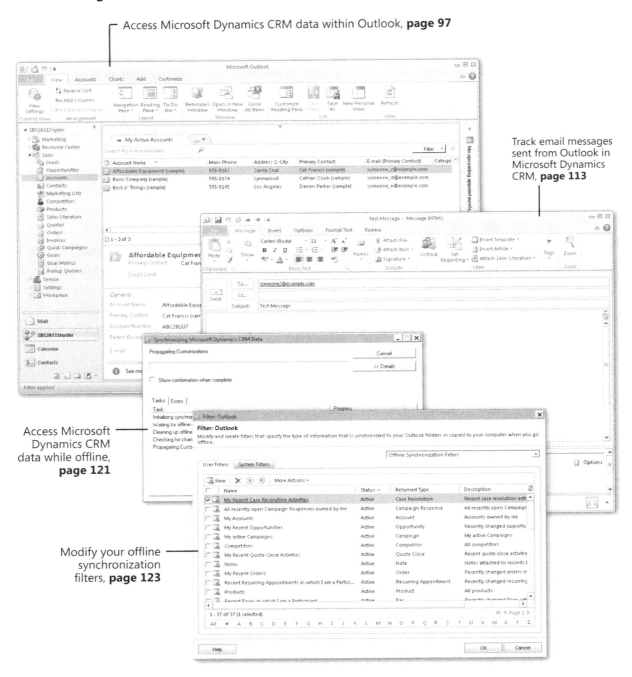

5 Using Microsoft Dynamics CRM for Outlook

In this chapter, you will learn how to

✔ Access CRM records within Microsoft Dynamics CRM for Outlook.

✔ Access CRM settings within Microsoft Dynamics CRM for Outlook.

✔ Synchronize contacts, tasks, and appointments between Microsoft Dynamics CRM and Outlook.

✔ Create and track CRM contacts, tasks, and appointments in Outlook.

✔ Use the Add Contacts wizard.

✔ Send and track email messages in Microsoft Dynamics CRM for Outlook.

✔ Delete records in Microsoft Dynamics CRM for Outlook.

✔ Go offline with Microsoft Dynamics CRM for Outlook.

✔ Configure your offline synchronization filters.

Microsoft Dynamics CRM offers a Microsoft Dynamics CRM for Outlook interface in addition to the web client interface. Without a doubt, the integration with Microsoft Outlook generates the most excitement and interest among Microsoft Dynamics CRM users. Information workers love the fact that they can work directly with their Microsoft Dynamics CRM data in Outlook without needing to open a second software application. More importantly, users do not need to learn a new software application to perform their day-to-day functions. The Microsoft Dynamics CRM for Outlook user experience closely matches the rest of the functions that users already know how to perform in Outlook. This chapter will highlight many of the key steps and processes you'll use when working with Microsoft Dynamics CRM for Outlook.

> **Important** Before you can use Microsoft Dynamics CRM for Outlook, you or your system administrator must install the software on your computer. In this chapter, we assume that the Microsoft Dynamics CRM for Outlook software is already installed and connecting properly to your Microsoft Dynamics CRM server.

Your company can deploy one of two versions of the Microsoft Dynamics CRM for Outlook software:

- Microsoft Dynamics CRM for Outlook
- Microsoft Dynamics CRM for Outlook with Offline Access

Both versions offer almost identical functionality, but the Offline Access version allows you to work offline, disconnected from the Microsoft Dynamics CRM server. In this chapter, we will assume that you are using the Offline Access client.

In this chapter, you will learn how to use the integration between Microsoft Dynamics CRM and Outlook to create contacts, tasks, appointments, and email messages in Outlook and track them in Microsoft Dynamics CRM. You'll also learn how to work with Microsoft Dynamics CRM records while disconnected from the server.

> **Practice Files** The exercises in this chapter require only records created in earlier chapters; none are supplied with the book's practice files. For more information about practice files, see "Using the Practice Files" at the beginning of this book.

> **Important** The examples and exercises in this chapter use Microsoft Dynamics CRM for Outlook and Outlook 2010, but Microsoft Dynamics CRM also supports Outlook 2007 and Outlook 2003. If you are using Outlook 2007 or Outlook 2003, the exercises and steps might vary, because the user interface is different in Outlook 2010. In addition, some features and functionality are not available in Outlook 2007 or Outlook 2003.

> **Important** The images used in this book reflect the default form and field names in Microsoft Dynamics CRM. Because the software offers extensive customization capabilities, it's possible that some of the record types or fields have been relabeled in your Microsoft Dynamics CRM environment. If you cannot find the forms, fields, or security roles referred to in this book, contact your system administrator for assistance.

> **Important** You must know the location of your Microsoft Dynamics CRM website to work the exercises in this book. Check with your system administrator to verify the web address if you don't know it.

Accessing CRM Records Within Microsoft Dynamics CRM for Outlook

With Microsoft Dynamics CRM for Outlook, you can access CRM records and perform key actions directly within Outlook. Many users prefer to access their CRM data by using this technique instead of using the web client because they are already working in Outlook to manage email and perform other tasks. The Outlook client user interface is a little different from the web client, so here is a brief overview of the various components.

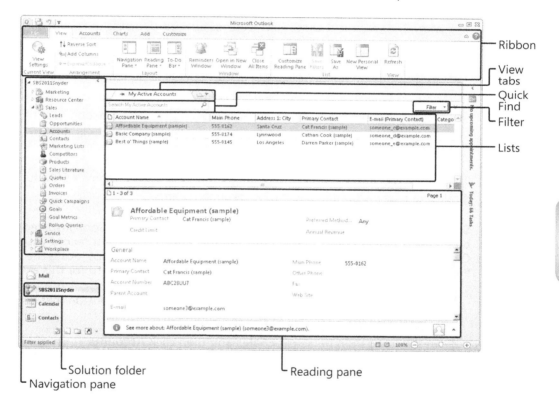

- **Solution folder** You will see this button in Outlook after you install the Outlook client. You click it to access additional Microsoft Dynamics CRM functionality. The name that appears in this button will match the name of the organization with which your Microsoft Dynamics CRM system is associated.

- **Ribbon** Just as in the web client, the ribbon displays different buttons and features depending on the context. For example, if you're viewing a list of accounts, the ribbon displays actions that you can take with account records. If you're viewing a list of contacts, the ribbon will display a different set of actions, those that are available for contact records.

- **View tabs** Use this area to select the data view you want to work with. In addition, you can use the view tabs to pin views that you want to quickly access in the future.

- **Lists** Similar to the grid in the web client, this area displays a list of records. Microsoft Dynamics CRM for Outlook filters the records displayed in the list depending on the view selected on the view tab.

- **Quick Find** Just as in the web client, you can enter a search term in the Quick Find field to search for specific records. However, unlike the web client version of Quick Find, the Outlook client Quick Find only searches for records in the currently displayed view. The web client Quick Find searches for records across the entire database.

- **Filter** You can use this to filter the records in the displayed view.

- **Reading pane** The reading pane in the Outlook client behaves like the reading pane you use when working with Outlook contacts, email, and so on. Selecting a record in the list updates the reading pane to show additional information about that record. Note that the reading pane is for display only; you cannot edit records within the reading pane.

In this exercise, you will familiarize yourself with Microsoft Dynamics CRM for Outlook by displaying a new view and navigating through records.

SET UP Open Outlook with Microsoft Dynamics CRM for Outlook installed before beginning this exercise. You need the Sonoma Partners account record you created in Chapter 3, "Working with Accounts and Contacts." If you cannot locate the Sonoma Partners record in your system, select a different account record for this exercise.

1. In the Outlook navigation pane, click the solution folder button that displays the name of your Microsoft Dynamics CRM organization.

2. In the navigation pane, click **Sales** and then click **Accounts**. A list of Microsoft Dynamics CRM accounts is displayed.

3. Click the top record in the list. The reading pane displays information about that account.

4. On the keyboard, press the Down arrow. Microsoft Dynamics CRM highlights the next account record in the list, and the record displayed in the reading pane updates accordingly.

5. In the **Quick Find** area, type ***Sonoma Partners***, and then press Enter. This should display the **Sonoma Partners** sample record you created in Chapter 3. If you didn't create that record, you can perform this exercise with any account in this list.

6. Double-click the **Sonoma Partners** record in the list. Microsoft Dynamics CRM launches the account record in the web client. Within this window, you can make any record edits necessary.

7. On the ribbon, click the **Save and Close** button.

Next you will display a new account view within Microsoft Dynamics CRM for Outlook.

8. In the view tabs area, click the new tab icon located to the right of the open tab. A list of available system and personal views appears.

9. Click **Active Accounts**. Microsoft Dynamics CRM adds a second tab and displays a list of active accounts within Microsoft Dynamics CRM for Outlook.

10. Now click the pin icon located on the left side of the **Active Accounts** tab. When you do so, Microsoft Dynamics CRM for Outlook keeps this tab open so that you can quickly access it in the future.

> **Tip** If you want to remove a tab, simply click the X located on the right side of the tab. Microsoft Dynamics CRM will remove the tab.

11. Microsoft Dynamics CRM for Outlook also lets you personalize the appearance of the user interface. Let's assume that you want to turn off the reading pane and replace it with a chart. Click the **Reading Pane** button, and select **Off** on the submenu that appears. Microsoft Dynamics CRM for Outlook removes the reading pane for the current entity you're working with (accounts).

12. On the ribbon, click the **Charts** tab, click the **Chart Pane** button, and select **Right** from the submenu that appears.

Microsoft Dynamics CRM displays a chart to the right of the list. Within this chart area, you can choose to display different charts. You can select the chart you want to display by clicking the chart name at the top of the chart pane.

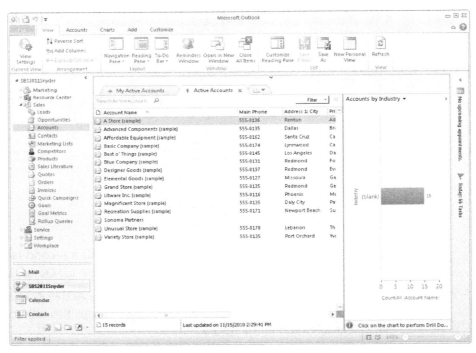

13. Finally, let's assume that you want to log an activity for one of the accounts in the list. As in the web client, you could use the Add tab on the ribbon to access the buttons you need. However, Microsoft Dynamics CRM for Outlook also provides a menu that allows you to log activities directly from the list. To access this menu, right-click any account in the list and click **Create**. Microsoft Dynamics CRM for Outlook opens a list of actions you can take against the record, allowing you to create activities, run a mail merge, add a note, and more.

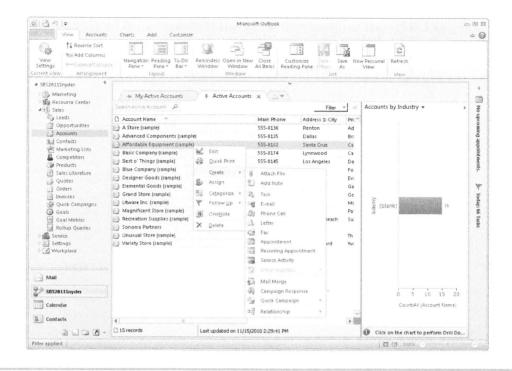

> **Tip** In addition to creating Microsoft Dynamics CRM records from this menu, you can also assign categories and set follow-ups.

Accessing CRM Settings Within Microsoft Dynamics CRM for Outlook

Now that you have worked with the basic user interface of Microsoft Dynamics CRM for Outlook, let's take a quick look at how to access the settings area. You should not need to access this area very often, but it is important to know where the settings information is located. Some of the key actions you might take in this area include:

- Setting personal options.
- Modifying your synchronization and offline data filters.
- Importing contacts.

In this exercise, you will access the CRM settings within Microsoft Dynamics CRM for Outlook.

SET UP Start Outlook with Microsoft Dynamics CRM for Outlook installed, if necessary, before beginning this exercise.

1. On the Outlook ribbon, click the **File** tab.

2. In the left pane, click **CRM**.

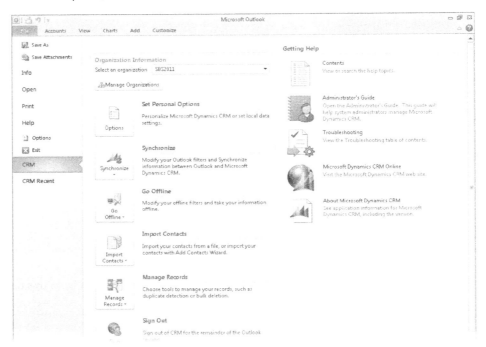

Synchronizing Contacts, Tasks, and Appointments

One of the main benefits of Microsoft Dynamics CRM for Outlook is that the software will automatically synchronize your contacts, tasks, and appointments between Outlook and Microsoft Dynamics CRM. Therefore, if you create a new contact in the Microsoft Dynamics CRM web client, the software can automatically download a copy of that contact into Outlook. Likewise, if you update a contact's information (with a new address or phone number, for example) in Outlook, the software will automatically update the Microsoft Dynamics CRM database. If other users of your system synchronize the updated contact to their Outlook file, they will receive your updates in the next sync process. This bi-directional update of contact information between Outlook and Microsoft Dynamics CRM means that you and other users can always access the latest information. In addition to synchronizing contacts, Microsoft Dynamics CRM for Outlook can perform similar updates for Outlook appointments and tasks. If you use a mobile device and synchronize it with Outlook, you will be able to access Microsoft Dynamics CRM contacts, appointments, and tasks on your mobile device.

> **Important** Microsoft Dynamics CRM can also synchronize other activities—such as phone calls, letters, and faxes—to Outlook. Regardless of the activity type (phone call, letter, fax, or task) in Microsoft Dynamics CRM, the synchronization software will copy all of the activities into Outlook as tasks.

Microsoft Dynamics CRM for Outlook does not synchronize *all* of the contacts, appointments, and tasks from your Outlook file; rather, it synchronizes only the records that you track in Microsoft Dynamics CRM. If you have personal records in Outlook that you do not want to copy into the Microsoft Dynamics CRM database, you do not need to track those records in Microsoft Dynamics CRM. You can determine whether a particular record is tracked in Microsoft Dynamics CRM by opening the record and looking for the CRM tracking pane located at the bottom on the record. If there is a tracking pane, the record is part of the Microsoft Dynamics CRM for Outlook synchronization process.

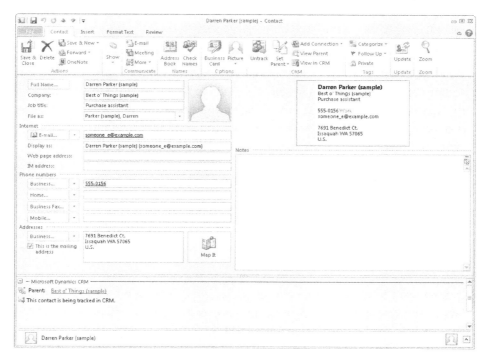

> **Tip** A tracked record can also be identified by the presence of the Untrack button in the CRM group on the record's ribbon.

In addition, records tracked in Microsoft Dynamics CRM will display a special icon when you view a list of records in Outlook.

When you first install Microsoft Dynamics CRM for Outlook, the software uses its default settings for the synchronization process. One of these settings sets the software to perform the synchronization process in the background every 15 minutes. This automatic background sync provides you with the convenience of not having to remember to explicitly sync your records. If you want, you can change your options to increase the amount of time between automatic synchronizations, but you cannot make it less than 15 minutes.

> **Tip** When you are connected to the server, changes made to contacts, tasks, and appointments in Outlook synchronize to the Microsoft Dynamics CRM server when the record is saved. However, changes made to the Microsoft Dynamics CRM server in the web client will not appear in Outlook until the completion of the next synchronization process.

If don't want to wait for the next scheduled synchronization interval, you can manually launch the synchronization process. In this exercise, you will manually synchronize Outlook records with the Microsoft Dynamics CRM server.

SET UP Start Outlook with Microsoft Dynamics CRM for Outlook installed, if necessary, before beginning this exercise.

1. In the Outlook navigation pane, click the **Contacts** button.

2. On the ribbon, click the **CRM** tab, and then click the **Synchronize with CRM** button. A progress indicator appears. When the software completes the synchronization process, the window closes.

> **See Also** As a reminder, you can create contacts in Microsoft Dynamics CRM by using either Microsoft Dynamics CRM for Outlook or the web client. This chapter shows you how to use Microsoft Dynamics CRM for Outlook, but you can also refer to Chapter 3 for an explanation on how to create contacts by using the web client.

Creating and Tracking Contacts

Microsoft Dynamics CRM can synchronize your existing contacts from the Microsoft Dynamics CRM server so that they display in your Outlook contacts file. However, as you continue to work with the system, you will want to create and track new contact records. To create contacts in Outlook and track them in Microsoft Dynamics CRM, create the record in Outlook as you normally would, click the Track button, and then save the contact. Doing so will create the contact record in Microsoft Dynamics CRM and include the record as part of future data synchronizations. When creating contacts in Outlook, you also can link the contact record to a parent account in Microsoft Dynamics CRM by clicking the Set Parent button on the Contact tab of the ribbon in Outlook.

> **Tip** Microsoft Dynamics CRM does allow you to specify a contact record as a parent record for another contact, but most organizations use account records as parents for contact records. For the purposes of this book, we'll assume that you'll use accounts as parent records for contacts.

As is the case when you create a contact in the web client, when you create a new contact in Outlook, track it in Microsoft Dynamics CRM, and link it to an existing parent account, the mapped fields (such as address and phone) in the contact record will *not* automatically update with information from the parent account. However, if you link a contact to a parent account from Microsoft Dynamics CRM, Microsoft Dynamics CRM for Outlook can save the parent account name in the Company field on the Outlook contact.

> **Troubleshooting** Filling out the Company field in the Outlook contact record will not automatically link the contact to that company's account record in Microsoft Dynamics CRM. For new contacts that you create in Outlook and track in Microsoft Dynamics CRM, you must explicitly link the record to a parent account.

When you track a contact in Microsoft Dynamics CRM, you can access additional information about the record from Outlook by clicking one of the following links in the contact record's ribbon:

- **View In CRM** This link will open the contact record in the Microsoft Dynamics CRM web client. This allows you to view all of the details and related records that you're tracking in Microsoft Dynamics CRM.

- **View Parent** This link will open the account record of the parent account. Typically the parent is the company for which the contact works.

In this exercise, you will create two new contacts (one from Outlook and one from the web client) to see how the different options impact the contact data. You will also update the contact records and manually kick off the synchronization process.

> **SET UP** Start Outlook with Microsoft Dynamics CRM for Outlook installed, if necessary, before beginning this exercise. You need the Sonoma Partners account record you created in Chapter 3. If you cannot locate the Sonoma Partners record in your system, select a different account record for this exercise.

1. In the Outlook navigation pane, click **Contacts**. On the ribbon, click **New Contact** to open the new contact form.

2. Enter *Chris Perry* as the contact name.

3. Click the **Track** button.

4. Click the **Set Parent** button and, on the menu that appears, click **Account**.

   A Microsoft Dynamics CRM lookup window opens.

5. In the text field, enter *Sonoma Partners*, and then press the Enter key to search for the account in Microsoft Dynamics CRM. Select the appropriate account in the results, and then click **OK**.

> **Important** If you cannot locate the Sonoma Partners account in your system, you can use any account for this exercise.

The Sonoma Partners account name appears in the Company field of the Chris Perry Outlook contact.

> **Troubleshooting** If the parent account name does not appear in the Company field, check your preference setting in the Microsoft Dynamics CRM for Outlook options. To update this preference, access the CRM settings as you did in the exercise earlier in this chapter, and click Set Personal Options. On the Synchronization tab of the Options window, locate the Update The Company Field For Outlook Contacts section and make sure that the check box is selected. This will allow you to automatically update the Company field with the parent account name.

6. On the ribbon, click the **Save and Close** button.

This record is now tracked in Microsoft Dynamics CRM, as indicated by the CRM tracking pane.

7. Open Windows Internet Explorer and browse to the address of your Microsoft Dynamics CRM system.

8. Navigate to the account records and open the **Sonoma Partners** account or other parent account selected in step 5.

9. In the navigation pane, click **Contacts**.

The Chris Perry record appears and is linked to this account.

10. Double-click the **Chris Perry** record to open it. In the **Business Phone** field, enter *(312) 555-1212*.

11. On the ribbon, click the **Save and Close** button. Microsoft Dynamics CRM closes the window and returns you to the list of contacts associated with the account.

12. In the entity navigation pane of the account record, click **Contacts**. Then on the ribbon of the account record, click the **Add New Contact** button to launch the **New Contact** form.

13. In the **First Name** field, enter *Jose*. In the **Last Name** field, enter *Curry*.

Note that, because you created this contact from the account, the contact record includes the mapped fields such as address and phone number from the parent account record.

14. Click the **Save and Close** button.

15. Close Internet Explorer.

16. In Outlook, click the **File** tab, and then click **CRM**. Click the **Synchronize** button, and then click the **Synchronize** option that appears on the submenu.

A window opens, indicating that Microsoft Dynamics CRM for Outlook is updating data.

17. In the Outlook navigation pane, click **Contacts**. In the search box, enter ***Jose Curry***.

The contact you created in the web client now appears in your Outlook file (with the mapped fields from the account).

18. In the search box, enter ***Chris Perry***.

Outlook shows the **Chris Perry** record, which now includes the phone number that you entered in the web client.

> **Important** Creating contacts from the account record in the web client will map fields such as address and phone number to the contact. However, creating a contact in Outlook and tracking it to an account will only map to the account name but not the other data fields.

Using the Add Contacts Wizard

You just learned how to add and track contacts in Microsoft Dynamics CRM one record at a time. However, you might already have a lot of contacts in your Outlook file that you would like to track, and you probably don't want to link them one record at a time, especially if you have hundreds of contacts. Fortunately, Microsoft Dynamics CRM for Outlook includes an Add Contacts wizard that helps you quickly and easily add your existing Outlook contacts to Microsoft Dynamics CRM.

Before you use the Add Contacts wizard, you might want to create different folders for your contacts to separate them into different groups, such as business contacts and personal contacts. When you work through the wizard, you can select the contact folders to use. If you don't have any contact folders, the Add Contacts wizard will include all of your contacts in the process.

Alternatively, instead of creating new folders, you can assign your existing Outlook contacts to different categories by using Outlook's category functionality. During the Add Contacts wizard import process, you can choose the categories of contacts to add to Microsoft Dynamics CRM.

In this exercise, you will use the Add Contacts wizard to load existing Outlook contacts into Microsoft Dynamics CRM.

 SET UP Start Outlook with Microsoft Dynamics CRM for Outlook installed, if necessary, before beginning this exercise.

1. On the ribbon, click the **File** tab and in the left pane, click **CRM**.

 2. Click the **Import Contacts** button, and click **Add Contacts** on the submenu.

   Microsoft Dynamics CRM for Outlook launches the Add Contacts wizard.

3. Click **Next**.

   If you have created multiple contact folders, the Choose Contact Folders step appears. (If you don't have multiple folders, the wizard skips this step.)

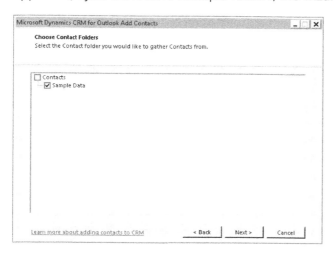

4. Select the folder you want to use for this process and click **Next**.

The wizard analyzes the contacts and displays the Choose Contact Groups dialog box.

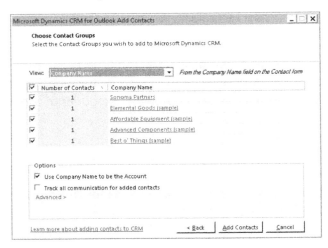

On this screen, you can choose which contacts to add to Microsoft Dynamics CRM. You can group the contacts by company name, email domain, or category. If you want to see the contacts in any of the groups, click the group name hyperlinked in blue to display a new window that lists the contacts.

You can choose the groups of records to import by selecting the check boxes of the records that you want to add to Microsoft Dynamics CRM.

5. For this exercise, select a group of records to import.

> **Tip** It is recommended that you only select one or two groups to test that the import works as you expect.

You might notice that the Number Of Contacts column includes color coding in the form of red, yellow, or green bars. These colors indicate the following:

○ **Green** 100 percent of the contacts already exist in Microsoft Dynamics CRM.

○ **Yellow** At least 50 percent of the contacts already exist in Microsoft Dynamics CRM.

○ **Red** At least one contact already exists in Microsoft Dynamics CRM.

6. In addition to adding contacts to Microsoft Dynamics CRM, the Add Contacts wizard can also import email messages and appointments associated with the imported contacts. To enable this option, select the **Track all communications for added contacts** check box.

7. By default, the wizard will automatically create new accounts in Microsoft Dynamics CRM linked to the imported contacts. To disable this option, clear the **Use Company Name to be the Account** check box.

> **Troubleshooting** If your system administrator has enabled the duplicate checking settings for Microsoft Dynamics CRM, the Add Contacts wizard might not create account and contact records during the import process. Check with your system administrator to see if this applies to your system.

Alternatively, Microsoft Dynamics CRM might already include account records that match the contacts you're importing. If you run the Add Contacts wizard with the default settings, it will import and create the contacts, but it won't link your imported contacts to the existing accounts automatically. Instead, you can choose to manually match the contacts you're importing to existing Microsoft Dynamics CRM accounts.

8. To do this, click the **Advanced** link. Two new columns appear. In the **Set Account** column, click in the box to display a new menu.

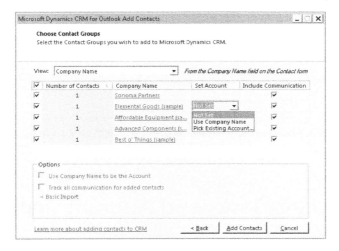

9. From this menu, click **Pick Existing Account.**

   The account lookup record dialog box appears. Select the account you want to manually link the contact to.

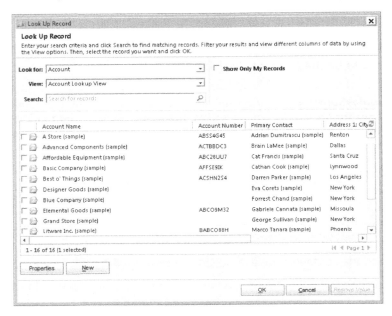

10. For this exercise, select any account, and then click **OK** to return to the wizard.

11. Click **Add Contacts**.

    The Add Contacts wizard runs through the process and displays a final confirmation screen, which includes a listing of any errors that might have occurred during the import process.

> **Tip** You can run the Add Contacts wizard as often as necessary, to import new contacts at a later time.

Creating and Tracking Tasks and Appointments

In addition to synchronizing contacts, Microsoft Dynamics CRM for Outlook can synchronize tasks and appointments between Microsoft Dynamics CRM and Outlook. The process of creating and tracking tasks and appointments follows the same rules as previously outlined for contacts. You can create the task and appointment records in Outlook by using the standard Outlook tools, and then click the Track button to save a copy to Microsoft Dynamics CRM. As you learned in previous chapters, you can also specify a Regarding value for activities such as tasks and appointments.

If you create tasks or appointments in the web client, Microsoft Dynamics CRM for Outlook can also synchronize those records from the server into your Outlook file.

> **Important** You can modify many of the Microsoft Dynamics CRM for Outlook synchronization settings. To access the personal settings page, click CRM on the Outlook ribbon, and then select Options. You can view the sync settings on the Synchronization tab.

Sending and Tracking Email Messages in Microsoft Dynamics CRM for Outlook

Even though you can create and send Microsoft Dynamics CRM email messages with the web client, most users prefer to create and reply to their email messages with Outlook. Copies of these Outlook email messages can be saved to Microsoft Dynamics CRM so that you can go back later and see a complete history of the communications. Much like creating contacts, tasks, and appointments in Outlook, you can create email messages as you normally would in Outlook and save a copy of each message to Microsoft Dynamics CRM by clicking the Track button. When processing an email message, Microsoft Dynamics CRM for Outlook reviews the list of message participants and automatically looks for matching email records in the Microsoft Dynamics CRM database. If it finds matching email addresses, the software appends the email message to the matching records as a completed email activity. This email matching process searches for matching email addresses across those record types that contain email addresses in Microsoft Dynamics CRM, such as contacts, accounts, leads, queues, users, and facilities/equipment.

In addition to linking an email message to the participants, Microsoft Dynamics CRM can be used to specify the record the email message is regarding. For example, you might send multiple email messages to a single customer, but one message might be about an existing order, whereas a different message might be about a customer service issue. By specifying the Regarding field of each message (one is regarding an order, and the other is regarding a service issue), you can split up the communication history to the appropriate records. This will save you time when you are viewing the activity history related to each record. Microsoft Dynamics CRM for Outlook saves a list of your recently used Regarding values so that you can quickly track email messages regarding recent topics.

In addition to tracking email messages sent from Outlook, Microsoft Dynamics CRM for Outlook allows you to track email messages that you receive. To track these types of messages, you can open the message and click the Track button, or you can select the email message in your Inbox and then click the Track button in the CRM group on the ribbon. You can set the Regarding value of the message by using the Set Regarding button on the ribbon.

> **Tip** You don't have to track email messages one at a time; you can select multiple email messages and click the Track button. Depending on your email system and your Microsoft Dynamics CRM tracking configuration, Microsoft Dynamics CRM can automatically track all of the email messages in a subject thread so that you don't have to manually track every message. Contact your system administrator to determine your exact system configuration.

> **See Also** For more information about tracking email messages and other activities in Microsoft Dynamics CRM, see Chapter 4, "Working with Activities and Notes."

When composing email messages with the Microsoft Dynamics CRM for Outlook client installed, you can also do the following:

- Insert a CRM email template.
- Insert a CRM knowledge base article.
- Attach sales literature stored in CRM.

These features allow you to save time and clicks because you can quickly access templates, articles, and attachments stored within Microsoft Dynamics CRM.

Microsoft Dynamics CRM for Outlook also allows you to access an Outlook address book that contains your Microsoft Dynamics CRM records. The Microsoft Dynamics CRM address book allows you to easily access the email addresses of your Microsoft Dynamics CRM records directly in Outlook, without requiring you to look up their email addresses from the web client. In addition, the Microsoft Dynamics CRM address book can include email information about non-contact records, which you cannot synchronize to Outlook.

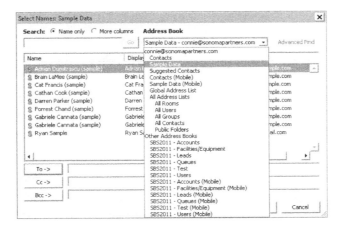

> **Tip** You can configure additional settings for the Microsoft Dynamics CRM address book in the Microsoft Dynamics CRM for Outlook options.

In this exercise, you will create an email message in Outlook, insert an email template, and track the message in Microsoft Dynamics CRM.

 SET UP Start Outlook with Microsoft Dynamics CRM for Outlook installed, if necessary, before beginning this exercise. You need the Sonoma Partners account record you created in Chapter 3. If you cannot locate the Sonoma Partners record in your system, select a different account record for this exercise.

1. On the ribbon, click the **Home** tab, and then click the **New E-Mail** button. A blank email message appears.

2. In the **To** field, enter any email address that does not already exist in your Microsoft Dynamics CRM database. (You need to use a new email address to complete steps 13 and 14 of this exercise.)

3. In the **Subject** field, enter *Test Message*.

4. On the ribbon, click the **Track** button. The CRM tracking pane will appear.

5. Click the **Set Regarding** button, and then select **More**.

   A Microsoft Dynamics CRM lookup window opens.

6. In the lookup window, click the **Look for** list to see the entities to which you can link the email message. Select **Account**.

7. In the search box, enter *Sonoma Partners*, and press the Enter key to search for the account in Microsoft Dynamics CRM. Select the appropriate account in the results, and then click **OK**.

   In the CRM tracking pane, you can see that Microsoft Dynamics CRM has updated the Regarding value to Sonoma Partners.

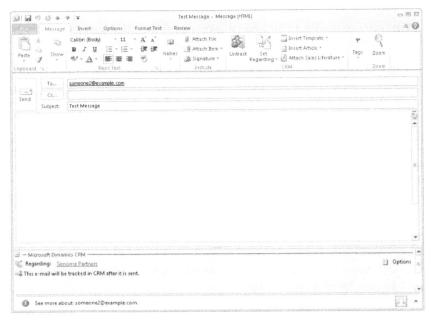

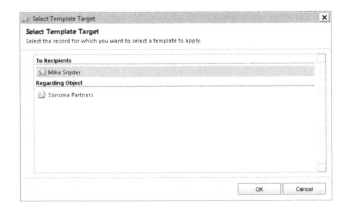

8. On the ribbon of the email message, click the **Insert Template** button, and then click **More Email Templates**.

> **Important** If your tracked email message has different types of records such as accounts, contacts, and leads, you will need to specify a template target when you insert a template, because the different record types can have different email templates available. If your email message is only regarding one type of record (like the one in this exercise), it will skip the Select Template Target dialog box.

Microsoft Dynamics CRM launches the Insert Template dialog box. This dialog box displays the global email templates plus the email templates related to the record you're sending a message to. For example, if you're sending an email message to a contact, you will see contact templates. If you're sending to a lead, you'll see lead templates. Because this email is regarding the Sonoma Partners account record, you'll see the Account templates in addition to the global templates.

9. For this exercise, click **Marketing communication unsubscribe acknowledgement**.

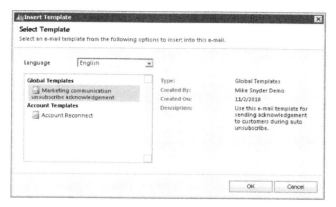

10. Click **OK**. Microsoft Dynamics CRM asks whether you want to override your existing email subject with the template subject. If you click **OK**, Microsoft Dynamics CRM will update your email subject to the subject associated with the email template. Instead, click **Cancel**, and Microsoft Dynamics CRM only inserts the selected email template into the body of your email.

11. Click the **Send** button.

12. Click the **Sent Items** link in the folder list to display a list of your sent email messages. Double-click the test email message you just sent.

Assuming that you entered an email address not already in your database, you will see in the CRM tracking pane that the sample email address is colored red. This record color indicates that Microsoft Dynamics CRM could not find a matching email address in your system.

13. To manually resolve this email message to a particular contact record, click the red email address. A menu will appear, from which you can choose to create the record as a contact or as a lead. For this exercise, click the **Create as contact** option.

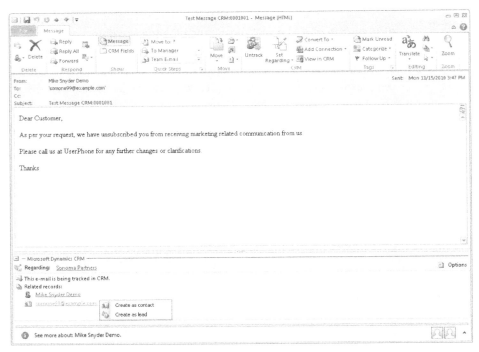

14. A blank contact form appears. Enter **Mike** as the **First Name** and **Snyder** as the **Last Name**. On the ribbon, click the **Save and Close** button. Now if you view the history of the **Mike Snyder** contact or the **Sonoma Partners** account, you can view a copy of this email message.

> **Tip** This exercise showed how to create a contact from an email message that you sent. For email messages and appointments that you receive from others, you can configure Microsoft Dynamics CRM for Outlook to automatically create records (either contacts or leads) when you click the Track button. You can access this setting by clicking the Options link in the CRM tracking pane.

Deleting Records in Microsoft Dynamics CRM for Outlook

After Microsoft Dynamics CRM for Outlook completes its initial synchronization process with your Outlook file, special rules apply to how the synchronization process handles deleted records. For example, deleting a contact record in Outlook will *not* delete that contact record in Microsoft Dynamics CRM. Conversely, deleting a contact in Microsoft Dynamics CRM removes the synchronized contact from Outlook for all users except for the Outlook user who owns the record in Microsoft Dynamics CRM.

With respect to deleted records, Microsoft Dynamics CRM for Outlook follows a set of rules and conditions to determine how the synchronization process should update Outlook and Microsoft Dynamics CRM. Microsoft Dynamics CRM for Outlook processes deleted records as outlined in the following table.

Record Type	Action	Record State	Result
Contact	Delete in Microsoft Dynamics CRM	Any	Deleted from Outlook for all users except contact owner. Remains in contact owner's Outlook file.
Contact	Delete in Outlook	Any	No change in Microsoft Dynamics CRM.
Task	Delete in Microsoft Dynamics CRM	Pending (not completed in Outlook)	Deleted from Outlook.
Task	Delete in Microsoft Dynamics CRM	Past (completed in Outlook)	Remains in Outlook.
Task	Delete in Outlook	Pending (open in Microsoft Dynamics CRM)	Deleted from Microsoft Dynamics CRM.
Task	Delete in Outlook	Past (completed or canceled in Microsoft Dynamics CRM)	No change in Microsoft Dynamics CRM.
Appointment	Delete in Microsoft Dynamics CRM	Pending (open in Microsoft Dynamics CRM)	Deleted from Outlook if appointment start time is in the future.
Appointment	Delete in Microsoft Dynamics CRM	Past (completed or canceled in Microsoft Dynamics CRM)	Remains in Outlook.
Appointment	Delete in Outlook	Pending (open in Microsoft Dynamics CRM)	Deleted from Microsoft Dynamics CRM if deleted by appointment owner or organizer. Not deleted from Microsoft Dynamics CRM if deleted in Outlook by a non-owner or non-organizer.
Appointment	Delete in Outlook	Past (completed or canceled in Microsoft Dynamics CRM)	No change in Microsoft Dynamics CRM.

If you delete a contact in Outlook (which does not delete the contact from Microsoft Dynamics CRM) and then someone subsequently modifies that contact record in Microsoft Dynamics CRM, Microsoft Dynamics CRM for Outlook will recreate that contact in the your Outlook file, even though you previously deleted it.

On a related note, deactivating contact records in Microsoft Dynamics CRM does not remove the contacts from Outlook. You must manually delete the deactivated contacts from Microsoft Dynamics CRM if you don't want them to appear in your Outlook file any longer.

In this exercise, you will delete two records to see how the synchronization process treats each scenario.

 SET UP Start Outlook with Microsoft Dynamics CRM for Outlook installed, if necessary, before beginning this exercise. Confirm that you have permission to delete contact records in Microsoft Dynamics CRM. If you are not sure, contact your system administrator. You need the Sonoma Partners account record you created in Chapter 3 and the Chris Perry and Jose Curry contact records you created earlier in this chapter. If you cannot locate these records in your system, select different records for this exercise.

1. In the Outlook navigation pane, click **Contacts**.

2. In the search box, type **Chris Perry** to locate the contact record.

 3. Select the **Chris Perry** record and, on the ribbon, click the **Delete** button.

4. Open Microsoft Dynamics CRM in Internet Explorer and navigate to the account list. Locate the **Sonoma Partners** account and double-click it to open it.

5. Click **Contacts** in the entity navigation pane.

   A list of contacts associated with the account appears. Note that even though you deleted the Chris Perry contact from Outlook, Microsoft Dynamics CRM for Outlook did not delete the record on the server.

6. Click the **Jose Curry** record and click the **Delete** button on the ribbon. In the **Contact Delete Confirmation** dialog box, click the **Delete** button, and then click **OK** in the secondary confirmation dialog box.

7. Close Internet Explorer.

8. Open Outlook. On the ribbon, click the **File** tab and then click **CRM**. Click the **Synchronize** button, and select **Synchronize** from the submenu. Microsoft Dynamics CRM runs the synchronization process.

9. In the **Contact** search box, type **Jose Curry**. Outlook displays the matching contact record. Double-click the record to open the contact.

   Note that Microsoft Dynamics CRM for Outlook did not delete the contact from your Outlook file because you are listed as the owner of this record. However, this contact record is no longer tracked in Microsoft Dynamics CRM. If you delete a contact record owned by a different user, Microsoft Dynamics CRM for Outlook will remove that record from your Outlook file.

Going Offline with Microsoft Dynamics CRM for Outlook

If you install Microsoft Dynamics CRM for Outlook with Offline Access, you have the option to work with your Microsoft Dynamics CRM data when you are disconnected from the server. This feature is useful if you need to travel onsite to customer meetings, because you can look up your existing notes, add new notes, run reports, and much more without needing an Internet connection. The concept of disconnecting from the Microsoft Dynamics CRM server is known as *going offline*. When you go offline, Microsoft Dynamics CRM for Outlook copies a subset of the Microsoft Dynamics CRM database to your computer. While offline, you can perform almost all of the Microsoft Dynamics CRM functionality just the same as when you're online. When you are able to connect to the Microsoft Dynamics CRM server again, you go online to synchronize your offline database with the main Microsoft Dynamics CRM database. When you go online, Microsoft Dynamics CRM for Outlook will automatically determine which records it should upload to the Microsoft Dynamics CRM database and which records it needs to synchronize with your local database.

Because some Microsoft Dynamics CRM databases can get quite large, going offline does not copy *all* of the data to your computer. Instead, Microsoft Dynamics CRM for Outlook uses offline synchronization filters to determine which subsets of the database it should copy to the offline database. The use of offline synchronization filters provides better performance and faster synchronization times than if you were using the entire Microsoft Dynamics CRM database. Offline synchronization filters are discussed more thoroughly in the next section.

> **Tip** You can configure Microsoft Dynamics CRM for Outlook with Offline Access to perform a background update of your local data as often as every 15 minutes. Setting up this option in the Microsoft Dynamics CRM for Outlook options will allow you to go offline more quickly in the future, in addition to allowing you to access relatively updated offline data in case you forget to explicitly go offline.

In this exercise, you will go offline, open a record while disconnected from the Microsoft Dynamics CRM server, and then go back online.

SET UP Start Outlook with Microsoft Dynamics CRM for Outlook with Offline Access installed, if necessary, before beginning this exercise. In order to complete this exercise, you need the version of Microsoft Dynamics CRM for Outlook that allows you to go offline. Contact your system administrator if you need to have a different version of Microsoft Dynamics CRM for Outlook installed.

1. On the Outlook ribbon, click the **CRM** tab, and then click the **Go Offline** button.

   A progress window opens, showing you the status of the synchronization process.

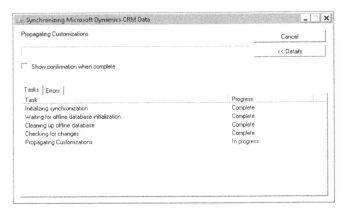

   When the process is complete, the Go Offline button will change to Go Online. This indicates that you are now working with data from the local database instead of data from the Microsoft Dynamics CRM server.

2. In the Outlook navigation pane, click the button with the name of your CRM organization, expand the **Sales** folder, and then click **Accounts**.

   You will see a list of accounts, just as if you were viewing them while connected to the Microsoft Dynamics CRM server. Depending on your offline synchronization filters, you might see only a subset of all of the Microsoft Dynamics CRM accounts.

3. To confirm that you are working offline, double-click an account record to open it. When the account record is open in Internet Explorer, press F11 on the keyboard.

   The Internet Explorer address bar appears. If you examine the web address of the account record, you will notice that it starts with *http://localhost:2525* instead of the typical web address that you use to access Microsoft Dynamics CRM. This localhost address references the offline version of Microsoft Dynamics CRM, so you know that you're working offline.

4. Click the **Go Online** button to reconnect to the Microsoft Dynamics CRM server.

Configuring Synchronization Filters

As you learned in the previous section, offline synchronization filters define which data Microsoft Dynamics CRM for Outlook with Offline Access will copy from the server to your offline database. During the installation process, Microsoft Dynamics CRM creates more than 35 different offline synchronization filters for the records in your system. If you plan to work offline frequently, you should examine these default offline synchronization filters to make sure you'll have access to the information you need when offline.

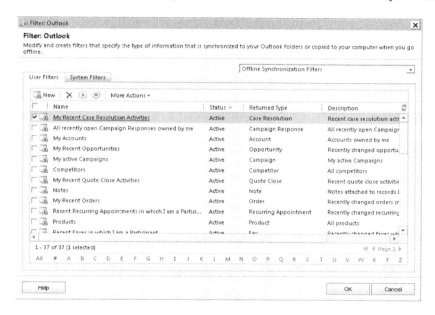

Two common modifications to the default local data groups are:

- Including all reports to run offline, because the default local data group downloads only the reports you own to the offline database.

- Including custom entities, because the default local data group does not include any custom entities.

> **Important** You can only modify your offline synchronization filter settings when you are online.

If your computer uses the online-only version of Microsoft Dynamics CRM for Outlook, your system still contains synchronization filters, but the software uses them for a different purpose. Online-only users of Microsoft Dynamics CRM for Outlook configure their Outlook synchronization filters to specify which types of records the software should copy from the server to your Outlook file. By default, Microsoft Dynamics CRM for Outlook includes Outlook synchronization filters that will copy contacts, phone calls, tasks, and other records that you own from the CRM server into your Outlook file.

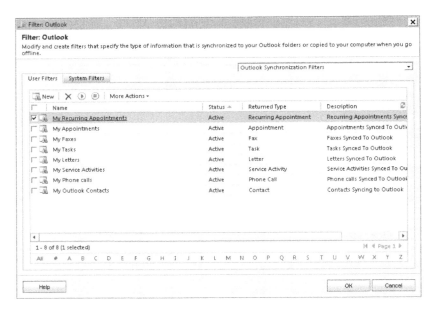

You can delete, deactivate, or modify synchronization filters, or add entirely new data groups if you want. Some users like to create synchronization filters so that Microsoft Dynamics CRM copies all of the contacts for the accounts and opportunities that they own.

In this exercise, you will modify the offline synchronization filters for Microsoft Dynamics CRM for Outlook with Offline Access to include contacts you modified in the past 30 days in your offline database.

> **Important** When you run reports offline, the reports will include only data from the offline database, which is typically a subset of the entire database. If you need to report on the entire database, make sure you go online first.

SET UP Start Outlook with Microsoft Dynamics CRM for Outlook with Offline Access installed, if necessary, before beginning this exercise.

1. On the Outlook ribbon, click the **File** tab, and then click **CRM**.

2. Click the **Synchronize** button, and then click the **Outlook Filters** option that appears on the submenu. The Outlook Filter dialog box appears.

3. In the picklist, select **Offline Synchronization Filters**.

4. In the grid toolbar, click the **New** button. The New Filter dialog box appears.

5. In the **Look For** picklist, select **Contact**.

6. Click the **Select** link, and choose **Modified By**.

7. Click the **Select** link again, click **Modified On**, and then click **On**. In the new pick-list that appears, choose the **Last X Days** option.

8. In the text field that appears, enter **30**.

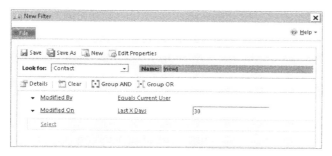

9. In the toolbar, click the **Save** button. A dialog box will appear, prompting you to name this filter. Type ***Contacts modified by current user in the last 30 days***. Then click the **OK** button.

10. Click the **Close** button in the upper-right corner to close the window.

11. Click **OK** to close the **Outlook Filter** window.

12. On the ribbon, click the **Go Offline** button. Microsoft Dynamics CRM will run with offline synchronization with this new filter in place. If you have modified contacts you don't own in the last 30 days, you will see those contacts downloading in the progress window.

CLEAN UP Go back online when you have finished this exercise.

Key Points

- Microsoft Dynamics CRM for Outlook provides integration between Outlook and Microsoft Dynamics CRM.

- Microsoft Dynamics CRM for Outlook is available in two versions: one for online use only, and one with offline access so that you can work while disconnected from the server.

- Microsoft Dynamics CRM for Outlook performs a bi-directional synchronization of tracked contacts, tasks, and appointments between Outlook and the Microsoft Dynamics CRM server.

- You can use the Add Contacts wizard to import contacts that already exist in Outlook into Microsoft Dynamics CRM. The wizard also gives you the option to automatically create new accounts and activities during the process. You can also link imported contacts to existing Microsoft Dynamics CRM accounts by using the Advanced option.

- To create contacts, tasks, and appointments in Outlook that will appear in the Microsoft Dynamics CRM database, simply click the Track button on the ribbon.

- You can create and reply to email messages in Outlook and track those communications to the appropriate Microsoft Dynamics CRM records by clicking the Track button.

- Synchronized records follow a unique set of processing rules regarding deletion, depending on their ownership, status, and other variables.

- Microsoft Dynamics CRM for Outlook with Offline Access allows users to copy data to a local database and work offline.

- Synchronization filters define which records are synchronized to your Outlook file. In offline mode, you can configure any record type that you want to access while offline. For online-only use, Outlook synchronization filters define the records that are synchronized to your Outlook file.

- You can create new synchronization filters or modify synchronization filters according to your needs.

Part 2

Sales and Marketing

6 Working with Leads and Opportunities. 129

7 Using Marketing Lists 151

8 Managing Campaigns and Quick Campaigns 177

9 Working with Campaign Activities
   and Responses 195

Chapter at a Glance

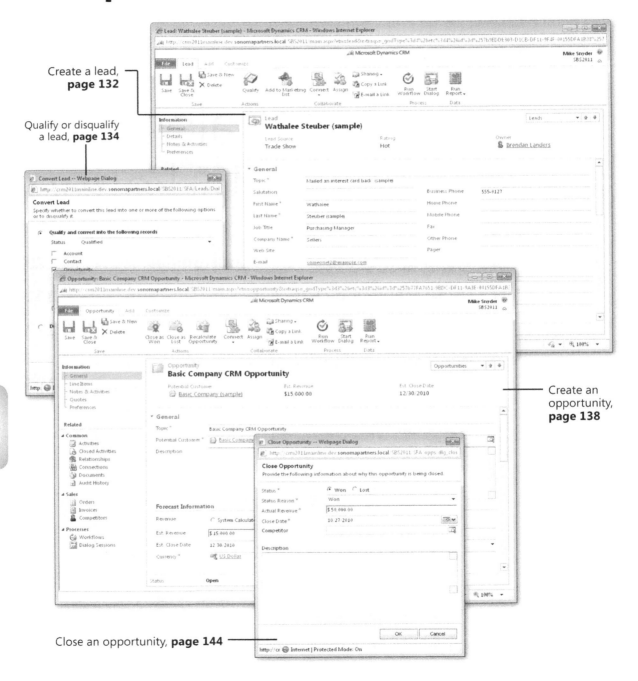

Create a lead, **page 132**

Qualify or disqualify a lead, **page 134**

Create an opportunity, **page 138**

Close an opportunity, **page 144**

6 Working with Leads and Opportunities

In this chapter, you will learn how to

- ✔ Understand the difference between leads and opportunities.
- ✔ Create a lead and track lead sources.
- ✔ Qualify a lead.
- ✔ Disqualify a lead.
- ✔ Create an opportunity.
- ✔ Use opportunities to forecast potential sales.
- ✔ Close an opportunity.
- ✔ Reopen an opportunity.
- ✔ Convert an email activity to a lead.

By now, you should understand many of the basics of Microsoft Dynamics CRM and how to navigate within the software. Microsoft Dynamics CRM includes three main modules: Sales, Marketing, and Service. This chapter will take a deeper look at some of the sales management capabilities in the software. As you would expect, the sales portion of Microsoft Dynamics CRM helps organizations track and manage revenue-generating activities such as lead management, opportunity forecasting, and quotes.

In this chapter, you will learn how to work with leads and opportunities in Microsoft Dynamics CRM so that you can manage your organization's sales data more efficiently.

> **Practice Files** The exercises in this chapter require only records created in earlier chapters; none are supplied with the book's practice files. For more information about practice files, see "Using the Practice Files" at the beginning of this book.

> **Important** The images used in this book reflect the default form and field names in Microsoft Dynamics CRM. Because the software offers extensive customization capabilities, it's possible that some of the record types or fields have been relabeled in your Microsoft Dynamics CRM environment. If you cannot find the forms, fields, or security roles referred to in this book, contact your system administrator for assistance.

> **Important** You must know the location of your Microsoft Dynamics CRM website to work the exercises in this book. Check with your system administrator to verify the web address if you don't know it.

Understanding Leads and Opportunities

Many CRM software systems use the terms *lead* and *opportunity* to describe different types of sales records, but sometimes these expressions can cause confusion for new users. Leads represent prospective customers that your sales representatives need to qualify or disqualify. Depending on your organization's sales and marketing processes, leads can come from many different sources—website requests, purchased lists, trade shows, or incoming phone calls, for example. Many organizations try to qualify or disqualify lead records as quickly as possible to determine whether they represent potential customers. Because lead records are not intended to be used for the long term, leads use a flat data structure in which the data about an individual and his or her company resides in a single record.

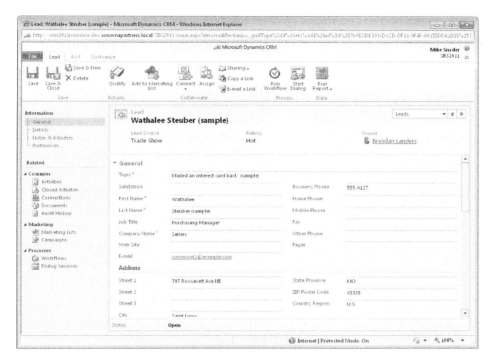

Each organization defines its own lead qualification criteria, but typical qualifying questions asked by businesses include:

- Is the lead located in a geographic region that we sell to?
- Does the lead fit the financial profile of customers that we sell to?
- Does the lead have a need or desire for our products or services?

If you determine that the lead meets your sales criteria, you convert the lead to one or more different types of records in Microsoft Dynamics CRM.

- Account
- Contact
- Opportunity

As you learned in Chapter 3, "Working with Accounts and Contacts," accounts represent businesses, and contacts represent people. By using accounts and contacts instead of leads to track prospects and customers, you can model additional relationships within Microsoft Dynamics CRM to capture the various people in each account.

Opportunities represent potential revenue-generating events for your organization. Most organizations track data about a potential sales opportunity, such as estimated close date, estimated revenue, sales representative, and sales stage. You link each opportunity to an account or a contact, depending on how you want to track the potential customer. Because a single customer might purchase multiple products or services from your organization, a single customer record can be linked to multiple opportunities. Each potential sale can have its own data about the sales opportunity, and you can even have different sales representatives pursuing different opportunities for the same contact or account record. Likewise, as you work with repeat customers over an extended period of time, you continue to create multiple opportunities to represent new sales opportunities while preserving the historical opportunity data.

> **Tip** Use leads to track prospects that need to be qualified or disqualified. Use opportunities to track potential sales to qualified prospects or existing customers. Not every organization uses leads. For example, businesses and organizations that sell their products and services to a small, defined customer base might not use lead records at all in Microsoft Dynamics CRM.

Creating a Lead and Tracking Lead Sources

Leads come from many different sources, depending on your sales and marketing processes. Your corporate website might generate leads automatically, or marketing personnel might import leads into Microsoft Dynamics CRM with a batch process. However, you can also manually create lead records. When working with a lead, you can use Microsoft Dynamics CRM activities such as tasks, phone calls, and email messages to track your inter-actions with the lead during the qualification process. The type of data that you capture about each lead depends on your business needs and any customizations your system includes, but most organizations track the person's name and address information.

> **See Also** If you need to create many leads at the same time by importing a data file, refer to Chapter 18, "Bulk Data Importing," for more details on that process.

Many organizations also want to capture the marketing source from which the lead origi-
nated. If your organization captures the *lead source* for each record, sales and marketing
managers can run reports to determine which lead-generation tactics are most effective.
For example, you might find that a lead source such as the trade show circuit generates a
large number of leads, but only a small percentage of them qualify as potential customers.
Meanwhile, another marketing tactic such as a website might generate a smaller number
of leads, but a high percentage of them qualify as potential customers. Understanding the
source of your leads will help your company make better decisions on where to invest in
future sales and marketing efforts.

In this exercise, you will create a lead to track a new prospect who found out about your
organization from a website.

SET UP Use the Windows Internet Explorer web browser to navigate to your
Microsoft Dynamics CRM website before beginning this exercise.

1. In the application area, click **Sales**.

2. In the application area, click the arrow on the **Leads** link, and then click **New** on the
   submenu that appears.

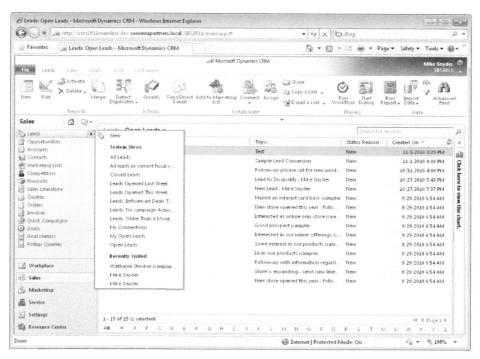

3. The **New Lead** form launches. In the **Topic** field, enter *New Lead – Mike Snyder*.

4. In the **First Name** field, enter *Mike*.

5. In the **Last Name** field, enter *Snyder*.

6. In the **Company Name** field, enter *Sonoma Partners*.

7. Scroll down the form to the **Details** group. In the **Lead Information** section, click the arrow in the **Lead Source** list. Select **Web**.

8. On the ribbon, click the **Save and Close** button.

> **Tip** Your system administrator can customize the list values for the Lead Source field, in addition to all of the other lead fields.

Qualifying a Lead

Leads represent potential customers that can be qualified or disqualified based on criteria set by your organization. After you work with a lead record and determine whether or not the potential customer fits your lead qualification criteria, you *convert the lead*. When you convert the lead, you specify whether or not the lead is qualified or disqualified.

When you qualify the lead, you create one or more of the following record types: Account, Contact, or Opportunity.

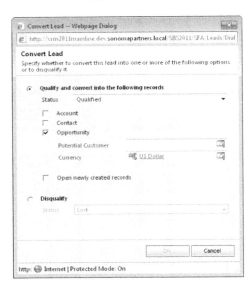

Your business process should dictate which of the records to create. For example, if your organization sells to businesses, you will probably want to create both an account and a contact. If your organization sells to individual consumers, you might not want to create an account. Likewise, you might not always create an opportunity when you qualify a lead. You might determine that a lead fits your qualification criteria but that an immediate sales opportunity does not exist.

In addition to creating a new opportunity, account, and contact all linked together, you can also convert a lead to a new opportunity that will be linked to an existing customer record in Microsoft Dynamics CRM. You might want to do this if a matching account or contact already exists in your Microsoft Dynamics CRM database.

When you qualify a lead, you can select a check box to open the newly created records, which will open the new account, contact, or opportunity records created during the lead conversion process so that you can work with them right away, saving yourself a few clicks.

> **Tip** Microsoft Dynamics CRM will populate data fields in the account, contact, and opportunity records you create from a qualified lead, based on the mapped data fields.

In this exercise, you will convert a lead as qualified and create a new account, contact, and opportunity.

 SET UP Use the Internet Explorer web browser to navigate to your Microsoft Dynamics CRM website, if necessary, before beginning this exercise. You need the Mike Snyder lead you created in the previous exercise.

1. Open the **Mike Snyder** lead you created in the previous exercise.

2. On the ribbon, click the **Qualify** button. A new dialog box opens.

3. Select the check boxes next to **Account**, **Contact**, and **Opportunity**.

4. Select the **Open newly created records** check box.

5. Click **OK**.

   Microsoft Dynamics CRM closes out the lead and creates three new records in new windows.

Disqualifying a Lead

Not every lead will meet your qualification criteria, so you will need to disqualify leads from time to time. Disqualifying a lead does not delete the record from your system. Instead, it deactivates the lead to indicate that no one needs to follow up with it. Likewise, converting a lead as qualified does not delete the record; it deactivates the lead record and creates an Account, Contact, or Opportunity record for further follow-up.

> **Tip** Converting a lead to Qualified or Disqualified status does not delete the lead record; rather, it deactivates the record so that it no longer appears in anyone's active leads list.

When you disqualify a lead, you can select a reason to indicate why you decided to disqualify the record. Again, your administrator can customize the disqualification reasons, but the default values include Lost, Cannot Contact, No Longer Interested, and Canceled.

Just as recording a lead source provides valuable sales and marketing data, recording a disqualification reason also provides data that you can analyze to optimize your sales and marketing processes. Cross-referencing the lead source data with the disqualification data can provide valuable insights. For example, you could discover that your sales team disqualified 50 percent of the leads from a purchased list because of invalid contact information. Sales and marketing managers can use this information to make educated purchases of future lists, or perhaps stop purchasing lists altogether. To obtain this kind of insight, each sales representative must accurately record the disqualification reasons.

In this exercise, you will create a lead and disqualify it.

SET UP Use the Internet Explorer web browser to navigate to your Microsoft Dynamics CRM website, if necessary, before beginning this exercise.

1. In the application area, click **Sales**.

2. In the application navigation pane, click the arrow on the **Leads** link, and then click **New** on the submenu that appears. A blank lead record opens.

3. In the **Topic** field, enter *Lead to Disqualify – Mike Snyder*.

4. In the **First Name** field, enter *Mike*.

5. In the **Last Name** field, enter *Snyder*.

6. In the **Company Name** field, enter *Sonoma Partners*.

7. Scroll down the form to the **Details** group. In the **Lead Information** section, click the arrow in the **Lead Source** list. Select **Web**.

8. On the ribbon, click the **Save** button.

9. On the ribbon, click the **Qualify** button to open the **Convert Lead** dialog box.

10. Select **Disqualify**.

11. Click the arrow in the **Status** list, and select **Cannot Contact**.

12. Click **OK** to update the lead's status to Disqualified and mark it inactive.

Creating an Opportunity

Opportunities represent potential sales, and many organizations carefully monitor their opportunity data to help them:

- Understand the sales pipeline.
- Evaluate the performance of individual sales representatives.
- Forecast future demand.

When you work with an opportunity, you can track all of the activities related to the potential sale, such as tasks, phone calls, and email messages.

By default, you can track the potential customer's name, estimated close date, estimated revenue, probability, and rating for each sales opportunity. Many organizations customize the opportunity form to track additional data about the potential sale, depending on the products and services they provide.

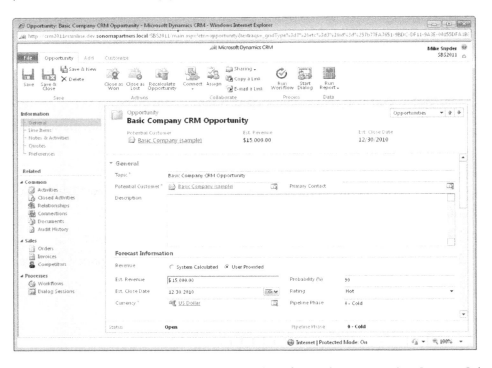

You can choose between two revenue settings for each opportunity: System Calculated and User Provided. If you select System Calculated, Microsoft Dynamics CRM will automatically calculate the estimated value of the opportunity by using a combination of the products attached to the opportunity and the selected price list. If you select User Provided, you can enter the dollar amount of the opportunity value directly into the

Est. Revenue field. Setting up products and price lists in Microsoft Dynamics CRM requires system administrator privileges, so the exercises in this chapter will utilize the User Provided option for revenue.

> **See Also** Your system administrator can enable and configure the product catalog in your deployment. Refer to the Microsoft Dynamics CRM online help for additional information on the specific configuration steps.

For the Est. Close Date field, enter the date when you expect to close the opportunity, either as a win or as a loss. The Probability field allows you to enter a percentage to indicate your confidence that you will win the opportunity. You can enter a whole number from 0 to 100 in the Probability field. For example, entering 50 in this field means that you're 50 percent confident that you will win the opportunity. Rating is another measure of the opportunity. The default values are Hot, Warm, and Cold. Some organizations use the Rating field to indicate their perception of the customer's interest, and other organizations use Rating to record how interested they themselves are in pursuing the opportunity.

> **Tip** Many organizations use the Microsoft Dynamics CRM workflow feature to automate the Probability and Rating values based on their unique business rules. Creating and designing workflow rules is beyond the scope of this book, but you can learn more about it in Working with Microsoft Dynamics CRM 2011, by Mike Snyder and Jim Steger (Microsoft Press, 2011).

Earlier in this chapter, you learned how to create an opportunity record by converting a lead. You will also want to create opportunities for existing accounts and contacts, so you also need to know how to create opportunities outside of the lead qualification process.

In this exercise, you will create an opportunity for the Sonoma Partners account record created in a previous chapter.

 SET UP Use the Internet Explorer web browser to navigate to your Microsoft Dynamics CRM website, if necessary, before beginning this exercise. You need the Sonoma Partners account record you created in Chapter 3. If you cannot locate the Sonoma Partners record in your system, you can use any account for this exercise.

1. Navigate to the **Accounts** view and open the **Sonoma Partners** account record.

2. In the entity navigation pane, click **Opportunities**.

3. On the ribbon, click the **Add New Opportunity** button. A blank opportunity record opens.

4. In the **Topic** field, enter *Sonoma Partners Sample Opportunity*.

5. For the **Revenue** data field, select **User Provided**. The Est. Revenue field becomes editable.

6. In the **Est. Revenue** field, enter *50,000.00*.

7. In the **Est. Close Date** field, enter *12/31/2011*.

8. In the **Probability** field, enter *50*.

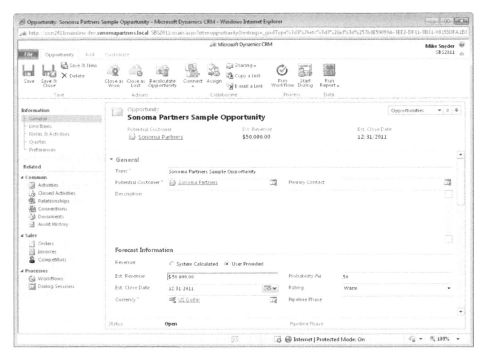

9. On the ribbon, click the **Save** button.

Using Opportunities to Forecast Potential Sales

One of the main reasons that organizations track opportunities in Microsoft Dynamics CRM is to allow managers and executives to forecast upcoming and future business. As you saw in the previous section, you can record the potential customer's name, the products or services they're interested in purchasing, the estimated close date, estimated revenue, and probability for each opportunity. By using these data points, sales managers can review the open opportunities to ensure that orders can be fulfilled and understand which sales representatives are generating new sales pipelines.

> **Tip** To record the sales representative pursuing the opportunity, assign the sales representative as the owner of the opportunity record.

Microsoft Dynamics CRM includes several system views for opportunities, including:

- Opportunities closing next month.
- Opportunities opened last week.
- Opportunities opened this week.

You can use the Advanced Find tool to modify these views, or you can create new views to analyze your opportunity information. Refer to Chapter 16, "Using Advanced Find," for more information about creating new views.

In addition to opportunity views, Microsoft Dynamics CRM provides additional reports, charts, and dashboards that you can use to analyze your sales information, such as the following:

- The Sales Activity dashboard
- The Sales Performance dashboard
- The Top Customers chart
- The Sales Leaderboard chart
- The Deals Won vs. Deals Lost chart
- The Sales Pipeline report
- The Lead Source Effectiveness report
- The Competitor Win Loss report

If none of these reports or analysis tools meet your needs, you can create new reports, charts, and dashboards yourself. Refer to Chapter 13, "Working with Filters and Charts," for more information on charting capabilities; and refer to Chapter 14, "Using Dashboards," for information on how you can set up and create your own dashboards. Refer to Chapter 15, "Using the Report Wizard," for information about creating reports by using this feature.

Lastly, you can perform ad hoc opportunity reporting and forecasting by exporting your opportunity data into Microsoft Excel. Chapter 17, "Reporting with Excel," explains how to create reports and perform analyses by using static and dynamic Excel worksheets.

In this exercise, you will open the Sales Activity dashboard and then view the Sales Pipeline chart.

 SET UP Use the Internet Explorer web browser to navigate to your Microsoft Dynamics CRM website, if necessary, before beginning this exercise. Your reports will appear different than the images in this exercise, because your Microsoft Dynamics CRM database contains different opportunities.

1. In the application area, click **Workplace**.

2. Under **My Work** in the application area, click **Dashboards**.

3. Click the arrow in the view selector and select **Sales Activity Dashboard**. The dashboard will update to show various charts and lists related to sales activity at your organization.

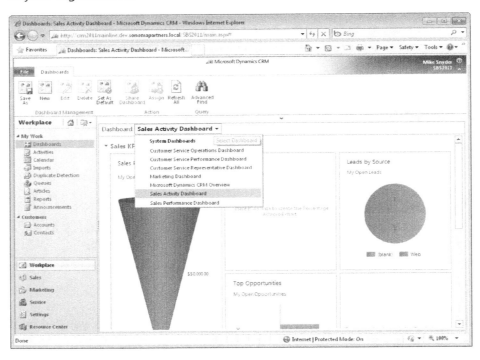

4. In the application area, click **Sales**, and then click **Opportunities**.

5. If the chart is not already displayed, click the arrow at the top of the chart section to display the chart.

6. Click the chart name to view a list of available charts, and select **Sales Pipeline**.

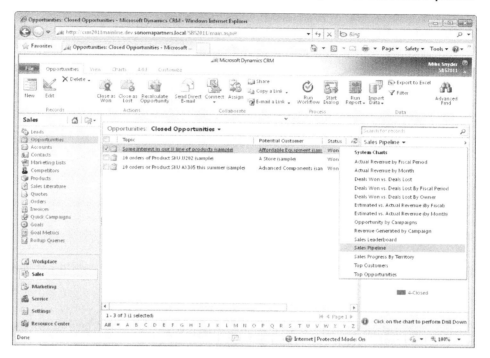

Microsoft Dynamics CRM displays the sales pipeline chart. Note that the data displayed in the chart varies depending on the selected view in the Opportunity grid.

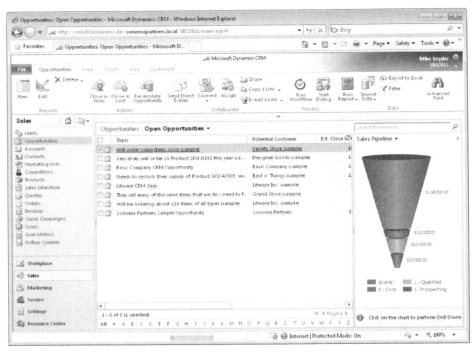

7. To update the chart, click the view name and select a different view, such as **My Open Opportunities**.

> **See Also** Refer to Chapter 13 for more information about how to use charts for more detailed analysis and reporting.

Closing an Opportunity

After you work with a prospect or customer to determine whether he or she wants to purchase from your organization, you close the opportunity record to indicate what the customer decided. Closing an opportunity does not delete the record; Microsoft Dynamics CRM just deactivates the record and updates its status so that it no longer appears in the active opportunities list. A *won* opportunity is one in which the customer decided to purchase from you, and a *lost* opportunity is one in which there was no purchase.

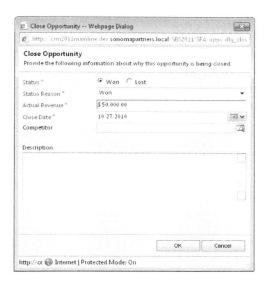

A lost opportunity does not necessarily mean that the customer purchased from someone else. You might close the opportunity as lost if the customer canceled the purchase decision or put it on indefinite hold. As with lead disqualification, your administrator can customize the reasons for marking an opportunity as lost so that you can report this type of data. Furthermore, if you lost the opportunity to a competitor, you can record which competitor you lost to for reporting and analysis.

> **Tip** As with all records in Microsoft Dynamics CRM, the software automatically logs date and time stamps for changes to the opportunity record. If you ever need to find out when someone closed an opportunity, you can access this information by navigating to the audit history located in the entity navigation pane and then filtering on the Status field.

In this exercise, you will close an opportunity as won.

SET UP Use the Internet Explorer web browser to navigate to your Microsoft Dynamics CRM website, if necessary, before beginning this exercise. You need the Sonoma Partners Sample Opportunity record you created earlier in this chapter. You can also perform this exercise with any other open opportunity record in your system.

1. Open the **Sonoma Partners Sample Opportunity** record.

2. On the ribbon, click the **Close as Won** button.

   The Close Opportunity dialog box appears, with a default status value of Won. Microsoft Dynamics CRM automatically populates the Actual Revenue field with the value from the Est. Revenue field from the opportunity. It also uses today's date as the close date by default.

3. Click **OK**. Microsoft Dynamics CRM closes the opportunity and updates its status as Won.

> **Tip** To close an opportunity as lost, you would follow a similar procedure but would start the process by clicking the Close As Lost button on the ribbon.

Reopening an Opportunity

The previous section mentioned that you could close an opportunity as lost if the customer delays the purchase decision. If you later find out that the customer would like to reopen discussions about the potential sale, you do not need to create a new opportunity record. Instead, you can *reopen* the closed opportunity and use that record to continue tracking the sale. When you reopen a closed opportunity, you can access all of the previously created activity history and notes attached to the opportunity.

In this exercise, you will reopen a closed opportunity.

SET UP Use the Internet Explorer web browser to navigate to your Microsoft Dynamics CRM website, if necessary, before beginning this exercise. You need the Sonoma Partners Sample Opportunity record you closed in the previous exercise.

1. Navigate to the **Opportunities** view.

2. Click the **View** list and select **Closed Opportunities**.

3. Find the **Sonoma Partners Sample Opportunity** record and double-click it to open the record.

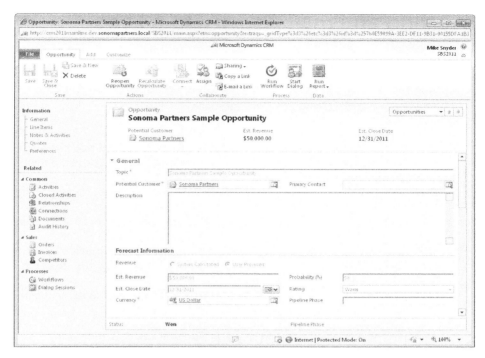

Notice that all of the fields in the opportunity are unavailable; you cannot edit any of the values.

4. On the ribbon, click the **Reopen Opportunity** button.

Microsoft Dynamics CRM prompts you with a dialog box to confirm that you want to reopen the opportunity.

5. Click **OK**.

Microsoft Dynamics CRM reopens the opportunity record so that you can edit its data fields and continue working with the record.

Converting an Email Activity to a Lead

Earlier in this chapter, you learned how to manually create a new lead. Another technique that you can use to create a new lead is to convert an email activity into a lead. You might want to do this if you receive an email message from a prospect that isn't currently recorded in your Microsoft Dynamics CRM database.

> **Tip** In addition to converting an email activity into a lead, you can also convert an email activity into an opportunity or a case by using the Convert Activity button on the email record.

In this exercise, you will create an email activity and convert it into a lead.

 SET UP Use the Internet Explorer web browser to navigate to your Microsoft Dynamics CRM website, if necessary, before beginning this exercise.

1. On the ribbon, click the **File** tab. Then click **New Activity** and select **E-mail** to launch a blank email form.

2. In the **E-Mail Subject** field, enter *Sample Lead Conversion*.

3. On the ribbon, click the **Save** button.

4. On the ribbon, click the **Convert E-mail to Lead** button.

   The Convert E-Mail To Lead dialog box appears. You use this dialog box to enter information about the lead, such as name, email address, and company. If you want, you can also select the check boxes to open the new lead and close the email form. Leave the default values selected.

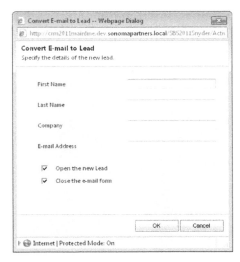

5. In the **First Name** field, enter *Jim*.

6. In the **Last Name** field, enter *Steger*.

7. In the **Company** field, enter *Sonoma Partners*.

8. In the **E-mail Address** field, enter *someone@example.com*.

9. Click **OK**.

   Microsoft Dynamics CRM closes the email record and creates a new lead with the values you entered.

> **Tip** This exercise showed how to convert an email to a lead by using the web client. Microsoft Dynamics CRM for Outlook also allows you to convert a Microsoft Outlook email into a lead, case, or opportunity. You can access these features from the Convert To button on the ribbon of a tracked email message.

Key Points

- Leads represent potential customers that sales representatives need to qualify or disqualify. Opportunities represent revenue-generating events such as potential sales linked to qualified prospects or existing customers.

- You can track activities such as tasks, phone calls, email messages, and appointments related to leads and opportunities.

- You convert leads to mark them as qualified or disqualified.

- When you qualify a lead, you can choose to create Account, Contact, and Opportunity records that Microsoft Dynamics CRM will populate with data from the Lead record.

- When you disqualify a lead, you can choose a reason for the disqualification, which will allow you to perform reporting and analysis in the future.

- An opportunity includes data about the potential sale such as sales representative, estimated close date, probability, and estimated revenue.

- Microsoft Dynamics CRM includes multiple sales reporting tools such as dashboards, charts, views, out-of-the-box reports, and the ability to export to Excel.

- You close an opportunity as won or lost to indicate whether or not the customer decided to purchase your products or services.

- You can reopen an opportunity after closing it.

- You can convert email activity records to create new leads, cases, and opportunities.

Chapter at a Glance

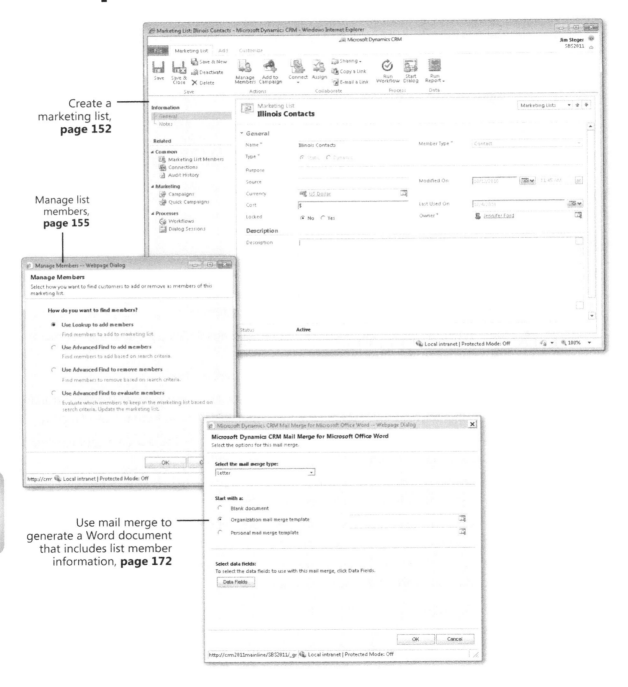

Create a marketing list, **page 152**

Manage list members, **page 155**

Use mail merge to generate a Word document that includes list member information, **page 172**

7 Using Marketing Lists

In this chapter, you will learn how to

- ✔ Create a static marketing list.
- ✔ Add members to a list by using a lookup.
- ✔ Add members to a list by using Advanced Find.
- ✔ Remove members from a list by using Advanced Find.
- ✔ Evaluate members included in a list by using Advanced Find.
- ✔ Remove selected members from a list individually.
- ✔ Create a dynamic marketing list.
- ✔ Copy members to another marketing list.
- ✔ Create opportunities from list members.
- ✔ Use mail merge to generate a Word document that includes list member information.

Organizations rely on effective communication with their customers and prospects. Marketing is often described as a process by which an organization creates the communication and mechanisms to convince customers to purchase its products or services. Marketing typically uses numerous communication channels—direct mail, email, seminars, on-site visits, outreach programs, and phone calls, for example—to communicate with customers and prospects. Firms use lists of customers and prospects to articulate the benefits of their products and services to their target audience. For example, a company might send an email to all prospects within a city about an exciting promotion occurring at a local store. Or a firm might send a renewal notice to all customers whose contracts expire in the next 30 days.

Marketing professionals can use Microsoft Dynamics CRM to execute marketing strategies and segment customer lists. Marketing lists are groups of accounts, contacts, and leads that can be used in marketing campaigns and for various other business purposes. For example, a sales representative can create a marketing list of her new accounts to quickly send proposal letters and create new sales opportunities in Microsoft Dynamics CRM.

In this chapter, you will learn how to use Microsoft Dynamics CRM to create both a static and a dynamic marketing list, manage list members, and create a mail merge document that includes marketing list member data.

> **Practice Files** There are no practice files for this chapter.

> **Important** The images used in this book reflect the default form and field names in Microsoft Dynamics CRM. Because the software offers extensive customization capabilities, it's possible that some of the record types or fields have been relabeled in your Microsoft Dynamics CRM environment. If you cannot find the forms, fields, or security roles referred to in this book, contact your system administrator for assistance.

> **Important** You must know the location of your Microsoft Dynamics CRM website to work the exercises in this book. Check with your system administrator to verify the web address if you don't know it.

Creating a Static Marketing List

The true value of a customer relationship management system lies in the quality of its data. Marketing lists provide a convenient mechanism for grouping account, contact, and lead records. Before you add members to a list, you must first define the list itself. By default, Microsoft Dynamics CRM requires you to enter a name for the list, choose a marketing list type, and choose a member type. The marketing list type will either be Static or Dynamic. The member type must be either Account, Contact, or Lead; each list can have only one member type. Additional information can be captured, such as the source, cost, and purpose of the list. You can also configure custom attributes to further define your list.

> **See Also** Microsoft Dynamics CRM provides the ability to import marketing lists, allowing you to quickly create multiple marketing lists by using a simple import wizard. Although you can import using the wizard, you will still need to add members by using the techniques described in this chapter. For more information on importing data into Microsoft Dynamics CRM, see Chapter 18, "Bulk Data Importing."

In this exercise, you will create a static marketing list of customer contacts who reside in the state of Illinois.

 SET UP Use the Windows Internet Explorer web browser to navigate to your Microsoft Dynamics CRM website before beginning this exercise. You need a user account that has the Marketing Manager security role or another role with privileges to create marketing lists.

 1. In the **Marketing** area, click **Marketing Lists**.

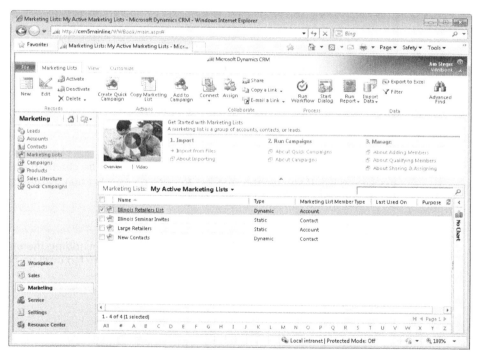

 2. Click the **New** button to open the Marketing List form.

3. In the **Name** field, enter ***Illinois Contacts***. In the **Member Type** field, choose **Contact**. Leave the **Type** field as **Static**.

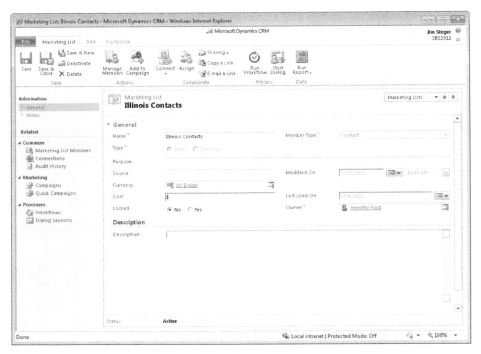

> **Troubleshooting** The type and member type cannot be changed after you save the marketing list. If you want to market to both prospects and customers, you should create multiple marketing lists.

> **Important** The Locked attribute prevents anyone from adding members to or removing them from your list. Leave this attribute set to No until you have added the members you want to your list.

4. Click the **Save and Close** button.

Adding Members to a List by Using a Lookup

The primary purpose of a marketing list is to associate multiple list members for use in one or more marketing campaigns. For example, you might want to have a list that contains all prospects you plan to invite to a seminar and another that contains all preferred customers. After you have saved a marketing list, you need to add list members to it. Microsoft Dynamics CRM provides a few ways to add members to a marketing list. You can add members individually or use Microsoft Dynamics CRM's Advanced Find feature to add multiple list members who share a common interest or attribute.

Adding members individually by using a lookup is the most straightforward approach to adding members to a list. Because you specifically select each member, you retain the greatest level of control over your list. Furthermore, using a lookup allows you to create a list of records that do not share common data, which is not the case with Advanced Find. For instance, imagine you have a pre-existing group of registrants for an upcoming seminar. You can create a new marketing list to track all the confirmed registrants. After a customer confirms his or her registration for the event, you can manually select the registrant's contact record and add it as a member to your seminar's confirmation list.

In this exercise, you will add members to an existing marketing list one at a time by using the standard lookup approach.

 SET UP Use the Internet Explorer web browser to navigate to your Microsoft Dynamics CRM website, if necessary, before beginning this exercise. You need a user account that has the Marketing Manager security role or another role with privileges to add members to a marketing list.

1. In the **Marketing** area, click **Marketing Lists**.

2. Double-click the **Illinois Contacts** marketing list created in the previous section.

3. In the entity navigation pane, click **Marketing List Members** to add members to the list.

Manage
Members

4. Click the **Manage Members** button to launch the **Manage Members** dialog box.

> **Tip** If you do not see the Manage Members button, check to make sure that you have not locked the list. Locking a marketing list prevents any members from being added or removed.

5. In the **Manage Members** dialog box, click **Use Lookup to add members**.

6. Click **OK** to close the **Manage Members** dialog box.

The Look Up Records dialog box opens.

7. In the **Look Up Records** dialog box, the **Look for** field is automatically set to the member type specified for the marketing list. Select one or more records and click **Add** to add them to the **Selected records** list.

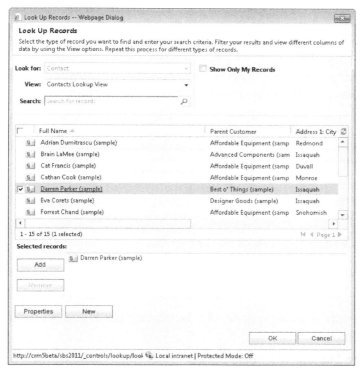

8. When you have finished selecting the records you want to add, click **OK**. The records will be added to the marketing list, and the **Look Up Records** dialog box will close.

Adding Members to a List by Using Advanced Find

Most lists members have something that relates them to the other members in the list—for example, a list might contain only those contacts who reside in the state of Illinois or all accounts with a preferred customer status. The Advanced Find feature allows you to easily search for records that share a specified attribute and add either all of them or a selected set from the query results as members to your marketing list.

> **See Also** For more information on searching for data with the Advanced Find feature, see Chapter 16, "Using Advanced Find."

In this exercise, you will add all active contacts with an Illinois address as members to the Illinois Contacts marketing list created in the previous section.

> **Tip** Microsoft Dynamics CRM will not add duplicate members to a list. If your query results contain a record that already exists in the marketing list, Microsoft Dynamics CRM will ignore the duplicate record.

SET UP Use the Internet Explorer web browser to navigate to your Microsoft Dynamics CRM website, if necessary, before beginning this exercise. You need a user account that has the Marketing Manager security role or another role with privileges to add members to a marketing list.

1. In the **Marketing** area, click **Marketing Lists**.

2. Double-click the **Illinois Contacts** marketing list created earlier in this chapter.

3. In the entity navigation pane, click **Marketing List Members** to view the members of the list.

4. Click the **Manage Members** button to launch the **Manage Members** dialog box.

5. In the **Manage Members** dialog box, click **Use Advanced Find to add members**.

6. Click **OK**. In the **Add Members** dialog box, set your query to find contacts as shown in the following screen shot.

> **Important** If your organization typically enters the full state name instead of an abbreviation or does not have any contact records with an IL address, enter a different state or other criterion instead to ensure that results are returned in your search.

> **Tip** Save your Advanced Find query to quickly add additional member records in the future.

7. Click **Find**. Verify that at least one contact is returned in the results. Then, below the results view, click **Add all the members returned by the search to the marketing list**.

8. Click **Add to Marketing List** to add all of the contacts returned by the search to the marketing list.

Removing Members from a List by Using Advanced Find

Members added to a marketing list will remain on the list until you manually remove them. As when you add members to a list, you can remove members individually or use the Advanced Find feature to remove a group of members. Using an Advanced Find query allows you to quickly remove multiple members based on common selection criteria.

In this exercise, you will use an Advanced Find query to remove contacts that do not have a city populated from your Illinois Contacts marketing list.

> **Important** This action only removes records from the list. It does not delete the actual records. To undo this change, you will need to re-add the members to your list.

 SET UP Use the Internet Explorer web browser to navigate to your Microsoft Dynamics CRM website, if necessary, before beginning this exercise. You need a user account that has the Marketing Manager security role or another role with privileges to manage marketing lists.

1. In the **Marketing** area, click **Marketing Lists**.
2. Double-click the **Illinois Contacts** marketing list created earlier in this chapter.
3. In the entity navigation pane, click **Marketing List Members**.
4. Click the **Manage Members** button to launch the **Manage Members** dialog box.
5. Click **Use Advanced Find to remove members**.
6. Click **OK**. In the **Remove Members** dialog box, create a query that checks to see whether the **Address1:City** field does not contain data.

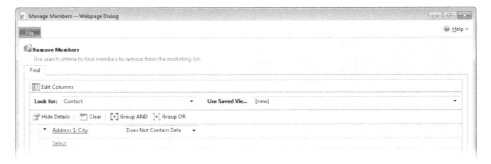

7. Click **Find** to execute the search.

> **Important** If your list does not return any contacts, use different search criteria to ensure that your query returns at least one contact record in the results. If no records are returned and you click the Remove From Marketing List button, you will receive an error.

8. Verify that at least one contact is returned in the results. Then, below the results view, click **Remove all the members returned by the search from the marketing list**.

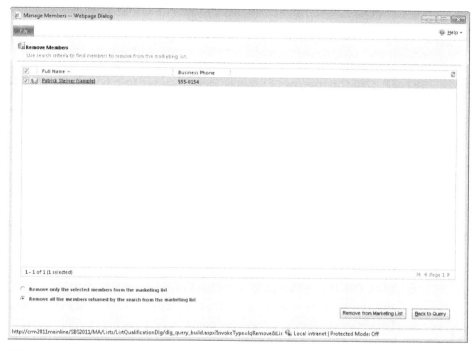

9. Click **Remove from Marketing List** to remove all of the contacts returned by the search from the marketing list.

Evaluating Members Included in a List by Using Advanced Find

Just as you can add and remove multiple members to and from a list by using an Advanced Find query, you can also use this same technique to evaluate which members should be kept on a list. The evaluation option provides you with the ability to easily update a marketing list based on a query. This option does not add new members based on the results, but it does remove any members from the list that don't match the search criteria.

For instance, let's assume you have a list of all contacts who reside in the state of Illinois. If some of the members added previously have moved and no longer live in Illinois, you will need to remove them from the list manually.

In this exercise, you'll evaluate the marketing list members for the Illinois Contacts list to ensure that only those contacts with an Illinois address are included in the list.

SET UP Use the Internet Explorer web browser to navigate to your Microsoft Dynamics CRM website, if necessary, before beginning this exercise. You need a user account that has the Marketing Manager security role or another role with privileges to manage marketing lists.

1. In the **Marketing** area, click **Marketing Lists**.

2. Double-click the **Illinois Contacts** marketing list created earlier in this chapter.

3. In the entity navigation pane, click **Marketing List Members**.

4. Click the **Manage Members** button to launch the **Manage Members** dialog box.

5. In the **Manage Members** dialog box, click **Use Advanced Find to evaluate members**.

6. Click **OK**. In the **Evaluate Members and Update Marketing List** dialog box, create the same query used in a previous section to find all active contacts who reside in Illinois.

7. Click **Find** to execute your search.

8. Verify that at least one contact is returned in the results. Then, below the results view, click **Keep all the members returned by the search from the marketing list**.

9. Click **Update Marketing List** to update the marketing list to remove any contacts that do not meet the criteria specified in the **Advanced Find** results.

Removing Selected Members from a List

As mentioned previously, marketing list members are not updated dynamically in the same way that lead, contact, and account records are updated in the system; members stay on the list until you manually remove them. In addition to removing records by using the options discussed earlier, with Microsoft Dynamics CRM, you can remove members from a list individually by using the Remove From Marketing List command.

In this exercise, you will remove individual members from your Illinois Contact list.

SET UP Use the Internet Explorer web browser to navigate to your Microsoft Dynamics CRM website, if necessary, before beginning this exercise. You need a user account that has the Marketing Manager security role or another role with privileges to manage marketing lists.

1. In the **Marketing** area, click **Marketing Lists**.

2. Double-click the **Illinois Contacts** marketing list created earlier in this chapter.

3. In the entity navigation pane, click **Marketing List Members**.

4. Without opening the marketing list member record, select at least one member to remove from the list.

5. On the ribbon, click the **Remove from Marketing List** button.

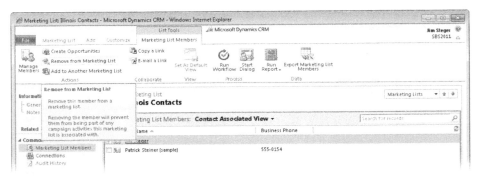

A confirmation page appears.

6. In the **Remove Members** dialog box, click **OK** to remove the selected member from the list.

Important This action permanently removes the member from the list. If you want to undo the change, you will need to re-add the member to your list.

Creating a Dynamic Marketing List

You can also create a marketing list whose membership is based on a query. The marketing list members would therefore be dynamically generated, based on the most recent set of results of that query. The ability to define your members based on the latest data means that you don't have to worry about explicitly managing the member list yourself. This approach can be useful for lists such as all contacts that live in a certain territory, all contacts who haven't ordered a product or service in the last six months, and similar lists.

In this exercise, you will create a dynamic marketing list of all the current customer contacts who still reside in the state of Illinois.

 SET UP Use the Internet Explorer web browser to navigate to your Microsoft Dynamics CRM website, if necessary, before beginning this exercise. You need a user account that has the Marketing Manager security role or another role with privileges to create marketing lists.

1. In the **Marketing** area, click **Marketing Lists**.

2. Click the **New** button.

3. In the **Name** field, enter *Current Illinois Contacts*. In the **Member Type** field, choose **Contact**. Change the **Type** field to **Dynamic**.

> **Troubleshooting** The type cannot be changed after you save the marketing list. If you want to change a dynamic marketing list to a static one, you can easily do so by clicking the Copy To Static button on the ribbon.

> **Important** The Locked attribute does not apply to dynamic marketing lists.

 4. Click the **Save** button. An alert appears at the top of the marketing list, indicating that the marketing list members are dynamically selected.

5. On the ribbon, click the **Manage Members** button.

The Manage Members dialog box opens, allowing you to create the query to determine the list members.

6. In the **Manage Members** dialog box, create the active Illinois contact query as shown in the following screen shot.

7. Click the **Find** button to examine the results of your query.

8. Click the **Use Query** button to associate the query to the dynamic marketing list. The Marketing List Members view will display the most recent results of the query.

Copying Members to Another Marketing List

You might sometimes want to quickly copy list members from one list to another. For example, let's assume that you have a list of leads who confirmed that they would attend your recent sales event. You decide to lock this particular list to ensure that you have a history of the individuals who responded prior to the event. However, you need to create another list of prospects who actually attended the event, so that your sales team can follow up with them. This new list of attendees will contain many of the same members as the RSVP list, but it will also contain some individuals who did not confirm ahead of time, and it will exclude those prospects who registered but did not attend the event. Microsoft Dynamics CRM provides a simple mechanism to copy marketing list members from one list to another.

In this exercise, you will copy the Illinois Contacts marketing list created earlier in this chapter to a new marketing list called Illinois Seminar Invites.

SET UP Use the Internet Explorer web browser to navigate to your Microsoft Dynamics CRM website, if necessary, before beginning this exercise. You need a user account that has the Marketing Manager security role or another role with privileges to manage marketing lists.

1. In the **Marketing** area, click **Marketing Lists**.

2. Double-click the **Illinois Contacts** marketing list created earlier in this chapter.

3. In the entity navigation pane, click **Marketing List Members** to view the members of the list.

> **Tip** Microsoft Dynamics CRM limits your selection to the maximum number of records displayed in the view. For information about changing the number of records returned per page, see Chapter 2, "Getting Around in Microsoft Dynamics CRM."

4. Without opening a list member record, select at least one member to copy to your new list.

5. In the ribbon's **Actions** group, click the **Add to Another Marketing List** button.

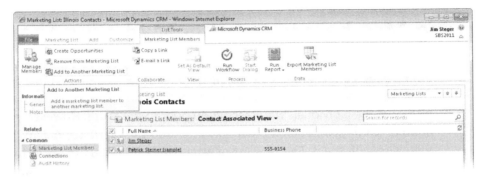

6. In the **Look Up Record** dialog box, the **Look for** field will automatically be set to **Marketing List** and will display any available static marketing lists with the same member type. At the bottom of the **Look Up Record** dialog box, click **New** to create a new marketing list.

> **Tip** Microsoft Dynamics CRM only displays static marketing lists, because the members of dynamic marketing lists are derived from a query.

7. In the **New Marketing List** form, in the **Name** field, enter *Illinois Seminar Invites*. In the **Member Type** field, choose **Contact**. Leave the **Type** field as **Static**.

8. Click the **Save and Close** button to create the marketing list.

The Look Up Record dialog box now displays the Illinois Seminar Invites marketing list.

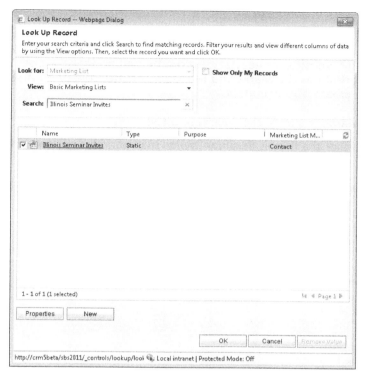

9. Select the **Illinois Seminar Invites** marketing list, and then click **OK** to add the selected members to the new list.

Creating Opportunities from List Members

Microsoft Dynamics CRM also allows you to easily create new opportunities directly from the members grid of a marketing list that has account or contact members. You can select up to the number of records displayed in the grid, but each opportunity created with this approach will have the same entered values (such as New Opportunity for the Opportunity Topic field). For lists that contain lead members, you can convert leads to opportunities by using the Convert Lead action.

In the example from earlier in this chapter, a marketing manager could use this feature to create opportunities for the sales team to track each prospect that attended the sales event.

In this exercise, you will create new opportunities for selected members of a marketing list.

SET UP Use the Internet Explorer web browser to navigate to your Microsoft Dynamics CRM website, if necessary, before beginning this exercise. You need a user account that has the Marketing Manager security role or another role with privileges to create opportunities.

1. In the **Marketing** area, click **Marketing Lists**.

2. Double-click the **Illinois Seminar Invites** marketing list created in the previous section.

3. In the entity navigation pane, click **Marketing List Members**.

4. In the grid, manually select the individual members for which you will create new opportunities.

5. In the ribbon's **Actions** group, click the **Create Opportunities** button.

> **Tip** The Create Opportunities ribbon button will be available only for lists that contain account or contact members. For lists that contain lead members, the ribbon will display the Qualify button and will make the Create Opportunities button unavailable.

6. In the **Create Opportunity for Marketing List Members** dialog box, complete all required fields.

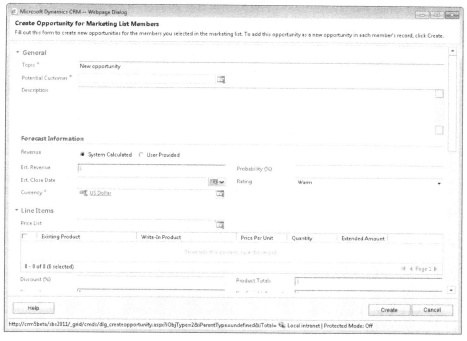

7. Click **Create** to create opportunities for all selected contacts.

> **Tip** Just as when you use the edit multiple records tool, all values entered in the Create Opportunity For Marketing List Members dialog box will be the same across all the newly created opportunities. The Potential Customer field will automatically populate with each account or contact selected in the marketing list.

Using Mail Merge to Generate a Word Document That Includes List Member Information

Marketing and service organizations often utilize direct mail as a critical communication strategy with their customers and prospects. They might send a special offer letter to all prospects, encouraging them to purchase a product; or they might distribute a customer service notification to all existing customers. The mail merge capabilities of Microsoft Dynamics CRM provide a convenient way to quickly generate these documents with personalized data directly from a marketing list.

In this exercise, you will create a mail merge letter with data from a marketing list.

> **Important** To complete this exercise, you must have access to the Reconnect With Contacts template for Microsoft Word that is included in every Microsoft Dynamics CRM installation. To verify that you have access to this template, in the Settings area, click Templates, and then click Mail Merge Templates. Change the view to Active Mail Merge Templates, and check to see if the Reconnect With Contacts template appears in the list. If the template does not appear, you can select another template or contact your system administrator.

SET UP Use the Internet Explorer web browser to navigate to your Microsoft Dynamics CRM website, if necessary, before beginning this exercise. You need a user account that has the Marketing Manager security role or another role with privileges to manage marketing lists and mail merge templates.

1. In the **Marketing** area, click **Marketing Lists**.

2. Double-click the **Illinois Seminar Invites** marketing list created earlier in this chapter.

Mail Merge on List Members

3. On the ribbon, click the **Add** tab, and then click the **Mail Merge on List Members** button.

4. In the **Microsoft Dynamics CRM Mail Merge for Microsoft Office Word** dialog box, select **Letter** for the mail merge type. Then choose **Organization mail merge template**, and click the now-available **Look Up** button.

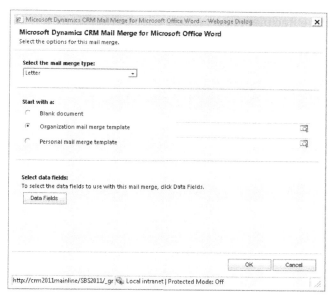

5. In the **Look Up Records** dialog box that opens, displaying the available mail merge templates, select the **Reconnect with Contacts** template, and then click **OK**.

> **Tip** Microsoft Dynamics CRM includes numerous mail merge templates. You can edit these templates or create your own.

6. Back in the **Microsoft Dynamics CRM Mail Merge for Microsoft Office Word** dialog box, click **OK**.

7. In the **File Download** dialog box, click **Open** to view the file in Word. If you want, you can click **Save** instead to save the mail merge to your computer.

> **Important** The next steps assume that you are using Word 2007 or Word 2010 and have the Microsoft Dynamics CRM for Outlook client installed. The CRM button on the Add-Ins tab will appear only if the Microsoft Dynamics CRM for Outlook client is installed on your computer.

8. In Word, click the **Add-Ins** tab, and then click the **CRM** button.

9. The **Mail Merge Recipients** dialog box opens. This lists all of the recipients that will be used in your mail merge. Click **OK** to include all of the recipients.

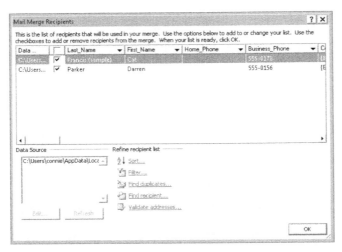

10. At this point, you can update the text of the letter and add information. After you have completed your edits, click **Next: Preview your letters** in the **Mail Merge** pane.

11. Preview the final information for each recipient and update the recipient list as necessary. Then click **Next: Complete the merge** when you are finished.

12. In the final step, you can print the resulting letters or edit each individual letter.

Key Points

- Marketing lists provide a convenient way to group accounts, contacts, or leads for use in marketing or outreach campaigns. Marketing lists can help you keep track of key customers, prospects invited to an event, all companies located in a particular geographic region, and more.

- Microsoft Dynamics CRM restricts marketing lists members to accounts, contacts, or leads.

- Because attributes can vary between accounts, contacts, and leads, each marketing list can contain only one member type. If you want to send a letter to both customers and prospects, you will need to create multiple lists.

- You must manually keep your marketing list members current for static marketing lists.

- Dynamic marketing lists membership will be based on the most recent results of the query associated with the list.

- You can easily copy the current members of a dynamic marketing list to a static marketing list by using the Copy To Static functionality.

- For static marketing lists, you can add, remove, or update members from a list by using an Advanced Find query.

- Locking a static marketing list prevents members from being added to or removed from the list.

- You can use the members of a marketing list to quickly create opportunities or targeted distribution lists for mail merge documents.

Chapter at a Glance

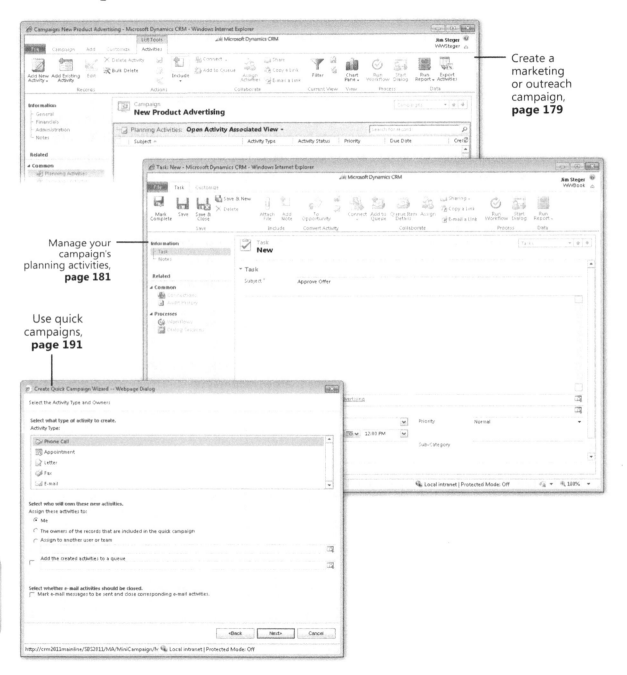

Create a marketing or outreach campaign, **page 179**

Manage your campaign's planning activities, **page 181**

Use quick campaigns, **page 191**

8 Managing Campaigns and Quick Campaigns

In this chapter, you will learn how to

- ✔ Create a campaign.
- ✔ Add planning activities.
- ✔ Select target marketing lists.
- ✔ Add target products and sales literature.
- ✔ Relate campaigns.
- ✔ Create campaign templates.
- ✔ Copy campaign records.
- ✔ Use quick campaigns.

In Chapter 7, "Using Marketing Lists," you learned how to use marketing lists to group your customers and prospects into lists. However, marketing lists make up just a small piece of a marketing strategy. After you've defined your customer or prospect groups, you can use marketing campaigns in Microsoft Dynamics CRM to communicate with each group and track the responses.

> **See Also** Chapter 9, "Working with Campaign Activities and Responses," discusses how to execute a campaign and track the results with campaign activities and responses, and covers several reports to measure campaign performance, compare campaigns, and track campaign activities.

A marketing campaign is a series of activities intended to increase awareness of your company, products, or services. As any marketer knows, a properly executed marketing campaign requires coordination of many parties, literature, and tasks. Microsoft Dynamics CRM provides a convenient way to manage marketing campaigns and their associated activities, tasks, and information.

For instance, suppose you want to launch a new customer loyalty program. This program will reward customers for repeat purchases of your product and entitle them to special discounts and promotions. To initiate the campaign, you plan to send a welcome letter and follow-up email to all qualifying customers, informing them of the program. Some of your activities might include:

- Determining the anticipated costs and expected results of the campaign.
- Creating and approving the copy for the welcome letter and email message.
- Defining customers to be included in the loyalty program.
- Coordinating the graphics and delivery of the letters and email messages with vendors or your IT staff.
- Actually sending the campaign-related content to your customers.
- Tracking the responses for follow-up activities and analysis.

In this chapter, you will learn how to create a campaign and then associate planning activities, customer lists, products, and sales literature to it. In addition, you will create campaign templates that can be reused in future campaigns. Finally, you will learn how to use the Quick Campaign Wizard in Microsoft Dynamics CRM to quickly create campaign activities for a selected set of leads, contacts, or accounts.

> **Important** There are no practice files for this chapter.

> **Important** The images used in this book reflect the default form and field names in Microsoft Dynamics CRM. Because the software offers extensive customization capabilities, it's possible that some of the record types or fields have been relabeled in your Microsoft Dynamics CRM environment. If you cannot find the forms, fields, or security roles referred to in this book, contact your system administrator for assistance.

> **Important** You must know the location of your Microsoft Dynamics CRM website to work the exercises in this book. Check with your system administrator to verify the web address if you don't know it.

Creating a Campaign

Microsoft Dynamics CRM allows you to track marketing or outreach program information on a campaign record. You can track the offer, type, schedule, and financial information about the campaign. For instance, you might have a campaign that coordinates the advertising activities planned for the launch of a new product.

By default, the fields described in the following table are tracked on campaigns and campaign templates in Microsoft Dynamics CRM.

Field	Description
Name	This field contains the title of the campaign.
Status Reason	This denotes the status of the campaign for reporting purposes. The default statuses are Proposed, Ready To Launch, Launched, Completed, Canceled, and Suspended.
Campaign Code	This can be either a user-entered or system-generated code for the campaign.
Campaign Type	This provides a category for the campaign, such as Advertisement, Direct Marketing, Event, or Co-branding. This field is useful in reporting.
Expected Response	This allows you to record the expected response for a campaign as a percentage from 0 to 100.
Total Cost of Campaign Activities	In this field, Microsoft Dynamics CRM automatically totals the costs of all campaign activities.
Miscellaneous Costs	This field records miscellaneous costs associated with the campaign.
Total Cost of Campaign	This field contains the sum of the total cost of campaign activities and miscellaneous costs.

In this exercise, you will create the campaign record that will be used to coordinate the advertising activities of your new product launch.

SET UP Use the Windows Internet Explorer web browser to navigate to your Microsoft Dynamics CRM website before beginning this exercise.

1. In the **Marketing** area, click **Campaigns**.

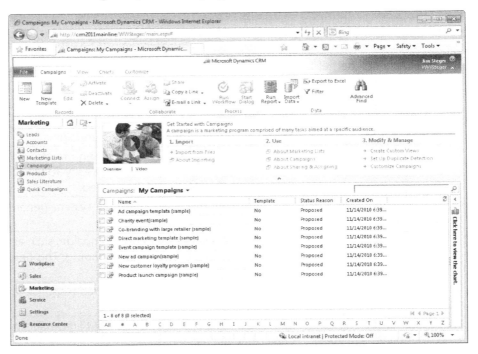

2. On the ribbon, click the **New** button.

The New Campaign form opens.

3. In the **Name** field, enter **New Product Advertising**. Leave the default values in the **Status Reason**, **Campaign Type**, and **Expected Response** fields. Finally, in the **Offer** field, enter **This is my new product advertising campaign.**

> **Tip** The campaign code will be completed automatically by Microsoft Dynamics CRM if you do not enter a value. The campaign code cannot be changed after you save the record.

Save

4. Click the **Save** button to create the campaign.

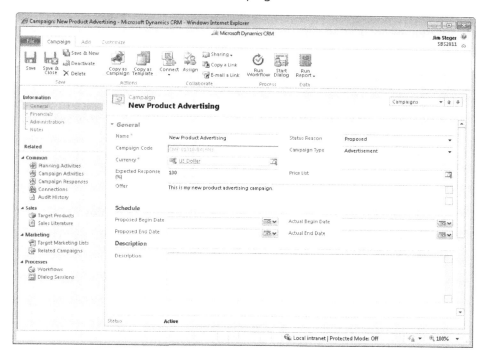

Adding Planning Activities

For each campaign, you can track the to-do list of activities that need to be completed to execute the campaign. These activities might include:

- Contacting your direct mail vendor.
- Creating and approving copy.
- Creating a target list.
- Printing literature.
- Approving the offer.

With Microsoft Dynamics CRM, you can manage these activities by using the planning activities area of a campaign. Planning activities are Microsoft Dynamics CRM activities that are associated with a campaign.

In this exercise, you will create a planning activity task to approve the offer for the new product advertising campaign created in the previous section.

 SET UP Use the Internet Explorer web browser to navigate to your Microsoft Dynamics CRM website, if necessary, before beginning this exercise.

1. In the **Marketing** area, click **Campaigns**.

2. Open the **New Product Advertising** campaign you created in the previous exercise, if it is not already open.

3. In the entity navigation pane, click **Planning Activities**.

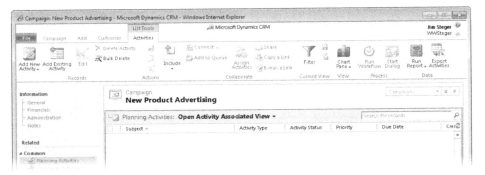

 4. On the ribbon, click the **Add New Activity** button, and then click **Task** on the submenu.

5. In the **Subject** field, enter **_Approve Offer_**. In the **Due** field, enter a date two weeks from today. In the **Duration** and **Priority** fields, leave the default values of **30 minutes** and **Normal** selected.

6. Click the **Save and Close** button to create the planning task.

> **See Also** For more information about working with activities, see Chapter 4, "Working with Activities and Notes."

Selecting Target Marketing Lists

You can use marketing lists to group accounts, contacts, and leads in Microsoft Dynamics CRM and then associate one or more of the lists with each campaign.

Marketing lists link your customers or prospects to your campaign, which is critical when working with and distributing campaign activities. Campaign activities are special activities—such as letters, faxes, and phone calls—within Microsoft Dynamics CRM that are created and associated with campaigns. Campaign activities contain campaign-specific information and must be distributed to create the individual activities for users to perform.

> **See Also** For more information about working with campaign activities, see Chapter 9.

In this exercise, you will add the Illinois Contacts marketing list from Chapter 7 to the New Product Advertising campaign.

SET UP Use the Internet Explorer web browser to navigate to your Microsoft Dynamics CRM website, if necessary, before beginning this exercise. You need the Illinois Contacts marketing list you created in Chapter 7. If you cannot locate the Illinois Contacts marketing list in your system, select a different marketing list for this exercise. You must have at least one marketing list available to associate with the campaign.

1. In the **Marketing** area, click **Campaigns**.

2. Open the **New Product Advertising** campaign record you created in the previous exercise, if it is not already open.

3. In the entity navigation pane, click **Target Marketing Lists**.

4. On the ribbon, click the **Add Existing Marketing List** button.

   The Look Up Records dialog box opens. The Look For field is automatically set to Marketing List.

5. Look for the **Illinois Contacts** list created in Chapter 7, or select another marketing list to add to your campaign. After you select your marketing lists, click the **Add** button.

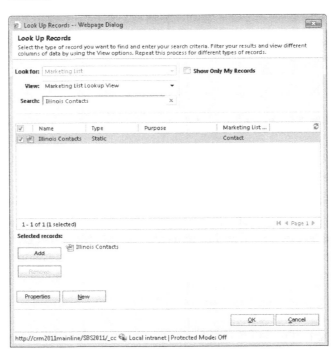

> **Tip** You can create a new marketing list directly from the Look Up Records dialog box by clicking the New button. To view additional details about a selected available record, click the Properties button.

> **See Also** For more information about creating marketing lists, see Chapter 7.

6. When you have finished selecting the marketing lists you want to add to your campaign, click **OK**.

7. You will be prompted to specify whether you want to add the marketing lists to undistributed campaign activities. If you want to add the members of these lists to your campaign activities, leave the check box selected.

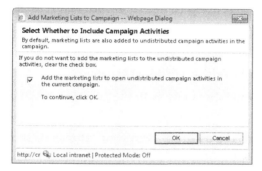

8. Click **OK** to add the selected marketing lists to the campaign and the campaign's open undistributed campaign activities.

Adding Target Products and Sales Literature

Campaigns can be used to promote your organization's products or services or to create awareness of a new program or outreach effort. For campaigns involving products or services, you can specify the target products or services within the campaign.

> **Tip** Products and services are configured by using the Product Catalog feature of Microsoft Dynamics CRM, which is located in the Settings area. Consult with your system administrator to properly set up a product or service.

In addition to tracking products and services, you can also relate relevant sales and marketing literature to a campaign. These documents might include presentations, product and pricing sheets, marketing literature, and company manuals. Microsoft Dynamics CRM uses the Sales Literature functionality to store one or more documents for use with marketing campaigns and products.

In this exercise, you will attach a product and sales literature about the product to your campaign.

SET UP Use the Internet Explorer web browser to navigate to your Microsoft Dynamics CRM website, if necessary, and have at least one product created before beginning this exercise.

1. In the **Marketing** area, click **Campaigns**.

2. Open the **New Product Advertising** campaign record you created earlier in this chapter, if it is not already open.

3. In the entity navigation pane, click **Target Products**.

4. On the ribbon, click the **Add Existing Product** button.

   The Look Up Records dialog box opens, with the Look For field automatically set to Product.

5. Select one or more products to associate with your campaign, and then click **OK**.

   The Target Products window opens, showing the product you selected.

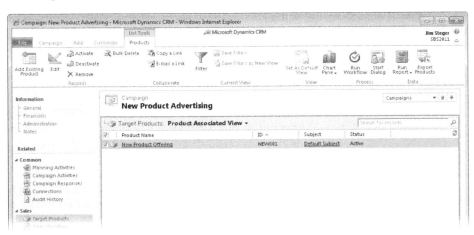

6. In the entity navigation pane, click **Sales Literature**.

7. On the ribbon, click the **Add Existing Sales Literature** button.

The Look Up Records dialog box opens, with the Look For field automatically set to Sales Literature.

8. Click **New** to create a new sales literature record.

> **Tip** You will create a basic sales literature record for the purposes of this exercise. You can also upload one or more documents and associate specific products with a sales literature record.

9. In the **Title** field, enter *Product Pricing*, and choose a subject from the **Subject** field. Then, in the **Type** field, choose **Price Sheets**.

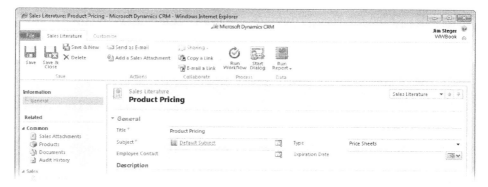

10. Click the **Save and Close** button.

The Product Pricing sales literature record now appears in the Look Up Records dialog box and is listed in the Selected Records area.

11. Click **OK** to associate the **Product Pricing** sales literature record with your campaign.

Relating Campaigns

You can relate your marketing campaign to other campaigns for reporting and tracking purposes. For instance, assume you have a global branding campaign. The initial branding campaign is comprised of multiple child campaigns, such as a direct mail campaign, an email campaign, and radio and television spots. In Microsoft Dynamics CRM, you can create a campaign record for each and relate all of them to a parent campaign. This allows you to track results for each campaign channel and aggregate multiple campaigns to measure the effectiveness of the entire branding effort.

In this exercise, you will create a related campaign to track co-branding efforts with a partner retailer as part of your new product advertising campaign.

> **Tip** When you relate two campaigns, Microsoft Dynamics CRM creates a one-way relationship. For instance, suppose you have campaigns A and B. With campaign B as the active campaign, you relate campaign A to campaign B. When you open campaign A, you will not see a relationship to campaign B, but you will see campaign A listed as a related campaign in campaign B.

 SET UP Use the Internet Explorer web browser to navigate to your Microsoft Dynamics CRM website, if necessary, before beginning this exercise.

1. In the **Marketing** area, click **Campaigns**.

2. Open the **New Product Advertising** campaign you created earlier in this chapter, if it is not already open.

3. In the entity navigation pane, click **Related Campaigns**.

4. On the ribbon, click the **Add Existing Campaign** button.

   The Look Up Records dialog box opens, with the Look For field automatically set to Campaign.

5. Click the **New** button to create a new campaign.

6. In the **New Campaign** form, in the **Name** field, enter *Co-branding with the large retailer 'More Bikes!'*.

7. Click **Save and Close** to create the new campaign.

8. Back in the **Look Up Records** dialog box, select the new **Co-branding with the large retailer 'More Bikes!'** campaign, and click **OK** to relate it to the parent campaign.

   The related campaign is displayed in the Related Campaigns area of the parent campaign.

 CLEAN UP Close the campaign record.

Creating Campaign Templates

Suppose you are the marketing manager for your company's monthly product catalog. Most of the planning activities for the catalog are the same each month. Rather than leaving you to recreate all of the common information for your campaign each month, Microsoft Dynamics CRM lets you create a campaign template that can be used as the starting point for your new campaign.

The campaign template stores core details and related information about the campaign and can be used to quickly launch a similar campaign. In Microsoft Dynamics CRM, campaign templates work just like campaigns.

In this exercise, you will create a new campaign template.

 SET UP Use the Internet Explorer web browser to navigate to your Microsoft Dynamics CRM website, if necessary, before beginning this exercise.

1. In the **Marketing** area, click **Campaigns**.
2. On the ribbon, click the **New Template** button to launch the **New Campaign (Template)** form.
3. In the **Name** field, enter **_TEMPLATE: Product Advertising_**.
4. Click **Save**.

Copying Campaign Records

Marketing campaigns can be very involved, and for complex campaigns, it can take considerable effort to enter the correct information in Microsoft Dynamics CRM. Campaign templates provide a common starting point for future campaigns and can save you time and duplication of effort when you are creating campaigns. Microsoft Dynamics CRM also provides two actions, Copy As Campaign and Copy As Template, to quickly duplicate information from an existing campaign or template. The copy action replicates all of the planning activities, campaign activities, marketing lists, products, and sales literature to your new campaign or template.

The Copy As Campaign and Copy As Template actions work similarly and can be used from either a campaign or campaign template. The key difference is the resulting output. When you use Copy As Campaign, the output will be a campaign ready for use. The Copy As Template action will produce a campaign template that can be used to create a campaign in the future. The following table can help you decide which copy action is appropriate.

Scenario	Appropriate Copy Action
You have an existing campaign that you want to preserve for future use.	From the campaign record, use Copy As Template to create a template record that can be used for a later campaign.
You want to create a campaign that's similar to an existing campaign for immediate use.	From the campaign record, use Copy As Campaign to create a new campaign record that can be used immediately.
You want to create a new campaign from an existing campaign template.	Open the campaign template and use Copy As Campaign to create the new campaign record.
You want to create a similar campaign template from an existing template.	Open the campaign template and use Copy As Template to create a new template record.

In this exercise, you will create a new campaign from the campaign template created in the previous section.

SET UP Use the Internet Explorer web browser to navigate to your Microsoft Dynamics CRM website, if necessary, before beginning this exercise.

1. In the **Marketing** area, click **Campaigns**.

2. Open the **TEMPLATE: Product Advertising** campaign template you created in the previous exercise.

3. On the ribbon, click the **Copy as Campaign** button.

   A campaign record opens, with a copy of all of the information from the originating campaign.

   > **Troubleshooting** Microsoft Dynamics CRM allows campaign and campaign template records to have the same name. Be sure to rename your new campaign (or campaign template) to avoid confusion.

Using Quick Campaigns

As you have seen, you can plan and track your marketing efforts with campaigns in Microsoft Dynamics CRM. But sometimes you might want to simply distribute a campaign activity (such as a letter, phone call, or email) to an ad-hoc list without the extra overhead and tracking of a full campaign. A quick campaign is a simplified version of a campaign in Microsoft Dynamics CRM that allows you to distribute a single campaign activity to a group of accounts, contacts, leads, or marketing lists.

In this exercise, you will create a quick campaign to track follow-up tasks for a group of leads.

 SET UP Use the Internet Explorer web browser to navigate to your Microsoft Dynamics CRM website, if necessary, and have multiple lead records already created and available before beginning this exercise.

1. In the **Marketing** area, click **Leads**.

2. Select a few lead records.

> **Tip** You can select multiple records by holding the Ctrl key while clicking the records.

 3. Click the **Add** ribbon tab, then click the **Quick Campaign** button.

4. Choose **For Selected Records** from the submenu.

   The Create Quick Campaign Wizard form opens.

5. The first step of the **Create Quick Campaign Wizard** describes the steps you are about to take. Click **Next** to continue.

6. The next step asks you to enter a name for the quick campaign. In the **Name** field, enter *Our First Lead Quick Campaign*, and then click **Next**.

7. Now you will need to choose an activity type and user to whom the resulting activities should be assigned. If you choose to use an email activity, you also have the option of automatically sending and closing the email activity. In the **Activity Type** box, select **Phone Call**, and for the **Assign these activities to** option, choose **Me**.

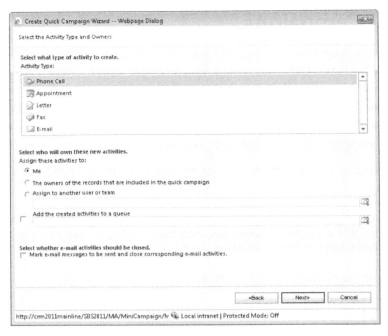

8. Click **Next**. The next step allows you to enter the content for the activity chosen in the previous step. Because you chose **Phone Call**, you will see the **Phone Call** form displayed. In the **Subject** and **Description** fields, enter *Follow-up call on leads*. In the **Due** field, chose the date you want the activity to be completed.

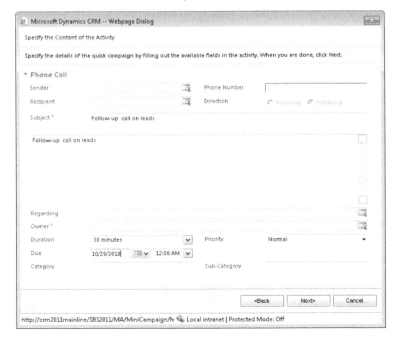

9. Click **Next**. The final step summarizes the choices made in the previous steps. If everything is correct, click **Create** to complete the quick campaign.

10. After completion, you can view your new quick campaign by clicking **Quick Campaigns** in the **Marketing** area.

11. Double-click the **Our First Lead Quick Campaign** record to see your quick campaign details, including the phone call activities created.

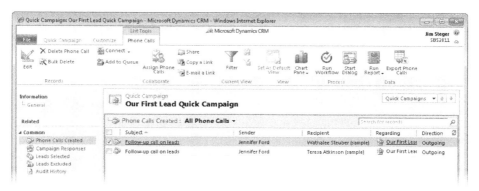

Key Points

- Campaigns allow you to track and communicate the schedules, costs, planning activities, lists, and responses related to your marketing and outreach efforts.

- Planning activities are common Microsoft Dynamics CRM activities in a campaign or quick campaign.

- Marketing lists associated with a campaign provide the names of customers targeted for campaign activities.

- You can track related products and sales literature to campaigns.

- You can copy a campaign and all of its related information to a campaign template or another campaign.

- You can quickly distribute campaign activities to ad-hoc lists of accounts, leads, contacts, or marketing lists by using the Quick Campaign Wizard.

Chapter at a Glance

Create a campaign activity, **page 196**

Distribute a campaign activity, **page 202**

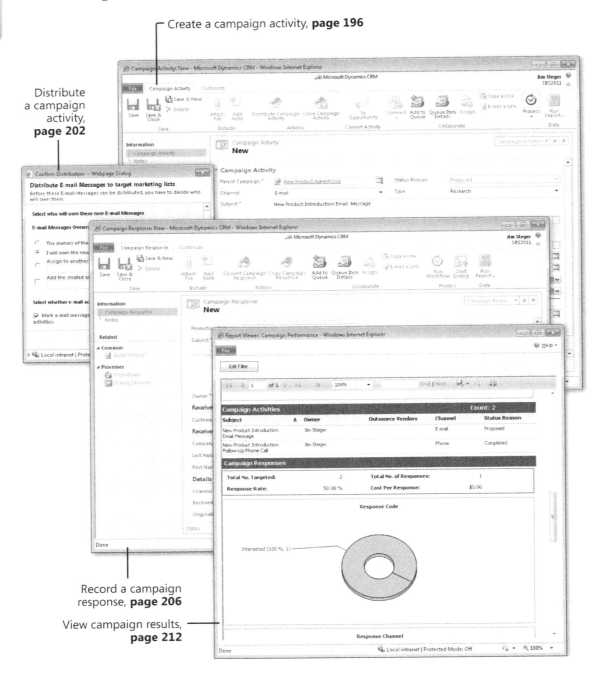

Record a campaign response, **page 206**

View campaign results, **page 212**

9 Working with Campaign Activities and Responses

In this chapter, you will learn how to

- ✔ Create a campaign activity.
- ✔ Associate a marketing list to a campaign activity.
- ✔ Distribute a campaign activity.
- ✔ Record a campaign response.
- ✔ Convert a campaign response to another record type.
- ✔ View campaign results.

In Chapter 8, "Managing Campaigns and Quick Campaigns," you learned how to use Microsoft Dynamics CRM to plan and prepare for a marketing campaign. Proper planning and setup of your campaign helps ensure successful execution and tracking. In addition to helping you prepare for a marketing campaign, Microsoft Dynamics CRM simplifies the execution of your marketing campaign by using campaign activities and campaign responses. This chapter introduces the concepts of campaign execution and tracking to help you successfully complete a marketing campaign.

A marketing campaign typically includes one or more communications to your target marketing list. For instance, assume that your marketing manager wants to send an email message that introduces a new product to all of the members in a marketing list. You would like your sales team to follow up on the email message with a phone call seven days later. When recipients of the communication respond to the campaign, you would like to record the responses and take additional actions that will vary depending on the character of each response. In Microsoft Dynamics CRM, campaign communications are recorded as campaign activities and member responses are recorded as campaign responses.

In this chapter, you will learn how to set up and distribute campaign activities. Additionally, you will learn how to record campaign responses and how to convert them to other record types. Finally, you will learn how to view the results of a marketing campaign to understand its effectiveness.

> **Practice Files** The exercises in this chapter require only records created in earlier chapters; none are supplied with the book's practice files. For more information about practice files, see "Using the Practice Files" at the beginning of this book.

> **Important** The images used in this book reflect the default form and field names in Microsoft Dynamics CRM. Because the software offers extensive customization capabilities, it's possible that some of the record types or fields have been relabeled in your Microsoft Dynamics CRM environment. If you cannot find the forms, fields, or security roles referred to in this book, contact your system administrator for assistance.

> **Important** You must know the location of your Microsoft Dynamics CRM website to work the exercises in this book. Check with your system administrator to verify the web address if you don't know it.

Creating a Campaign Activity

In the example introduced at the beginning of this chapter, we discussed a simple campaign with two communication points: an email message followed by a phone call. Microsoft Dynamics CRM allows you to set up these communication points as campaign activities. You can record information about a campaign activity for tracking and analysis across one or many campaigns. The following table describes the fields that are most often tracked for a campaign activity.

Field	Description
Channel	The communication method for the activity
Type	A way to categorize the activity
Subject	A high-level description of the activity
Owner	The user who has been assigned to the activity
Outsource Vendors	Any accounts or contacts related to the activity from an execution standpoint (not targets of the campaign)

Field	Description
Scheduled Start	The target start date for the activity
Scheduled End	The target end date for the activity
Actual Start	The actual start date for the activity
Actual End	The actual end date for the activity
Budget Allocated	The amount of budget allocated for the activity
Actual Cost	The actual cost of the activity
Priority	Prioritization of the activity
No. of Days	An anti-spam setting that lets you prevent too-frequent communication from a campaign

In this exercise, you will create two campaign activities to be distributed to your team to support your marketing campaign.

 SET UP Use the Windows Internet Explorer web browser to navigate to your Microsoft Dynamics CRM website before beginning this exercise. You need the New Product Advertising campaign you created in Chapter 8. If you cannot locate the New Product Advertising campaign in your system, select a different campaign for this exercise.

1. In the **Marketing** area, click **Campaigns**.
2. Open the **New Product Advertising** campaign.
3. In the entity navigation pane, click **Campaign Activities**.

   A list of any campaign activities associated with this campaign appears.

 4. On the ribbon, click the **Add New Campaign Activity** button.

The Campaign Activity form appears. You will notice that the Owner field defaults to your name, the Parent Campaign field is populated with the New Product Advertising campaign, and the type field defaults to Research.

5. In the **Subject** field, enter **New Product Introduction Email Message**.

6. In the **Channel** field, select **E-mail**.

This selection affects how an activity will be distributed. By selecting E-Mail, you are choosing to send an email message to the recipients.

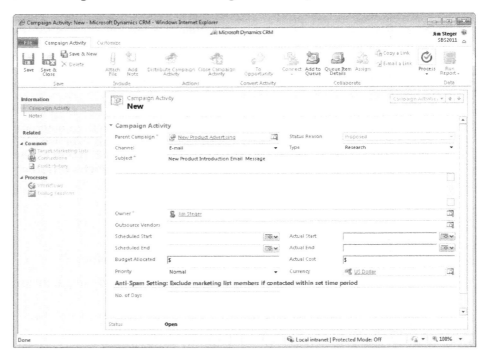

7. On the form ribbon, click the **Save and Close** button to create the campaign activity.

8. On the ribbon on the Campaign Activities screen, click the **Add New Campaign Activity** button.

9. In the **New Campaign Activity** form, enter *New Product Introduction Follow-Up Phone Call* in the **Subject** field.

10. In the **Channel** field, select **Phone**.

11. Click **Save and Close**.

Two campaign activities now appear in the list.

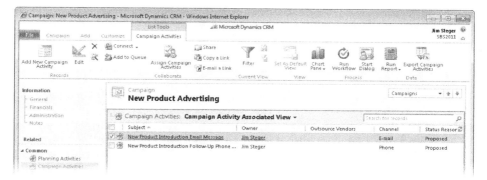

> **Tip** The channels available for the campaign activity directly relate to the activity types in Microsoft Dynamics CRM. The only exception is the Other channel, which exists to handle custom campaign activities that do not align with the native activity types. A campaign activity designated as Other serves as a record of the activity for scheduling and budgeting purposes only, and cannot be distributed to list members.

> **See Also** The Letter, Fax, and E-mail channels let you leverage the Microsoft Dynamics CRM mail merge feature. For more information about mail merge, see "Using Mail Merge to Generate a Word Document That Includes List Member Information" in Chapter 7, "Using Marketing Lists."

Associating a Marketing List to a Campaign Activity

In Chapter 8, you associated marketing lists to your campaign. As you might expect, when you create a campaign activity, the marketing lists associated with the campaign are automatically associated with the activity. As things change over the course of the campaign, you might decide that you do not want to distribute a campaign activity to all marketing lists. For example, suppose you have different activity templates for different industries, so that you can emphasize different benefits of your new product to different audiences. In this case, you could create specific campaign activities for each industry. Or consider the case in which you need to add another marketing list after a campaign activity has been set up. If you have additional marketing lists you would like to add to the campaign, you can automatically add the list to all pending campaign activities, or you can manually add the list to specific campaign activities, if you don't want to associate the list to all open activities.

In this exercise, you will add and remove marketing lists from a campaign activity.

SET UP Use the Internet Explorer web browser to navigate to your Microsoft Dynamics CRM website, if necessary, before beginning this exercise. You need the New Product Advertising campaign you created in Chapter 8. If you cannot locate the New Product Advertising campaign in your system, select a different campaign for this exercise.

1. In the **Marketing** area, click **Campaigns**.

2. Open the **New Product Advertising** campaign.

3. In the entity navigation pane, click **Target Marketing Lists**.

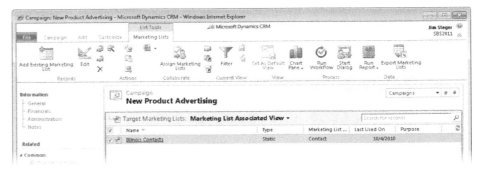

4. On the ribbon, click the **Add Existing Marketing List** button.

The Look Up Records dialog box appears.

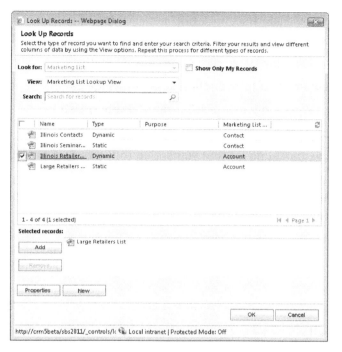

5. In the **Look Up Records** dialog box, select a marketing list. If no marketing lists exist, create a new one. Click **OK**.

> **Tip** If you need a refresher on creating a marketing list, see "Creating a Static Marketing List" in Chapter 7.

The Select Whether To Include Campaign Activities dialog box opens.

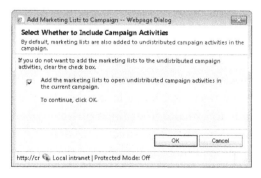

6. In the dialog box, clear the check box and click **OK** to indicate that you do not want to associate the marketing list to the open campaign activities.

7. In the entity navigation pane, click **Campaign Activities**.

8. Open the **New Product Introduction Email Message** campaign activity.

9. In the entity navigation pane, click **Target Marketing Lists**.

10. On the ribbon, click the **Add From Campaign** button.

11. Select the new marketing list that you added to the campaign, and then click **OK**.

   The additional marketing list has now been added to the campaign activity. When you distribute this campaign activity, the additional marketing list members will also be included in the activity.

> **Tip** Just as you can add a marketing list to a campaign activity, you can also remove a marketing list. To do so, select one or more marketing lists and click the Remove button on the ribbon.

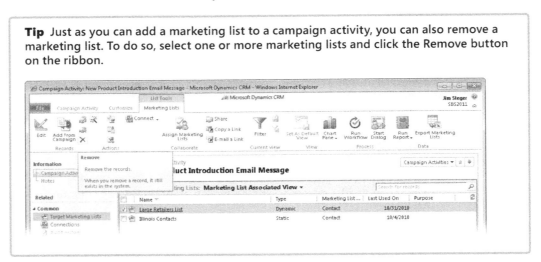

Distributing a Campaign Activity

When you have created and associated the appropriate marketing lists with your campaign activities, you have taken the necessary steps to prepare for the execution of the activity. Then, when you are ready to execute the campaign activity, you will distribute the activity. This action will create Microsoft Dynamics CRM activity records that will exist under the account, contact, or lead records specified in the target marketing lists.

Tip Most distributed campaign activities are distributed as open activities that need to be completed. The only exceptions to this rule are email campaign activities, because you can choose to automatically send an email when you distribute the email campaign activity.

In this exercise, you will distribute the email and phone call campaign activities you created earlier in this chapter.

 SET UP Use the Internet Explorer web browser to navigate to your Microsoft Dynamics CRM website, if necessary, before beginning this exercise. You need the New Product Advertising campaign you created in Chapter 8. If you cannot locate the New Product Advertising campaign in your system, select a different campaign for this exercise.

1. In the **Marketing** area, click **Campaigns**.
2. Open the **New Product Advertising** campaign.
3. In the entity navigation pane, click **Campaign Activities**.
4. Open the **New Product Introduction Email Message** campaign activity.

5. Click the **Distribute Campaign Activity** button. The **New E-mails** window opens.

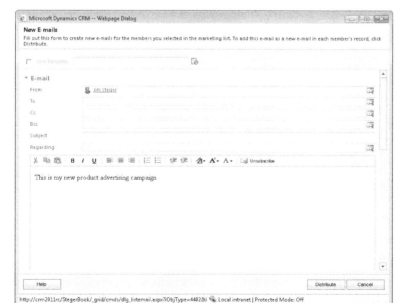

> **Important** The following steps will send an email message to the email addresses for all members included in the target marketing lists for this campaign activity. Make sure that your marketing lists do not include any customer email addresses, so that you do not send a test message to them!

6. The body text defaults to the text from the **Offer** field of the parent campaign. Enter a subject and update the body for your email message. Then click **Distribute**.

> **Tip** You can also save time by selecting a predesigned email template.

The Distribute E-Mail Messages To Target Marketing Lists dialog box appears. In this dialog box, you can select who will own the activity by choosing the record owners, yourself, another user, a team, or a queue. You can also specify whether the email message should automatically be sent and the corresponding activity marked as closed when the activity is distributed.

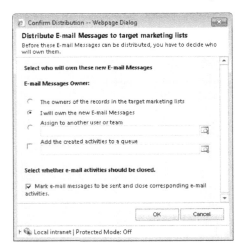

7. Leave the **Mark e-mail messages to be sent and close corresponding e-mail activities** check box selected, and click **OK**. The email messages are now sent.

8. In the campaign activity, click **Save and Close**.

9. Open the **New Product Introduction Follow-Up Phone Call** campaign activity.

10. On the form ribbon, click the **Distribute Campaign Activity** button.

The New Phone Calls window opens.

11. Enter a subject and a description, and change the due date to one week in the future.

12. Click **Distribute**.

The Distribute Phone Calls To Target Marketing Lists dialog box appears.

13. Under **Phone Calls Owner**, select **The owners of the records in the target marketing lists**, and then click **OK**.

You have successfully distributed your campaign activities. The New Product Introduction email message has been sent, and the New Product Introduction Follow-Up Phone Call activity has been created. Owners of the marketing list member records will see the activities in their activity lists with the due date you entered.

Microsoft Dynamics CRM allows you to create multi-step marketing campaigns and allows you to record campaign activities in many channels.

When you have distributed the activities, you can view the activities you created (both the successes and the failures) in the entity navigation pane of the campaign activity.

Recording a Campaign Response

After your campaign activities have been distributed and your target marketing list members have received the communication, you can record the responses you receive, both positive and negative. By tracking responses, you can take additional action to pursue the customer or prospect. For positive responses, you might schedule a follow-up phone call or other activity. For negative responses, you might remove members from a certain marketing list. Recording both positive and negative responses provides marketing managers with an overall understanding of the total response rate along with the positive response rate. There are several ways that you can record campaign responses in Microsoft Dynamics CRM. You can:

- Manually create a campaign response record.
- Close a campaign activity as a response.
- Automatically create a campaign response for email replies.
- Import campaign responses.

> **See Also** For more information about importing campaign responses and other record types, refer to Chapter 18, "Bulk Data Importing."

In this exercise, you will manually create a campaign response.

 SET UP Use the Internet Explorer web browser to navigate to your Microsoft Dynamics CRM website, if necessary, before beginning this exercise. You need the New Product Advertising campaign you created in Chapter 8. If you cannot locate the New Product Advertising campaign in your system, select a different campaign for this exercise.

1. In the **Marketing** area, click **Campaigns**.
2. Open the **New Product Advertising** campaign.
3. In the entity navigation pane, click **Campaign Responses**.
4. Click the **Add New Campaign Response** button.

The Campaign Response activity form appears. Many fields are available for capture in a campaign response, including the response code, who the response was received from, and other details about the response.

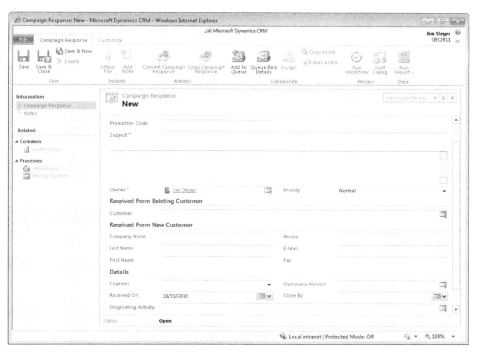

5. Enter a subject, select an existing customer, and then click the **Save** button.

Promoting a Campaign Activity to a Campaign Response

You might have noticed that one of the fields in the campaign response form, Originating Activity, lets you associate the campaign response with the original campaign activity. Microsoft Dynamics CRM also lets you create the campaign response from the original campaign activity, so you can track the effectiveness of each campaign activity in addition to understanding the effectiveness of the campaign overall. You can also convert campaign responses to other entities, as you will see in the next section.

In this exercise, you will promote a campaign activity to a campaign response.

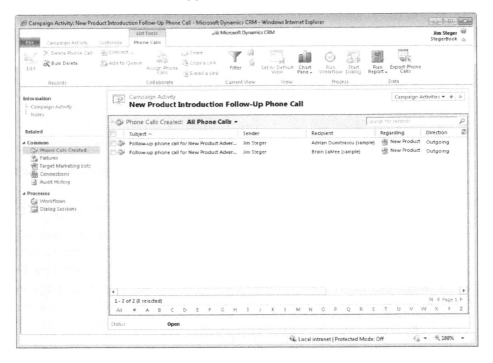

SET UP Use the Internet Explorer web browser to navigate to your Microsoft Dynamics CRM website, if necessary, before beginning this exercise. You need the New Product Advertising campaign you created in Chapter 8. If you cannot locate the New Product Advertising campaign in your system, select a different campaign for this exercise.

1. In the **Marketing** area, click **Campaigns**.

2. Open the **New Product Advertising** campaign.

3. In the entity navigation pane, click **Campaign Activities**.

4. Open the **New Product Introduction Follow-Up Phone Call** activity.

5. In the entity navigation pane, click **Phone Calls Created**.

   The Phone Calls Created list appears.

6. Open one of the phone call activities in the list.

7. On the ribbon, in the **Convert Activity** group, click the **Promote to Response** button.

The Campaign Response form appears. Notice that many of the fields are populated based on the campaign activity you used for the conversion.

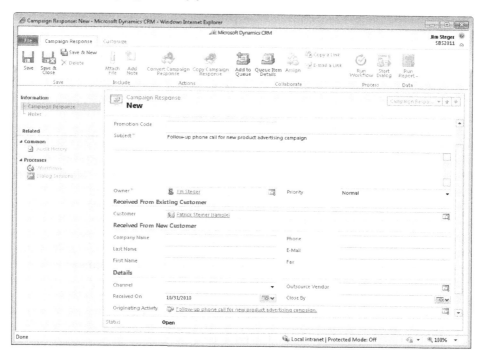

8. Update the subject and any other field, and then click the **Save** button.

Converting a Campaign Response

When you receive a positive response from a target marketing list member, you will probably want to pursue the customer or prospect further. Microsoft Dynamics CRM lets you close the campaign response and convert it into one of several different record types. The following table describes the types of record conversion you can choose.

Record Conversion Option	Reason for Use
Create new lead	The target member responds with interest in learning more, but the potential customer has not been qualified yet.
Convert an existing lead	The target member currently exists as a lead. As a result of the campaign response, the lead is qualified and therefore will be converted.
Create new record for a customer	The target member is an existing customer targeted for potential up-sale or cross-sale. You would like to create a new quote, order, or opportunity for the existing customer.

In this exercise, you will convert a campaign response into a new lead.

SET UP Use the Internet Explorer web browser to navigate to your Microsoft Dynamics CRM website, if necessary, before beginning this exercise. You need the New Product Advertising campaign you created in Chapter 8. If you cannot locate the New Product Advertising campaign in your system, select a different campaign for this exercise.

1. In the **Marketing** area, click **Campaigns**.

2. Open the **New Product Advertising** campaign.

3. In the entity navigation pane, click **Campaign Responses**.

   A list of all responses associated with the campaign appears.

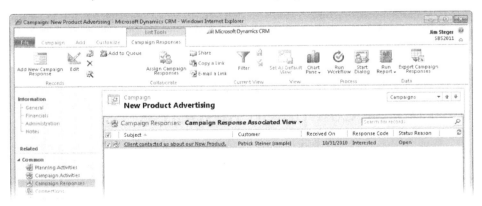

4. Open any open **Campaign Response** record.

5. On the form ribbon, click the **Convert Campaign Response** button.

   The Close And Convert The Response dialog box appears.

Convert Campaign Response

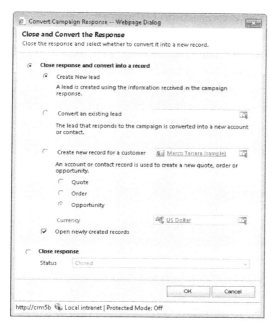

6. Leave the **Create New lead** option selected, and click **OK**.

   This action closes the campaign response and opens a new Lead form with the Topic populated from the campaign response.

You have successfully converted the campaign response to a lead record. From here, you can follow your normal sales processes to further pursue the record. If the lead record already existed when you chose to convert the lead, you would have been presented with the standard lead conversion dialog box. If you chose to create a new record for a customer, the specified record would be created with information populated from the campaign response (as when you converted the lead). Alternatively, you could select to close the response with a status of Completed or Canceled, without creating new records.

Viewing Campaign Results

While the campaign is being executed, you'll want to have visibility into the campaign activities and understand the results of the campaign. The speed with which activities have been closed, the activities that are still open, and the number of responses received are all very important data points. You might want to take additional actions based on these data points. For example, you could create an additional campaign activity for target members who have not responded, or you could follow up with the marketing team to ensure that the activities are taking place. Microsoft Dynamics CRM provides you with several reports you can use to view the results of marketing campaigns.

In this exercise, you will view the overall results of a marketing campaign by using the default campaign reports.

SET UP Use the Internet Explorer web browser to navigate to your Microsoft Dynamics CRM website, if necessary, before beginning this exercise. You need the New Product Advertising campaign you created in Chapter 8. If you cannot locate the New Product Advertising campaign in your system, select a different campaign for this exercise.

1. In the **Marketing** area, click **Campaigns**.

2. Open the **New Product Advertising** campaign.

3. On the ribbon, in the **Data** group, click the **Run Report** button and select **Campaign Performance** from the menu.

The Campaign Performance report is run. This report includes a view that combines information across the campaign record, including the target marketing lists, sales literature, related campaigns, planning tasks, campaign activities, campaign responses, and campaign finance.

> **Tip** The data in the following examples will reflect the campaign you have created and will vary depending on the size of the marketing lists selected. Therefore, you will likely see different data than the example provided.

In this example, four campaign activities have been created and three campaign responses have been received. The response rate is 50 percent.

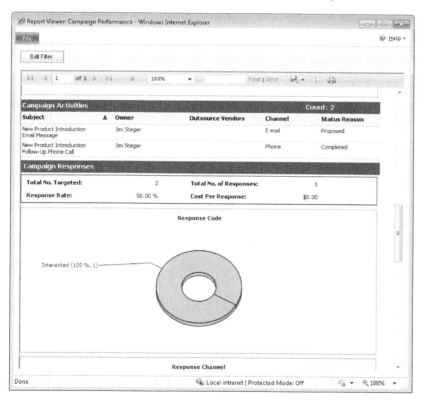

 CLEAN UP Close the Campaign Performance report.

Viewing Specific Campaign Information

In addition to viewing the results of a marketing campaign, you might want to view specific information about the status of campaign activities. The Campaign Activity Status report provides information related to the status of campaign activities.

In this exercise, you will view the status of a campaign activity by using the Campaign Activity Status report.

SET UP Use the Internet Explorer web browser to navigate to your Microsoft Dynamics CRM website, if necessary, before beginning this exercise. You need the New Product Advertising campaign you created in Chapter 8. If you cannot locate the New Product Advertising campaign in your system, select a different campaign for this exercise.

1. In the **Marketing** area, click **Campaigns**.

2. Open the **New Product Advertising** campaign.

3. In the entity navigation pane, click **Campaign Activities**.

4. Select the **New Product Introduction Follow-Up Phone Call** activity without opening the record.

5. On the ribbon, in the **Data** group, click the **Run Report** button, and then click **Campaign Activity Status**.

   The Select Records dialog box appears. This dialog box lets you specify whether to run the report for all campaign activities or only for those that were selected when the Run Report button was clicked.

6. Click **The selected records**, and then click **Run Report**.

The Campaign Activity Status report appears. Here you can see information about the campaign activity, including the status of the distributed campaign activities and assignment by activity owner.

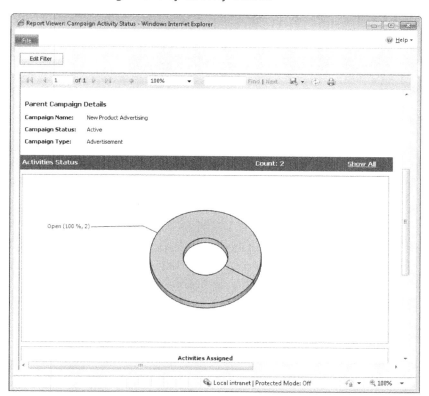

If you want to see the records that make up the charts in the report, you can click the Show All link or click the chart directly to see a list of the specific records.

 CLEAN UP Close the Campaign Activity Status report.

> **See Also** Chapter 16, "Using Advanced Find," discusses in detail the additional reporting capabilities available in Microsoft Dynamics CRM with Advanced Find and system views. Chapter 15, "Using the Report Wizard," provides more information about the additional reporting capabilities of the Report Wizard.

Key Points

- Campaign activities allow you to track the campaign-specific communications related to a marketing campaign.

- You can assign specific marketing lists to a campaign activity. Not all campaign marketing lists need to be used in a campaign activity.

- When you distribute campaign activities, the activities are created and assigned to the chosen users or teams to be completed.

- You can choose to send email campaign activities immediately when they are distributed.

- You can record a campaign response in several ways. In addition to manually creating a campaign response, you can record a response by converting a campaign activity, you can allow email responses to automatically create campaign activities, or you can import campaign responses by using the Import Data Wizard.

- Campaign responses can be converted to other Microsoft Dynamics CRM record types, such as leads, accounts, contacts, opportunities, quotes, or orders.

- Microsoft Dynamics CRM includes several reports that let you view the results of marketing campaigns and campaign activities. Two examples are the Campaign Performance report and the Campaign Activity Status report.

Part 3
Service

10 Tracking Service Requests 219

11 Using the Knowledge Base .235

12 Working with Contracts and Queues 255

Chapter at a Glance

Create a service request case, **page 220**

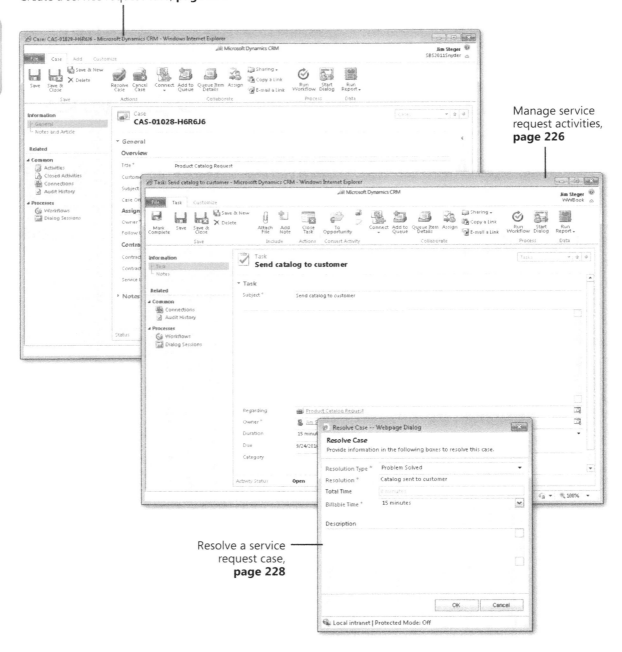

Manage service request activities, **page 226**

Resolve a service request case, **page 228**

10 Tracking Service Requests

In this chapter, you will learn how to

✔ Create and assign a service request case.

✔ Manage service request activities.

✔ Resolve a service request case.

✔ Cancel and reopen a service request case.

Many CRM system implementations are initiated by sales and marketing teams to build a shared, central repository of customer sales and order data. In the previous chapters of this book, you've learned how Microsoft Dynamics CRM can be used to manage marketing activities, prospective customers (leads), sales opportunities, and orders. Of course, after a sale is completed, your company's relationship with the customer does not end! To ensure that the customer is satisfied with the sale, customer service teams can use the information gathered during the marketing and sales processes to manage the post-sale relationship with the customer.

Consider the following scenario: You've just purchased a flight to your favorite vacation locale from a travel website. The day before you're scheduled to leave, you receive an email message indicating that your flight has been canceled and that you'll need to contact the travel website's customer service team for more information. You call the customer service number listed in the message, only to be routed through three customer service representatives, explaining your situation to each before someone finally books you on another flight.

Regardless of the purchase, this scenario is not uncommon when customer support issues are involved, which is why a system that allows customer service teams to share sales and support information is such a powerful concept. All communications regarding the support request can be captured in one location and viewed by everyone on the team to ensure a speedy resolution. As the archive of service requests accumulates, customer service managers can identify common issues and trends that can then be used to drive enhancements to the sales process, service, or product development.

In Microsoft Dynamics CRM, service requests are called cases. A case represents any request or support incident for a customer. Typically, a case includes a description of the service issue or problem reported by the customer and the related notes and follow-up activities that service representatives use to resolve the issue.

Providing an avenue for customers to submit requests or issues during and after the sales process is critical to ensuring that customers are satisfied and willing to do business with your company in the future.

In this chapter, you'll learn how customer service teams can create, update, and resolve cases in Microsoft Dynamics CRM.

> **Practice Files** There are no practice files for this chapter.

> **Important** The images used in this book reflect the default form and field names in Microsoft Dynamics CRM. Because the software offers extensive customization capabilities, it's possible that some of the record types or fields have been relabeled in your Microsoft Dynamics CRM environment. If you cannot find the forms, fields, or security roles referred to in this book, contact your system administrator for assistance.

> **Important** You must know the location of your Microsoft Dynamics CRM website to work the exercises in this book. Check with your system administrator to verify the web address if you don't know it.

Creating and Assigning a Service Request Case

Each case in Microsoft Dynamics CRM contains the details of a customer request or issue, as well as follow-up dates, resolution steps, and other details. Multiple cases can be tracked for each customer, and each case has its own follow-up dates and status value. Because of the flexibility of the case record and the ability to customize forms and fields in Microsoft Dynamics CRM, cases are often used to track more than just support requests. Examples of how we've seen cases used include the following:

- Resolving call center support requests from customers of a financial services firm
- Managing concierge requests for top-tier clients of a hospitality provider

- Tracking safety requests to fix potholes and replace broken streetlights for a municipal government

- Capturing end-user requests for the CRM system itself

- Tracking warranty requests for residential home sales

In this exercise, you'll create a new case for a customer who is requesting a product catalog. After creating the case with the appropriate details from the customer, you'll assign it to a customer service representative.

SET UP Use your own Microsoft Dynamics CRM installation in place of the CRM sample data shown in the exercise. Use the Windows Internet Explorer web browser to navigate to your Microsoft Dynamics CRM website before beginning this exercise.

1. In the **Service** area, click **Cases** to view the case list.

2. On the ribbon, on the **Cases** tab, click the **New** button to launch the **New Case** form.

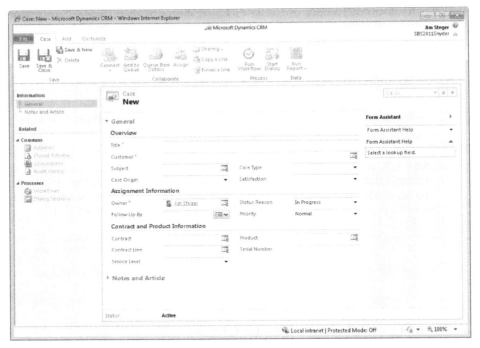

3. In the **Title** field, enter the following text description: ***Product Catalog Request***.

4. Click the **Lookup** button next to the **Customer** field, and select an account.

> **Tip** Each case must be related to a customer account or contact. In addition to customers, cases can also be related to service contracts and products.

5. Select a **Subject** category for the case.

6. Set the **Case Origin** field to **Phone** to indicate that the customer called with this request.

7. Set the **Case Type** field to **Request**.

8. On the **Case** tab of the ribbon, click **Save** to create the case.

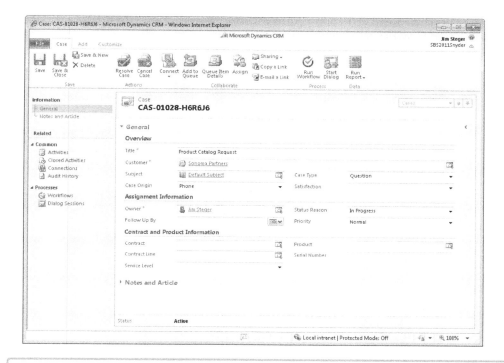

> **Tip** Microsoft Dynamics CRM automatically assigns a number to each case when it is first saved. Case auto-numbering can be configured by system administrators in the Administration section of the Settings pane. By default, each case will be created with a three-character prefix (CAS), a four-digit code, and a six-character identifier—for example, CAS-01028-H6R6J6.

9. On the **Case** tab of the ribbon, in the **Collaborate** group, click the **Assign** button to assign the case to a customer service representative.

10. In the **Assign to Team or User** dialog box, select **Assign to another user or team** and use the **Lookup** button to select another user record.

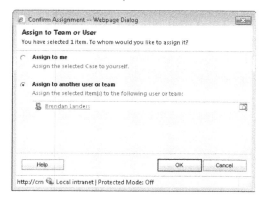

11. Click **OK** to assign the record to the selected user.

Configuring the Subject Tree

Subjects are categories that are used to organize products, sales literature, cases, and knowledge base articles in Microsoft Dynamics CRM. Consider the subject tree as an index of topics related to your business. A hierarchical subject tree can be used in Microsoft Dynamics CRM to categorize your business information. Because subject categories are applied across sales and service records, it's important to consider the best categories for your business when configuring your Microsoft Dynamics CRM system.

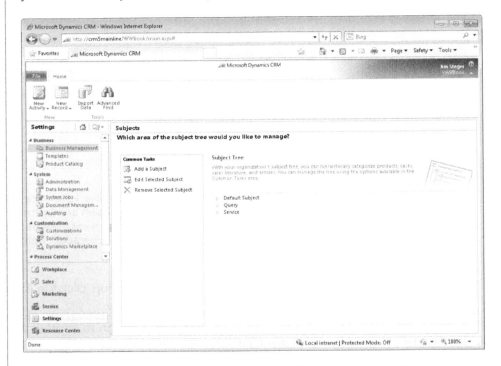

Your subject tree might be aligned to your products or business divisions, or perhaps you want to track customer invoicing questions without relating them to a specific product or service. The following table includes sample subject trees for different industries.

Business Type	Sample Subject Tree

Financial services firm	– Brokerage services
	   – Product A
	      + Client relations
	      + Confirmations
	      + Settlements
	   + Product B
	+ Financial planning
	+ Foreign exchange

Software consulting company	+ Billing
	– Product support
	   + Product A
	   + Product B
	+ Sales and marketing
	+ Service agreements
	– Services
	   + Application development
	   + Consulting

Residential real estate developer	+ Buyers
	– Conversion management
	   + Tenants
	+ Marketing materials
	– Projects
	   – Property A
	      + Units
	      + Other inventory
	      + Warranties
	   + Property B

The subject tree is accessed and updated from the Business Management section of the Settings area in Microsoft Dynamics CRM. Because the right to create, edit, and remove subjects for your organization is considered an administrator function, changing the structure of the subject tree is outside the scope of this book. For assistance with creating the subject tree in your Microsoft Dynamics CRM environment, contact your system administrator.

Managing Service Request Activities

Depending on the complexity of the customer request or issue, it might take a customer service representative just a few minutes to resolve a case, whereas more complicated cases might take days or even months before they are resolved. Because the workload of a customer service team is subject to the requests and support issues created each day, it's important for teams to continuously resolve issues and track progress on new issues as they're logged.

For example, the catalog request example in the previous section has a straightforward resolution: The customer service representative will create a task for the fulfillment clerk to send a catalog to the customer, and after this has been completed, no additional follow-up is required with the customer.

Many requests require more research, either internally or with the customer. After submitting an initial warranty claim for a malfunctioning stereo system, a customer might be asked to speak to a service representative on the phone several times and schedule an appointment at a service center before the stereo is fixed. And if it can't be fixed, the customer might be asked to ship the broken stereo to the manufacturer for replacement.

For customer service managers, tracking the steps taken during a case provides a way of identifying the best solution to frequently logged issues and managing the amount of time each representative spends on a case.

In this exercise, you'll log a follow-up activity for the case created in the previous section, creating a task activity to track time spent on the service request.

> **See Also** For more information about activities, see Chapter 4, "Working with Activities and Notes."

 SET UP Use the Internet Explorer web browser to navigate to your Microsoft Dynamics CRM website, if necessary, before beginning this exercise. You need the Product Catalog Request case you created in the previous exercise. Open the Product Catalog Request case.

   1. On the ribbon, click the **Add** tab to display additional options for the case.

2. In the **Activity** group, click **Task** to create a new task related to the case.

> **Note** Activities can also be created from the Activities view accessed in the entity navigation pane of the Case form. See Chapter 4 for more information.

3. Enter the following in the **Subject** field: *Send catalog to customer*.

4. In the **Due** field, select a date three business days from today's date.

5. Set the **Duration** field on the **Task** form to **15 minutes**. The duration is the anticipated time the task will take to complete.

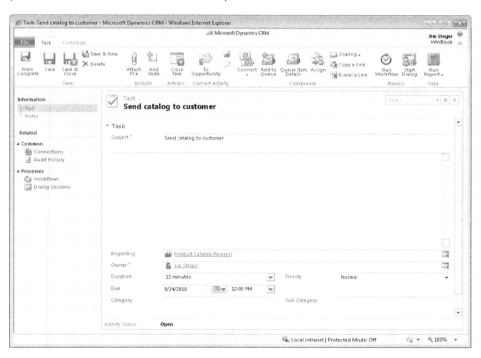

6. Click the **Mark Complete** button to mark the task as completed.

After the status of the task is updated to Completed, the Task form automatically closes.

Resolving a Service Request Case

As customer service teams work toward resolving service request questions and incidents, it's important to maintain an accurate status value for each case to ensure that new cases are addressed in a timely manner and worked on until a resolution is identified. When a case is resolved to the customer's satisfaction, customer service representatives can update the status of the case to Resolved, which will maintain the case record in the Microsoft Dynamics CRM database but remove it from the active case view.

Before a case can be marked as resolved, all open, related activities must be completed or canceled. The duration value of each completed activity regarding the case will be totaled when the case is resolved, so customer service managers can track the amount of time spent working on the case.

In this exercise, you'll mark the case created in a previous exercise as resolved.

 SET UP Use the Internet Explorer web browser to navigate to your Microsoft Dynamics CRM website, if necessary, before beginning this exercise. You need the Product Catalog Request case you created earlier in this chapter. Open the Product Catalog Request case.

1. On the **Case** tab of the ribbon, in the **Actions** group, click the **Resolve Case** button to resolve the case.

> **Important** A case cannot be resolved until all open activities regarding the case have been closed. Before resolving the case, make sure all activities for the case have been marked as Completed or Canceled.

2. In the **Resolve Case** dialog box, enter *Catalog sent to customer* in the **Resolution** field and leave *15 minutes* selected in the **Billable Time** field.

> **Note** By default, Microsoft Dynamics CRM includes only one status option for the Resolved case status: Problem Solved. This value will automatically appear in the Resolution Type field in the Resolve Case dialog box. The customization tools in Microsoft Dynamics CRM can be used to modify status reason values for cases to match your business needs. Contact your system administrator for assistance.

3. Click **OK** to update the case status to Resolved.

All fields will be saved and made read-only on the form. Microsoft Dynamics CRM automatically creates a Case Resolution activity that stores the details of the resolution in the case's closed activities.

4. In the entity navigation pane for the case, click **Closed Activities** to view the completed activities for the case.

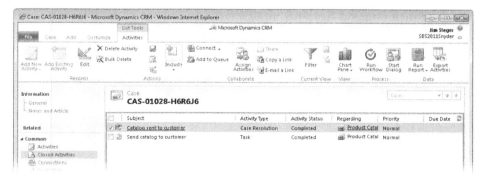

5. Open the **Case Resolution** activity. Note that the resolution and total time for the case are stored in the history for reporting and analysis.

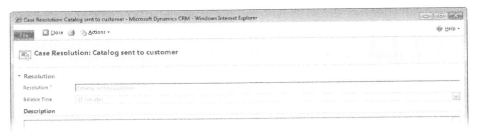

Canceling and Reopening a Service Request Case

There will be times when a case drops off the customer's priority list or the customer resolves an issue internally. Imagine a situation in which a customer submits a warranty claim for a refrigerator he recently purchased. The day after the case was logged with the appliance company's customer service team, the company issues a recall of the customer's refrigerator model, having seen several similar cases logged against it in previous months. The customer service team sets up a new case tracking category to manage recall requests and logs a new case under it for the customer. To prevent the initial case from remaining in the customer service team's active case list, the case is canceled. Canceled cases are deactivated so that all fields on the form are read-only, but these cases can still be searched and referenced as necessary. Sometimes the reverse happens—a case that was previously resolved or canceled is reopened if the issue reoccurs for the customer. Resolved and canceled cases can be reactivated in Microsoft Dynamics CRM so that customer service teams can continue working with them. Software development companies often have cases that require ongoing customer input; these cases might be canceled if no response is received from the customer for a long period of time. In this example, the case could be reopened in Microsoft Dynamics CRM if the customer contacts the support team at a later date.

In this exercise, you'll mark a case as Canceled and then reopen it.

SET UP Use the Internet Explorer web browser to navigate to your Microsoft Dynamics CRM website, if necessary, before beginning this exercise.

1. In the **Service** area, click **Cases**, and then in the on the **Cases** tab of the ribbon, click **New** to create a new case.

2. In the **New Case** form, type or select values in the required fields, as follows:

Field	Value
Title	***Unable to register new software licenses***
Customer	***Sonoma Partners***, or any account in your system
Subject	***Default Subject***, or any subject in your system

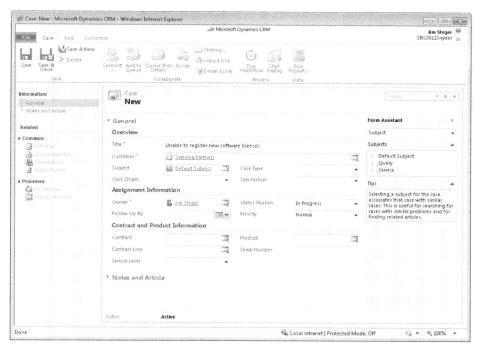

3. Click **Save** to create the case.

4. In the **Actions** group on the ribbon's **Case** tab, click the **Cancel Case** button.

5. In the **Case Cancel Confirmation** dialog box, select the appropriate status reason for the cancellation, and then click **OK** to confirm that you want to cancel the case.

After you click OK, the case will update to Canceled status and all fields on the case form will be read-only.

6. In the **Actions** group on the ribbon's **Case** tab, click the **Reactivate** button.

7. In the **Reactivate the Selected Case** dialog box, click **OK** to reactivate the case.

This will update the case to Active status, and all the fields in the form will again be editable.

 CLEAN UP Close the case record.

Key Points

- A case represents any service request or support incident for a customer in Microsoft Dynamics CRM. Customer service teams can use cases to manage customer requests and problems.

- Customer service managers can analyze case data to identify frequently occurring customer issues, improve product or service offerings, and streamline the time it takes service representatives to resolve issues.

- By default, Microsoft Dynamics CRM requires that a case be assigned a Subject value. The subject tree allows you to categorize sales and support records in Microsoft Dynamics CRM and should be configured by a system administrator.

- Follow-up activities ensure that steps are taken to resolve a case. A follow-up activity might be a simple task to send a catalog or update a customer's address, or it could be more involved, such as a series of phone calls with the customer, service appointments, or research tasks.

- By tracking activities to a case, customer service managers can add the duration of each completed activity to the total time spent on the case. This total is automatically calculated in the Resolve Case dialog box.

- Maintaining the status value of each case accurately is important to ensure that new issues are addressed in a timely manner and resolved as quickly as possible.

- Cases can be marked as Resolved or Canceled to remove them from the active case list. Updating a case to Resolved or Canceled status makes the case read-only in Microsoft Dynamics CRM; however, cases with these statuses can be reactivated as needed—for example, if the customer reports the problem again or if additional edits to the case are necessary.

Chapter at a Glance

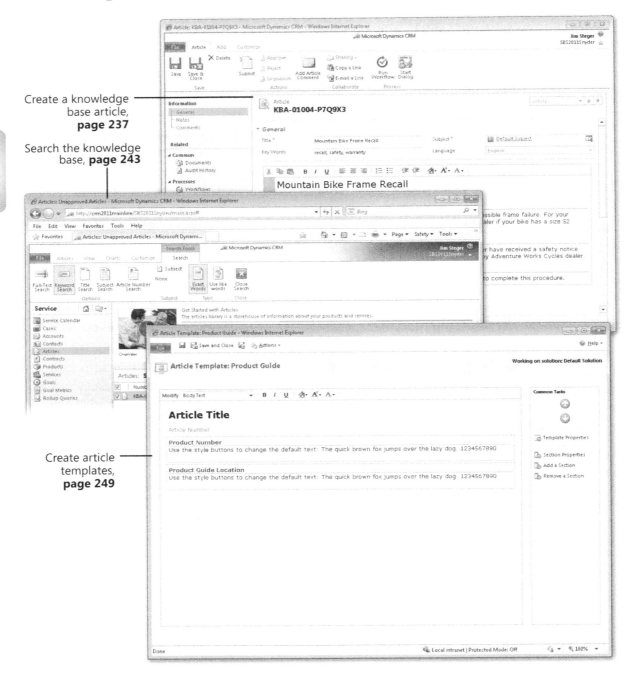

Create a knowledge base article, **page 237**

Search the knowledge base, **page 243**

Create article templates, **page 249**

11 Using the Knowledge Base

In this chapter, you will learn how to

- ✔ Create and submit a knowledge base article.
- ✔ Publish a knowledge base article.
- ✔ Search for a knowledge base article.
- ✔ Remove an article from the knowledge base.
- ✔ Create knowledge base article templates.

In the previous chapter, you learned how to manage service requests in Microsoft Dynamics CRM. Whether your organization tracks the questions, comments, and problems submitted by your customers as cases in Microsoft Dynamics CRM or elsewhere, over time there will probably be common themes or patterns in the service requests. This should make recurring cases easier to resolve, but often the organizational knowledge collected in service requests is lost in the sheer volume of cases managed by each representative. Another challenge in retaining experience and organizational knowledge on customer service teams is the high turnover common on many teams.

Beyond quantitative analysis of case-related metrics—such as the number of cases per customer or the average time it takes to resolve a case—customer service teams can benefit from a qualitative repository of case summaries, whittled down to include the information that will help the team respond to future service requests quickly and accurately. Combined, the qualitative and quantitative stores of data can become a powerful source for improving service to customers and driving sales, marketing, and product development processes to better meet customers' needs.

In this chapter, you'll learn how to build a knowledge base—a collection of articles in Microsoft Dynamics CRM that can be referenced by customer service representatives when they are answering questions about an organization's products or services. Articles are text based and can include product user guides, summaries of recurring problems and their solutions, and frequently asked questions (FAQs) assembled by the customer service team. Any information that can be used to quickly answer questions from customers, prospects, and other parties can be stored in your organization's knowledge base.

Like service request cases, knowledge base articles are assigned a subject, tying knowledge base articles to the same business categories used to group other sales and service records in Microsoft Dynamics CRM. For articles, subjects also provide the user with a quick way to search for information on a particular topic, even if the specific article title is not known. Because a subject value is required for each article, you should make sure that your subject tree is configured before you create an article. For assistance with creating the subject tree in your Microsoft Dynamics CRM environment, contact your system administrator.

> **See Also** For more information about subject trees, see the "Configuring the Subject Tree" sidebar in Chapter 10, "Tracking Service Requests."

> **Tip** Although many fields can be marked as optional instead of required in Microsoft Dynamics CRM forms, the Article form cannot be modified. However, during the installation process, a "default subject" value is created in the subject tree. You can select this default subject value on articles prior to configuring your subject tree, if necessary.

A well-organized knowledge base can reduce the amount of time customer service representatives spend searching for answers and reference documents on behalf of customers.

In this chapter, you'll learn how to build a knowledge base by creating, publishing, searching for, and modifying articles in Microsoft Dynamics CRM.

> **Practice Files** There are no practice files for this chapter.

> **Important** The images used in this book reflect the default form and field names in Microsoft Dynamics CRM. Because the software offers extensive customization capabilities, it's possible that some of the record types or fields have been relabeled in your Microsoft Dynamics CRM environment. If you cannot find the forms, fields, or security roles referred to in this book, contact your system administrator for assistance.

> **Important** You must know the location of your Microsoft Dynamics CRM website to work the exercises in this book. Check with your system administrator to verify the web address if you don't know it.

Creating and Submitting a Knowledge Base Article

In addition to a subject value, each article contains a title, a list of search keywords, and the content, which varies by article template. You'll learn more about configuring article templates later in this chapter. For this first exercise, you'll use one of the templates included with Microsoft Dynamics CRM.

Knowledge base articles are not assigned to customers; instead, the information contained in each article is typically applicable to a subset of customers—or even all customers. In this exercise, you'll create a new article detailing a product recall and then submit it to the customer service manager for review.

 SET UP Use the Windows Internet Explorer web browser to navigate to your Microsoft Dynamics CRM website before beginning this exercise. You need a user account that has the CSR Representative security role or another role with privileges to create, read, and write knowledge base articles.

1. In the **Service** area, click **Articles** to view the knowledge base articles.

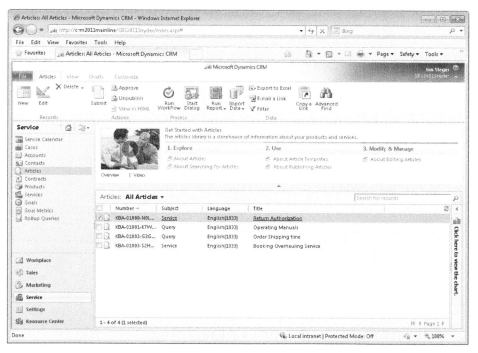

2. On the **Articles** tab of the ribbon, in the **Records** group, click the **New** button. The Select A Template dialog box appears.

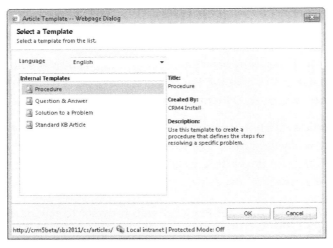

3. In the dialog box, select the **Procedure** template and then click **OK**.

4. In the **Title** field in the **New Article** form, enter *Mountain Bike Frame Recall*.

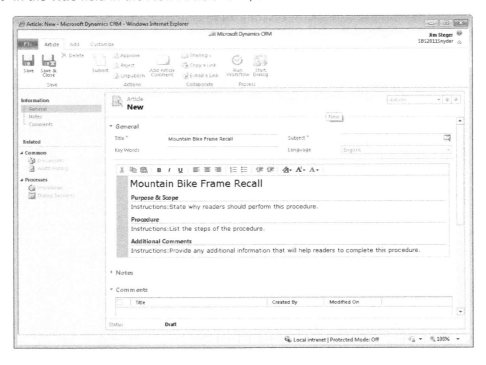

> **Tip** As you update the Title field, your title will automatically update in the article's text editor.

5. In the **Subject** field, select **Default Subject** or any other subject in your system.

> **See Also** For more information about subject trees, see the "Configuring the Subject Tree" sidebar in Chapter 10.

6. In the **Keywords** field, enter the following: ***recall, safety, warranty***.

> **Tip** Keywords allow users to quickly find articles. Even though Microsoft Dynamics CRM does not require you to provide keywords, consider entering common words or phrases relevant to your article.

7. In the article text editor, click the text under the **Purpose & Scope** section heading and enter the following: ***SAFETY NOTICE: All 52 Mountain Frames are being recalled due to possible frame failure. For your safety, contact Customer Service or any Adventure Works Cycles dealer if your bike has a size 52 mountain frame.***

> **Tip** The instruction text is automatically hidden when you begin typing in each section.

8. In the **Procedure** section, enter the following: ***Registered customers who provided a warranty card and serial number have received a safety notice about the recall. Bikes can be returned for a replacement frame at any Adventure Works Cycles dealer.***

9. Click the **Save** button to create the article.

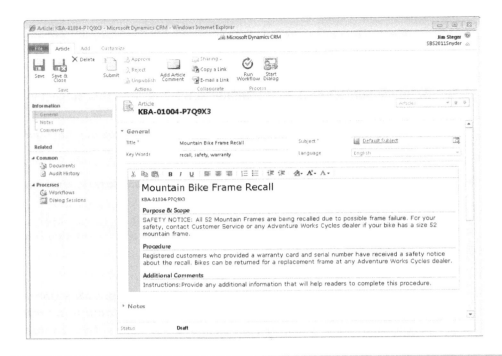

> **Tip** When an article is saved for the first time, it will automatically be assigned an article number. Article auto-numbering can be configured by system administrators in the Administration section of the Settings area. By default, each article will be created with a three-character prefix (KBA), a five-digit code, and a six-character identifier—for example, KBA-01004-P7Q9X3. If you have security rights to modify auto-numbering settings in your Microsoft Dynamics CRM system, you can modify the article prefix applied to each new article.

10. Click the **Submit** button in the **Actions** group on the **Article** ribbon tab to move the article into the **Unapproved** view so that it can be reviewed by a customer service manager.

CLEAN UP Close the new article record created in the exercise.

Publishing a Knowledge Base Article

After you have created a knowledge base article in Microsoft Dynamics CRM, the article is saved as a draft. When you submit the article, it is moved to an Unapproved article view so it can be reviewed by a customer service manager and either rejected for further revisions or approved into the searchable knowledge base. A knowledge base article cannot be searched by other users before it is published.

When first building your knowledge base, you might ask other members of your team to contribute articles. Microsoft Dynamics CRM allows users with the Customer Service Representative security role to create and submit knowledge base articles; however, additional security privileges are required to approve articles into the Published view, where they can be searched and referenced by other users.

> **Tip** The Publish Articles security privilege can be modified on the Service tab of any security role. To grant article publishing rights to a user, contact your system administrator.

The submit-and-publish process for articles allows many members of a team to contribute articles, but as a best practice, only a few team members should be able to review the articles and publish them into the knowledge base. Those with publishing rights should be tasked with making the articles as comprehensive and accurate as possible.

In this exercise, you'll publish the article submitted in the previous section into the knowledge base.

 SET UP Use the Internet Explorer web browser to navigate to your Microsoft Dynamics CRM website, if necessary, before beginning this exercise. You need a user account that has the CSR Manager security role or another role with privileges to publish knowledge base articles, and you need the Mountain Bike Frame Recall article you created in the previous exercise.

1. In the **Service** area, click **Articles**.

2. Select the **Unapproved Articles** view from the view selector, and then select the mountain bike frame recall article without opening it.

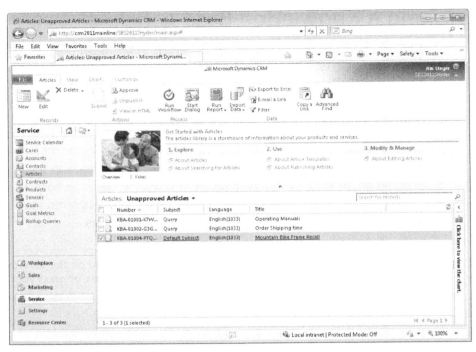

3. On the **Articles** tab of the ribbon, in the **Actions** group, click the **Approve** button to designate the article as approved.

> **Tip** You can approve multiple articles by selecting all of the articles you want to publish and then clicking the Approve button. Alternatively, you can also publish an individual article from a submitted Article form.

The Article Approval Confirmation dialog box appears.

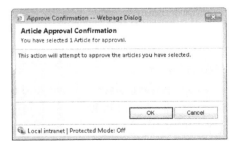

4. In the dialog box, click **OK**.

5. Change the view back to the **Published Articles** view and verify that the article is displayed there.

Searching for a Knowledge Base Article

Published articles can be searched for by article text, title, number, or keywords. Additionally, you can browse the subject tree to find all articles for a specific subject. The knowledge base search page can be accessed in two places in Microsoft Dynamics CRM:

- In the Service area, by clicking the Articles option in the entity navigation pane and then clicking the Search Tools tab on the ribbon

- In the Workplace area, by clicking the Articles option in the entity navigation pane and then clicking the Search Tools tab on the ribbon

From both locations, Microsoft Dynamics CRM provides the options shown in the following table to browse or search for specific articles in the knowledge base in your system.

Search Options	Description
Full-Text Search	Searches article content based on text you enter.
Keyword Search	Searches articles by the keyword field that the article author completed. This approach is useful for quickly finding relevant articles, but requires the author to properly complete the keywords field.
Title Search	Searches article titles based on the text you enter.
Subject Search	Searches articles based on the subject you enter.
Article Number Search	Searches based on the article number entered.

In this exercise, you'll submit a keyword search to retrieve the bike frame recall article published in the previous exercise.

SET UP Use the Internet Explorer web browser to navigate to your Microsoft Dynamics CRM website, if necessary, before beginning this exercise. You need a user account that has the Customer Service Representative security role or another role with privileges to read subjects and articles, and you need the Mountain Bike Frame Recall article you published in the previous exercise.

1. In the **Service** area, click **Articles** to view the article queue.

2. In the **Quick Find** field, enter *recall* as the keyword.

3. As you begin to enter text in the **Quick Find** search box, the **Search Tools** ribbon tab displays. Click the **Keyword Search** button. Leave the **Exact Words** button selected in the **Type** group.

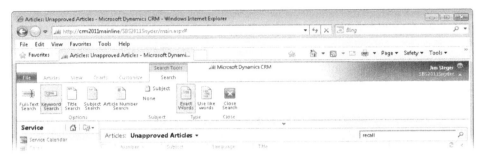

4. Back near the **Quick Find** field, click the **Search** button.

> **Tip** The Exact Words option limits your search to those articles that match your keyword exactly. For example, if you enter "recalls" in your search, Microsoft Dynamics CRM will not return an article that has "recall" listed in the keyword field. You can expand your search to include articles with keywords that match a portion of your search terms or a keyword that is similar to your search terms by clicking the Use Like Words button.

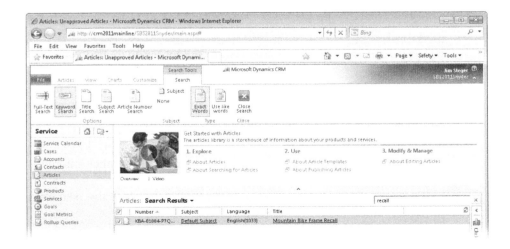

5. Double-click the bike frame recall article in the results pane to view the article. Note that the article is read-only and cannot be edited.

 CLEAN UP Close the knowledge base article.

Removing an Article from the Knowledge Base

After an article has been published to the knowledge base, it cannot be edited by any users, regardless of their security roles. So what happens when the product guide included in an article is updated or the recall period for a product ends? Articles can be unpublished from the knowledge base for updates or revisions, or they can be removed by being deleted from the database. Each knowledge base article must be in one of the three article views in Microsoft Dynamics CRM—Draft, Unapproved, or Published. Articles can move from one view to another as follows:

Article View	Available Actions to Remove Article from Queue	
Draft	Submit	Moves the article into the Unapproved view for management review
	Delete	Deletes the article record from Microsoft Dynamics CRM
Unapproved	Reject	Moves the article back to the Draft view for revisions
	Approve	Moves the article to the Published view so it can be searched and referenced by other users
	Delete	Deletes the article record from Microsoft Dynamics CRM
Published	Unpublish	Removes the article from the active knowledge base and returns it to the Unapproved view

Tip The availability of these actions varies based on the security privileges for each user. If you do not see one or more of the above options on the Article form's ribbon, you might not have the necessary security privileges to perform that action.

Tip As articles move through each view, users can add comments to indicate updates that need to be made or other notes about the article. The comments are available on a tab of the Article form so that users can quickly reference the notes for each article. However, the comments are not searchable.

In this exercise, you'll unpublish the article approved in the previous section and assign it back to the Draft view so it can be updated with additional information about the product recall.

 SET UP Use the Internet Explorer web browser to navigate to your Microsoft Dynamics CRM website, if necessary, before beginning this exercise. You need the Mountain Bike Frame Recall article created and approved earlier in this chapter.

1. Open the **Published Articles** view in Microsoft Dynamics CRM.

2. In the **Published Articles** view, locate the mountain bike frame recall article.

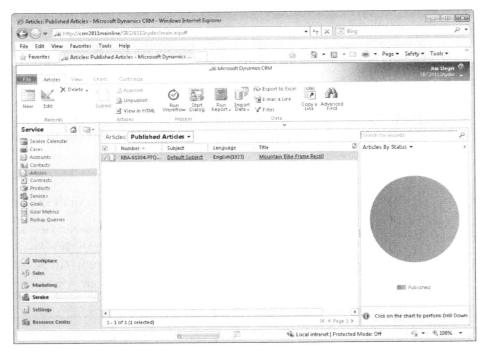

 3. Select the article and, in the **Actions** group of the **Articles** ribbon tab, click the **Unpublish** button.

   The Article Unpublish Confirmation dialog box appears.

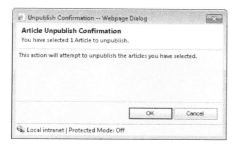

> **Tip** This dialog box appears only when you unpublish one or more articles from the list view.

4. Click **OK** to verify that you want to unpublish the article.

5. Go to the **Unapproved Articles** view and open the currently unapproved mountain bike frame recall article.

6. In the **Actions** group on the **Article** ribbon tab, click the **Reject** button to move the article to the **Draft** view so that a customer service representative can update it with additional recall information.

7. When the **Provide a Reason** dialog box appears, enter the following reason for rejecting the article: ***Update with serial numbers for recall information.***

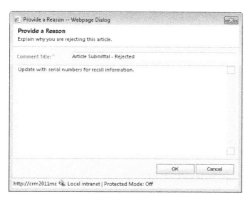

8. Click **OK** to reject the article and move it back to the **Draft** view.

9. In the **Article** form, click the **Comments** tab in the entity navigation pane to verify that the rejection note is displayed in the list, so that the customer service representative knows what updates are needed for the article.

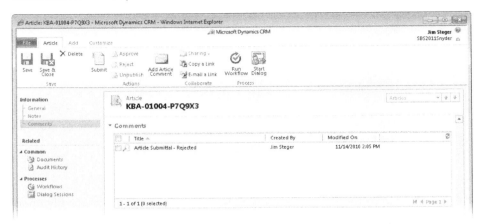

10. Double-click the comment to view the additional details about why the article was rejected.

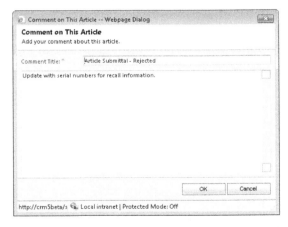

11. Click **OK** to close the **Comment on This Article** dialog box.

 **CLEAN UP** Close the article.

Creating Article Templates

Microsoft Dynamics CRM includes several templates for formatting knowledge base articles. Templates typically contain one or two sections, such as a Question section and an Answer section, which provide the people tasked with creating knowledge base articles with content and formatting guidelines for each article type. You might want to add a section to an existing template or even create a custom template to capture knowledge base information specific to your organization. Customer service managers can change section heading names and add instructional text to article templates, as well as modify the font style, size, and color.

For example, assume that the new customer service manager at the bike company wants to make sure that part numbers are included for all product articles. To ensure that this information is included in the knowledge base articles created by the customer service team, the manager will update each template with a new section called Product Number.

In this exercise, you'll create a new product guide template that includes a section specifically for the product number.

Important The CSR Manager security role in Microsoft Dynamics CRM has privileges to create and modify article templates. If the role has been altered in your environment or you do not have rights to modify the templates, contact your system administrator. Rights to modify article templates are configured on the Service tab of each security role.

Tip If you do not want your customer service team to use one of the templates included with Microsoft Dynamics CRM, you can remove the template from the Select A Template dialog box that displays when a new article is created. You do this by deactivating the template. To deactivate a template, click Templates in the Settings page, and then click Article Templates. Select the template you want to remove, and select the Deactivate option in the More Actions menu in the grid toolbar.

SET UP Use the Internet Explorer web browser to navigate to your Microsoft
Dynamics CRM website, if necessary, before beginning this exercise. You need a
user account that has the CSR Manager security role or another role with privileges
to create and update article templates.

1. In the **Settings** area, navigate to the **Templates** section, and then click **Article
Templates**.

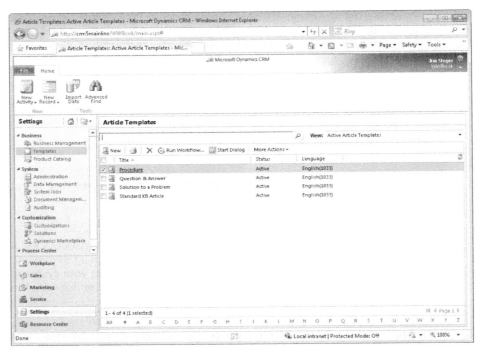

2. On the grid toolbar, click the **New** button to create a new article template.

> **Tip** The article template area does not display a contextual ribbon. You will access
> menu options for grid records through the grid toolbar.

3. In the **Article Template Properties** dialog box that appears, enter the following
values:

Field	Value
Title	*Product Guide*
Description	*Details and location of product guide*
Language	*English*

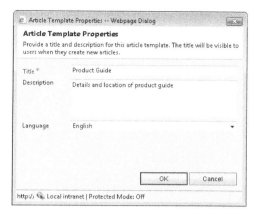

4. Click **OK**. The **New Article Template** form appears.

5. In the **Common Tasks** pane on the right side of the form, click the **Add a Section** button.

6. In the **Add a New Section** dialog box, enter the following values:

Field	Value
Title	*Product Number*
Instructions	*Specify the product number.*

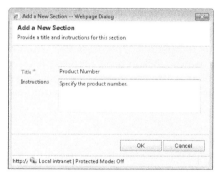

7. Click **OK**.

8. Click the **Add a Section** button again to add a second section to the template.

9. In the **Add a New Section** dialog box, enter the following values:

Field	Value
Title	*Product Guide Location*
Instructions	*Enter the URL for the product guide.*

10. Click **OK**.

11. Click the **Save** button to create the new article template.

> **Tip** The instructions entered in the template will be displayed when new articles are created from the template, so use the Instructions field to provide as much detail as possible for the people creating your articles. In addition to listing the desired content in the Instructions field, you might also consider providing sample formatting or other examples.

 CLEAN UP Close the article template.

Key Points

- The knowledge base in Microsoft Dynamics CRM is a store of useful product and service information and other resources relevant to your organization.

- One objective of the knowledge base is to capture the collective "know-how" of the customer service team so that it can be easily searched and referenced by other team members when they are answering common customer requests.

- Knowledge base articles can include any information that helps customer service representatives provide more timely and accurate customer service. Examples of article content include user guides, data sheets or schematics for products or services, frequently asked questions (FAQs), or summaries of recurring problems and their solutions.

- Articles are automatically moved through a workflow as they are published in Microsoft Dynamics CRM. As they are reviewed, articles are moved between three views: Draft, Unapproved, and Published.

- Only customer service managers have the right to publish articles into the knowledge base so that they can be searched by other users, but customer service representatives can contribute to the knowledge base by creating and submitting articles for management approval.

- Only published articles are available to other members of the organization. Articles with Draft or Unapproved status cannot be searched or accessed by other users.

- Knowledge base articles can be searched for by title, keywords, text, subject, and article number. The knowledge base search screen can be accessed from the Workplace or Service pages in Microsoft Dynamics CRM.

- Microsoft Dynamics CRM includes several templates that provide a framework for the layout and content of knowledge base articles. Customer service managers can create or modify article templates in the Settings section to tailor them to the requirements of their organization.

Chapter at a Glance

Create a contract template, **page 256**

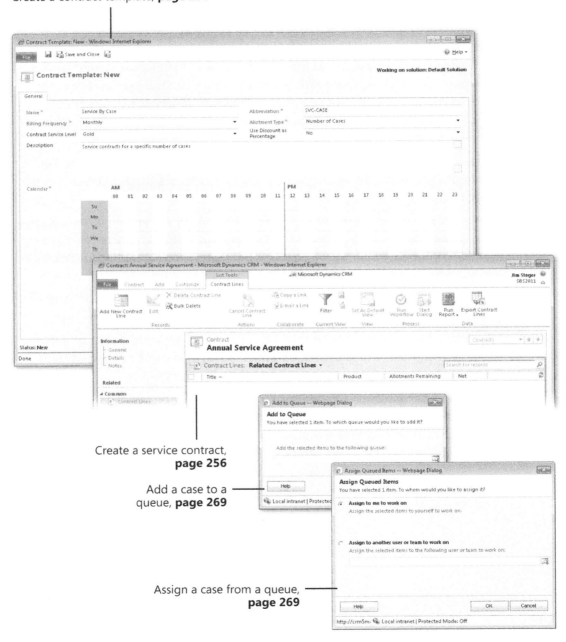

Create a service contract,
page 256

Add a case to a
queue, **page 269**

Assign a case from a queue,
page 269

12 Working with Contracts and Queues

In this chapter, you will learn how to

- ✔ Create a contract template.
- ✔ Create a service contract with a contract line.
- ✔ Activate and renew a contract.
- ✔ Create a queue and assign a case to it.
- ✔ Accept a case from a queue.

In previous chapters, you learned about cases and knowledge base articles, which capture the customer requests and product information used by customer service teams to address support issues. Most of the service requests your company receives are not likely to be resolved by referencing a single knowledge base article. Instead, each request is probably routed through an involved process that includes verifying a customer's information and service agreement terms, obtaining details about the problem, and escalating to the correct customer service representative to resolve the case. Large customer service teams typically have several tiers of support resources so that senior-level representatives can focus on complex or advanced issues while level-one representatives take calls from customers and verify basic information.

To facilitate the routing process of service requests, Microsoft Dynamics CRM allows customer service teams to manage multiple service agreement types and submit cases to service queues. Service contracts are agreements that define the support terms offered to a customer, either during a specified time period or for a specified number of cases or hours. Each contract contains one or more contract lines, which are the line-item details such as service term, pricing, and other conditions for the services specified in the contract. Contracts are valuable if your organization offers support services to its customers, because they allow customer service representatives to quickly identify each customer's eligibility for support.

After verifying that a customer is eligible for customer service, the level-one representative creates a case detailing the issue and submits it to the team's work queue so that another representative can research the solution. A queue is a holding bin of open cases and activities that need to be completed. Queues can be accessed by multiple members of a team so that individuals can accept new work items as they complete old ones.

Contracts and queues are used to manage customer service processes to ensure that customer requests are handled efficiently.

In this chapter, you'll learn how to create, activate, and renew service contracts for your customers and use queues to distribute cases to your customer service team.

> **Practice Files** The exercises in this chapter require only records created in earlier chapters; none are supplied with the book's practice files. For more information about practice files, see "Using the Practice Files" at the beginning of this book.

> **Important** The images used in this book reflect the default form and field names in Microsoft Dynamics CRM. Because the software offers extensive customization capabilities, it's possible that some of the record types or fields have been relabeled in your Microsoft Dynamics CRM environment. If you cannot find the forms, fields, or security roles referred to in this book, contact your system administrator for assistance.

> **Important** You must know the location of your Microsoft Dynamics CRM website to work the exercises in this book. Check with your system administrator to verify the web address if you don't know it.

Creating a Service Contract

Even if you don't work at a call center, your company probably provides some type of post-sale support to customers. To offset support costs within an organization, many companies sell service agreements to customers to ensure that the customer's questions or problems are addressed within predefined terms, such as response time, guarantee of resolution, availability, and so on. The terms of a service agreement vary for different organizations and industries. For example, a large manufacturing company might offer warranties on parts and repair calls, and a professional services firm might offer support for a predefined number of incidents or a specified period of time.

Microsoft Dynamics CRM provides you with the flexibility to set up several different types of contract templates, which provide the framework for service contracts. Each contract template has an allotment type that indicates the units of service, such as number of cases, time, or coverage dates. You can create as many templates as needed in your organization. The following table details the components of a contract template.

Field	Description
Name	The name of the contract template.
Abbreviation	An abbreviation of the template name. This is displayed with the name when you create a new contract.
Billing Frequency	The invoice frequency for the contract, such as monthly, bimonthly, quarterly, semiannually, or annually.
Allotment Type	The service units of the contract, which could be in number of cases, time, or coverage dates.
Contract Service Level	The rating of the customer service level. The default values are Gold, Silver, and Bronze.
Use Discount As Percentage	A configuration field in which you can set any applicable discount amount as a percentage or as a fixed dollar value.
Description	Additional comments or a description of the contract template.
Calendar	The hours of availability by day for the contract. This is typically set to include regular business hours but can be configured for 24-hour, 7-days-a-week support.

> **Tip** Because you can't create a contract without a contract template, Microsoft Dynamics CRM includes a default contract template named Service. You can access this template in the Templates section of the Settings area.

In Microsoft Dynamics CRM, each contract must be created from a contract template. The values from the contract template act as defaults for the content of each contract record, although some values—such as the service level and the discount type—can be overridden at the contract level. After creating a contract, customer service managers add line items (contract lines) to specify the details of the agreement. The following list describes some typical examples of contracts and contract lines:

- A local park district provides contracts to refreshment vendors to manage cleanup and facility maintenance requests. In this example, contract lines are allotted a number of minutes to be used toward maintenance.

- A plumber offers two types of service contracts, one to provide a one-year warranty on services and another to track incident-based requests. In this example, contract lines are allotted coverage dates for the first type of contract and a number of cases for the second type.

- A financial services firm offers incident-based support to large brokerage clients to ensure that preferred customers receive high-priority, 24/7 support. In this example, contract lines are allotted a number of cases.

- A medical supply provider manages setup and maintenance of home health care supplies for patients on behalf of hospitals and insurance companies. In this example, contract lines are allotted a fixed number of service calls for particular products.

In this exercise, you'll create a contract template for a case-based service agreement and then use it to create a contract that provides 20 service cases.

 SET UP Use your own Microsoft Dynamics CRM installation in place of the CRM sample data shown in this exercise. Use the Windows Internet Explorer web browser to navigate to your Microsoft Dynamics CRM website before beginning this exercise. You need the Sonoma Partners customer account you created in Chapter 3, "Working with Accounts and Contacts." If you cannot locate the Sonoma Partners account in your system, select a different customer account for this exercise. Also, use a user account that has the CSR Manager security role or another role with privileges to create contract templates, contracts, and contract lines.

1. In the **Settings** area, click **Templates**, and then click **Contract Templates** to view the available templates.

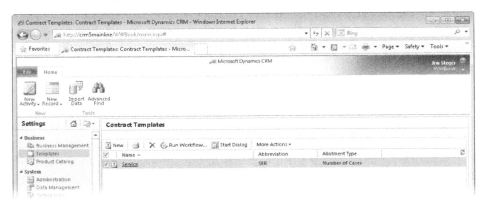

 2. Click the **New** button to launch the **New Contract Template** form.

> **Tip** The contract template area does not display a contextual ribbon. You will access menu options for grid records through the grid toolbar.

3. Complete the **New Contract Template** form with the following values.

Name	*Service By Case*
Abbreviation	*SVC-CASE*
Billing Frequency	Monthly
Allotment Type	Number of Cases
Contract Service Level	Gold
Use Discount as Percentage	No
Description	*Service contracts for a specific number of cases*

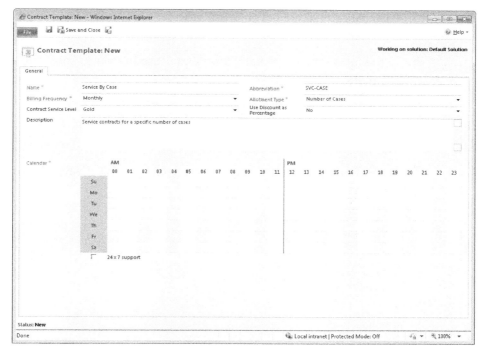

4. In the **Calendar** area, click the days and hours to designate the availability of service resources for the agreement from 9:00 A.M. until 5:00 P.M., Monday through Friday.

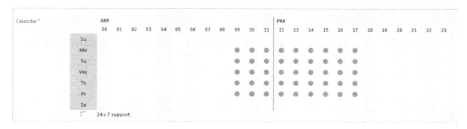

> **Tip** Note that the Calendar hours are based on a 24-hour day, so 5:00 P.M. displays as 17:00. When configuring the availability for your contract templates, you can click the day (row) or hour (column) headings in the Calendar area to toggle the settings for all cells of that value. For example, if you click the 08 column heading, all of the days will be set to available for 8:00 A.M. If you click the column heading again, you will toggle all of the days to unavailable at 8:00 A.M.

> **Important** At least one time slot must be marked for availability in the Calendar area before you can save a contract template. Green dots indicate the times that support is offered. If your organization does not limit when customer service is offered, select the 24 x 7 Support check box below the Calendar to mark all days as available. Calendar settings are not enforced when service requests are created.

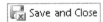

5. In the form toolbar, click the **Save and Close** button to finish creating the contract template.

6. Navigate to the **Service** area and click **Contracts**.

7. Click the **New** button to launch the **New Contract** form.

The Template Explorer dialog box opens.

8. In the **Template Explorer** dialog box, select the **SVC-CASE - Service By Case** template.

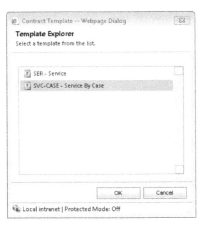

9. Click **OK** to close the dialog box and open the **New Contract** form. In the **General** section of the form, enter or select the following values.

Contract Name	*Annual Service Agreement*
Customer	*Sonoma Partners*
Contract Start Date	*9/1/2010*
Contract End Date	*8/31/2011*
Bill To Customer	*Sonoma Partners*
Billing Start Date	*9/1/2010*
Billing End Date	*8/31/2011*
Billing Frequency	Monthly
Discount	Amount
Service Level	Gold

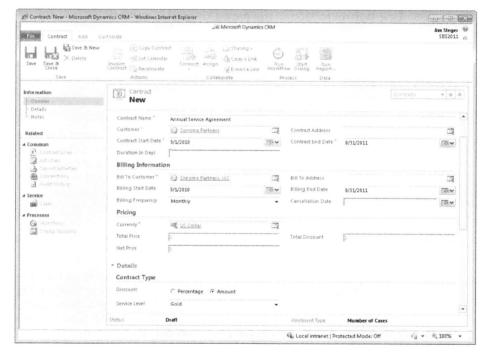

10. Click the **Save** button to create the contract.

> **Tip** Microsoft Dynamics CRM automatically assigns a unique identifying number to each contract when it is first saved. Similar to the auto-numbering for cases and knowledge base articles, contract numbering can be configured by system administrators in the Administration section of the Settings pane. By default, each case will be created with a three-character prefix (CNR), a five-digit code, and a six-character identifier—for example, CNR-01006-V7PQMB.

11. In the entity navigation pane of the new contract, click **Contract Lines**.

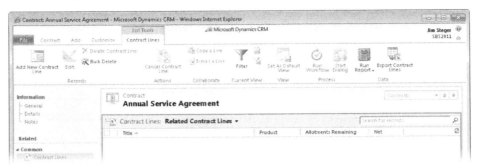

12. On the ribbon, on the **List Tools Contract Lines** tab, click the **Add New Contract Line** button to launch the **New Contract Line** form.

13. In the **General** section of the **New Contract Line** form, in the **Title** field, enter *FY2010-FY2011*.

14. Verify that the **Start Date** and **End Date** fields default to 9/1/2010 and 8/31/2011, respectively.

> **Important** Microsoft Dynamics CRM validates the start and end dates entered in the contract line to ensure that the end date does not occur in the past and that both the start and end dates are within the Contract Start Date and Contract End Date fields specified on the Contract form. If the end date of 8/31/2011 occurs in the past, you will need to change it to a future date to complete this exercise.

15. In the **Total Cases/Minutes** field, enter *20*.

> **Tip** For this example, the Total Cases/Minutes field will be required on the form, be-cause the associated contract template allots a number of cases to the contract. When a contract template with an allotment type of Coverage Dates is used, the Total Cases/ Minutes field will be read-only on the form, because the contract covers a time period rather than a specified number of cases or minutes.

16. In the **Total Price** field, enter *10,000*. In the **Discount** field, enter *2,500*.

17. Click **Save** to create the contract line.

> **Important** Each time the Contract Line form is saved, several fields are updated auto-
> matically based on system calculations. In the Allotment Details section, the total cases
> or minutes logged against the contract line is subtracted from the Total Cases/Minutes
> value to display the allotments remaining. In the Pricing section, the net charge is re-
> calculated based on the Total Price and Discount values, and a rate is calculated based
> on the Total Price and Total Cases/Minutes values.

18. Click **Save and Close** to save and close the contract line.

CLEAN UP Close the contract record.

Activating and Renewing a Contract

When a contract is created in Microsoft Dynamics CRM, the system assigns a default status of Draft to the contract. Only contracts in Draft status can be edited; after a contract has progressed to Invoiced or Active status, the fields in the contract are locked. When the contract is Active, service cases can be logged against the contract and a running tally of used cases or time is tracked against the total allotment specified in the contract line.

Given the need for a business to lock down the terms of a contract while still allowing for flexibility as the company's needs change, the life cycle of a contract can become complicated. Consider the following scenarios for why a service contract might change:

- A company's internal team takes over support for a software application, so it cancels its support agreement with a consulting firm.

- A customer service manager receives notification from her company's accounting department that a customer has several past due invoices for support services, so the manager places the customer's service contract on hold to prevent any new cases from being created until the balance is paid.

- Upon the expiration of a year-long service agreement, a customer decides to renew the contract for another year of service.

Not every contract will follow a fixed life cycle from start to finish, so it's important to understand how contract statuses are managed in Microsoft Dynamics CRM and what actions are allowed for each status. The following table provides an overview of contract statuses and available actions.

Status	Description	Actions
Draft	The default status when a contract is created.	Can be edited or deleted. No cases can be assigned. Cannot be placed on hold, canceled, or renewed.
Invoiced	Indicates that the contract has been accepted by the customer and has a pending start date. A contract cannot be moved to this status until it has at least one contract line.	Cannot be edited or deleted. No cases can be assigned. Can be placed on hold or canceled. Cannot be renewed.
Active	Indicates that the contract is within the specified start and end dates and is eligible for support cases. Each contract is automatically moved to this status on the specified start date.	Cannot be edited or deleted. Cases can be assigned. Can be placed on hold or canceled. Can be renewed.

Status	Description	Actions
On Hold	Indicates that the contract is on hold from Active status, typically for further review or negotiation with the customer.	No actions can be taken against the contract until the hold is released. No cases can be assigned.
Canceled	Indicates that the contract was canceled prior to the end date by the organization or the customer.	Cannot be edited or deleted. No cases can be assigned. Can be renewed.
Expired	Indicates that the contract has passed the specified end date without being renewed.	Cannot be edited. No cases can be assigned. Can be canceled. Can be renewed.

In this exercise, you'll move the contract created in the previous section to Active status, log a case against it, and then renew it.

SET UP Use your own Microsoft Dynamics CRM installation in place of the CRM sample data shown in this exercise. Use the Internet Explorer web browser to navigate to your Microsoft Dynamics CRM website, if necessary, before beginning this exercise. You need the contract you created in the previous exercise. Also, use a user account that has the CSR Manager security role or another role with privileges to create and edit contracts, contract lines, and cases.

1. In the **Service** area, click **Contracts**, and then double-click the contract created in the previous exercise.

2. On the **Contract** tab of the ribbon, in the **Actions** group, click the **Invoice Contract** button.

Because the start date is in the past, the contract automatically moves to the Active status and allows you to enter cases against it.

> **Important** When you select the Invoice Contract option, the contract's status is updated to either Invoiced (if the start date is in the future) or Active (if the start date is the current date or a past date). When a contract is in Invoiced or Active status, all fields on the contract are read-only.

3. In the entity navigation pane of the contract, click **Cases** to view the case manager for the contract.

4. On the ribbon, click the **New** button to open a new case against the contract.

5. In the **New Case** form, enter the following values.

Title	*Replace water line for company coffee machine*
Customer	*Sonoma Partners*
Subject	Default Subject
Case Type	Problem
Case Origin	Phone
Contract	**Annual Service Agreement** (created in the previous exercise)
Contract Line	FY2010-FY2011 (created in the previous exercise)

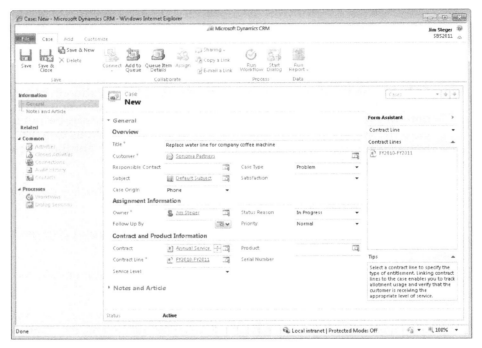

6. Click **Save** to create the case.

7. In the **Actions** group on the ribbon, click **Resolve Case** to mark the case as resolved.

> **Tip** Only resolved cases are counted against the total allotment specified on the contract line. For each resolved case, the remaining allotment is recalculated. For example, if a contract line has five cases specified in the Total Cases/Minutes field, it's possible to log six or more cases against it, as long as no more than five of those cases are in Resolved status.

8. In the **Resolve Case** dialog box, in the **Resolution** field, enter *Water line replaced.*

9. Click **OK** to mark the case as Resolved.

10. Click the browser window's **Close** button to close the case window.

11. In the **Contract** form, in the entity navigation pane, click **Contract Lines**. Then click the **Refresh** button, if needed, to verify that the **Allotments Remaining** value is updated to 19.

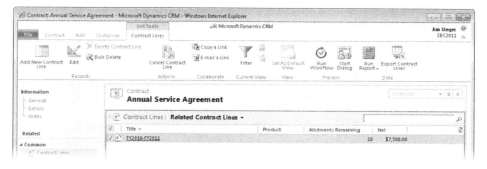

12. On the ribbon, click the **Contract** tab, and then in the **Actions** group, click **Renew Contract** to renew the contract for another term.

The Renew Contract dialog box appears.

> **Tip** You can update the status of a contract from the Contract tab of the ribbon. From this ribbon tab, you can also cancel or place a hold on a contract. The actions that are available vary depending on the current status of the contract.

13. In the dialog box, leave **Include canceled contract lines** selected, and then click **OK**.

> **Important** When a contract is renewed, Microsoft Dynamics CRM automatically creates a copy of the contract with updated start and end dates. The new contract will default to Draft status and will have the same contract number as the original.

14. Close the draft contract.

In the Service area, in the Contracts view, note that a new contract in Draft status has been created with the same number as the active contract.

15. Double-click the renewed contract in **Draft** status, and verify that the start and end dates are automatically calculated as an extension of the original contract.

> **Tip** Microsoft Dynamics CRM creates a link between the original contract and the renewed contract. You can find this information in the Originating Contract field on the Details section of the Contract form.

 CLEAN UP Close the contract record.

Working with Service Queues

In addition to using contracts to manage the number of cases or service hours billed to customers, customer service teams can use service queues to improve the routing of cases and ensure that each request is handled efficiently. In Microsoft Dynamics CRM 2011, a queue is a public listing of records, such as cases and activities. Queues are typically set up based on team assignments or subject matter expertise on a product or service.

When a case is added to a service queue, it is shared by the group of users that have access to the queue until it is accepted by or assigned to a customer service representative. When a record is added to a queue, Microsoft Dynamics CRM creates a queue item, associates the record to that queue item, and then displays queue items in the Workplace area. Customer service managers can create queues in the Business Management section in the Settings area.

Users can work on items from queues they have access to by assigning themselves to the queue items. After a record (such as a case) is assigned to a user, it is moved to the user's Items I Am Working On view and cannot be worked on by other team members until it is released.

Users can perform the following actions on items in a queue.

Action	Description
Routing	Moves a queue item from one queue to another. Each item can only be associated to one queue at a time. This action also allows a user to reassign the target records from the queue item during this process.
Work On	Assigns a queue item to a particular user or team. When a user works on an item, the queue item will be displayed in a special view for the user. Only one user or team can be assigned to work on a queue item at a time.
Release	Removes the user associated with the queue item.
Remove	Removes the queue item from the queue.
Queue Item Details	Displays additional information associated with the queue item.

In Microsoft Dynamics CRM 2011, most records—such as accounts and contacts—can be owned by users or teams. Although queues cannot own a record, Microsoft Dynamics CRM allows you to add a record to a queue. When you add a record to a queue, the owner of the record stays the same and will display in the queue, but other users can now choose to work on the record. When a user selects the record to work on it, Microsoft Dynamics CRM associates the queue item to that user, and the queue item then appears in the user's unique Items I Am Working On queue.

> **Important** Adding a record to a queue does not change the ownership of the record. A queue item can only belong to one queue at a time. Furthermore, a queue item can only be assigned to one user or team at a time.

If you enter an email address when you create a queue, you can have service requests received by that email address delivered directly to the queue. All inbound email messages to that address will then be created as email activity records in Microsoft Dynamics CRM and will be displayed in the queue so customer service representatives can accept each email message and follow up accordingly. When configuring email messages to automatically display in a queue, you can select options that determine which messages will be displayed. For example, you can display the following:

- All email messages sent to the specified address.
- Only those email messages that are sent to the specified address in response to messages sent from Microsoft Dynamics CRM.
- Only those email messages that are sent to the specified address from a lead, contact, or account in your Microsoft Dynamics CRM database.
- Only those email messages that match an address from a Microsoft Dynamics CRM record that is email enabled.

You do not need to supply an email address when setting up a queue, but this feature is helpful for customer service teams that receive a lot of service requests via email.

> **See Also** With Microsoft Dynamics CRM workflow, you can set up routing rules to automatically assign cases to the appropriate queue. Furthermore, you can configure workflow rules for the queue items, allowing for escalation within the queue itself. Although the workflow feature is beyond the scope of this book, you can learn more about it in Working with Microsoft Dynamics CRM 2011, by Mike Snyder and Jim Steger (Microsoft Press, 2011).

In this exercise, you'll create a service queue and route a case to it, then accept the case into your Items I Am Working On queue.

SET UP Use the Internet Explorer web browser to navigate to your Microsoft Dynamics CRM website, if necessary, before beginning this exercise. You need the Product Catalog Request case you created in Chapter 10, "Tracking Service Requests." If you cannot locate the Product Catalog Request case, select a different active case for this exercise. Also, ensure that your user account has the CSR Manager security role or another role with privileges to create queues and cases.

1. In the **Settings** area, click **Business Management**, and then click **Queues** to view the available queues.

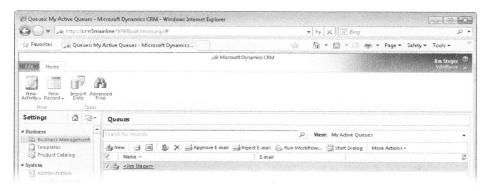

2. Click the **New** button to launch the **New Queue** form.

3. In the **New Queue** form, enter the following information:

Queue Name	*Catalog Request*
E-mail	*someone@example.com*
Owner	This will vary among individual systems, so select your user account.
Description	*Catalog fulfillment requests*
Convert to e-mail activities	All e-mail messages
E-mail access type - Incoming	None
E-mail access type - Outgoing	None

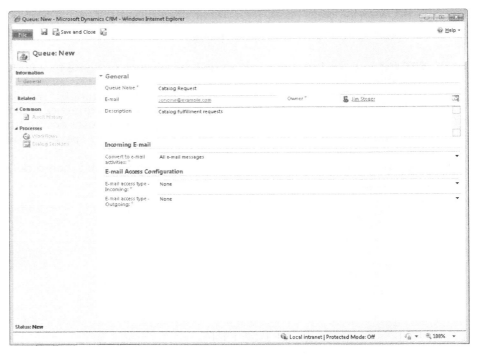

4. Click **Save and Close** to create the queue.

5. In the **Service** area, click **Cases** to view the case manager.

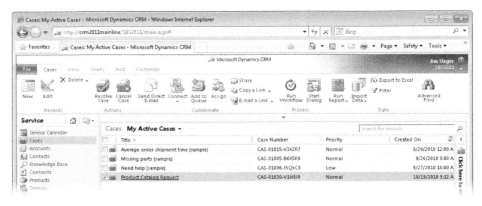

6. Locate the **Product Catalog Request** case, and then select the record in the grid (without opening it).

7. On the ribbon, in the **Collaborate** group on the **Cases** tab, click the **Add to Queue** button to associate the case to a queue.

The Add To Queue dialog box appears.

8. In the dialog box, click the **Lookup** button.

The Look Up Record dialog box appears.

9. In the **View** selector, change the view to **Queues: Primary E-mail (Pending Approval)**, select the **Catalog Requests** queue, and then click **OK**.

10. Click **OK** in the **Add to Queue** dialog box.

11. In the **Workplace** area, click **Queues**, and then select **Items available to work on** from the view selector. Then select the **Catalog Requests** queue to verify that the case you assigned appears.

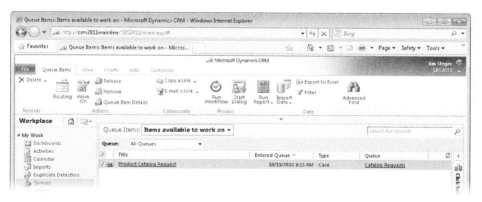

12. Make sure that the case is selected. Then, on the Queue Items tab of the ribbon, click the **Work On** button to assign the case into your personal queue.

The Assign Queued Items dialog box opens.

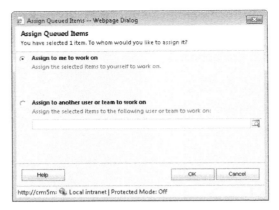

13. Click **OK** to verify that you are accepting the case.

14. In the view selector, click the **Items I am working on** queue, and verify that the case now appears.

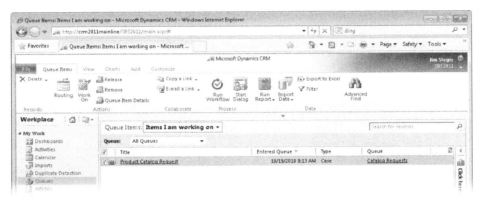

Key Points

- Service contracts can be used to manage support requests from customers. Each contract includes the duration of the agreement, the number of incidents or hours of service, pricing, and customer billing information. Multiple contract lines can be assigned to a contract to store the particular terms of each agreement.

- Customer service managers can create contract templates to establish the framework for service contracts. Each contract must be created from a contract template.

- Contracts can be edited only while in Draft status, so it's important that customer service representatives complete the contract terms as thoroughly and accurately as possible before moving the contract to Invoiced status.

- Each contract in Invoiced status is automatically moved to Active status on the specified start date and moved from Active to Expired status on the end date if the contract has not been renewed.

- Cases can be logged against only those contracts that are in Active status.

- A contract can be renewed while in Active, Canceled, or Expired status. When renewing a contract, Microsoft Dynamics CRM creates a copy of the original contract and stores a link to the originating contract on the new record.

- Contracts can be placed on hold or canceled to prevent new cases from being logged against them.

- Customer service teams can share records, such as cases, in queues to ensure that all service requests are routed to the correct people and resolved quickly.

- When a record is added to a queue, Microsoft Dynamics CRM creates a separate queue item and associates it to the queue and to the record.

- Records remain in a queue until they are accepted by a user, who assumes responsibility for handling the queue item or escalating it to another representative.

- Service requests submitted via email can be assigned to a queue automatically, if an email address was assigned to the queue during setup.

Part 4

Reporting and Analysis

13 Working with Filters and Charts 279

14 Using Dashboards 297

15 Using the Report Wizard 319

16 Using Advanced Find 343

17 Reporting with Excel. 363

Chapter at a Glance

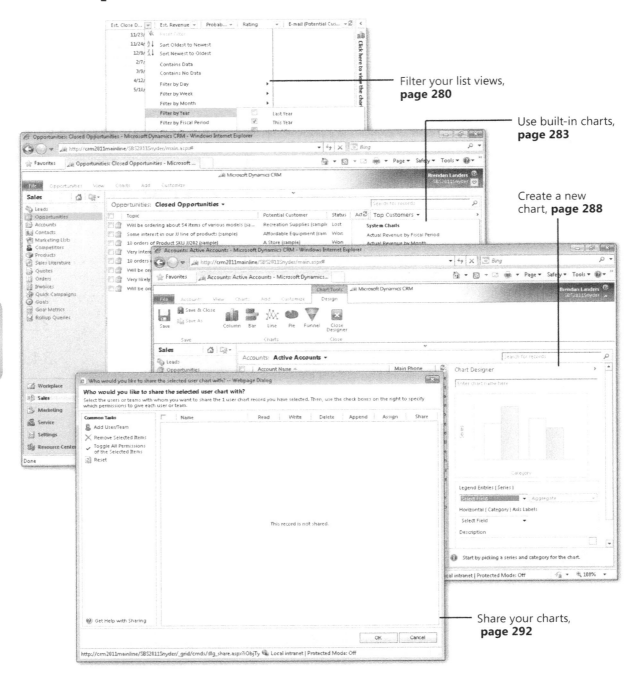

Filter your list views, **page 280**

Use built-in charts, **page 283**

Create a new chart, **page 288**

Share your charts, **page 292**

13 Working with Filters and Charts

In this chapter, you will learn how to

- ✔ Apply filters to your data and save filtered views.
- ✔ Set additional filters on a saved view.
- ✔ Use charts to analyze and interact with Microsoft Dynamics CRM data.
- ✔ Create new charts to view pertinent data visually.
- ✔ Share a chart with a co-worker.

Microsoft Dynamics CRM enables you to collect large amounts of data and provides tools that you can use to easily search through the data and find the records you need. In addition, the software offers several different reporting options that empower you to make business decisions based on the data within the reports. Often you might find yourself digging into data in unpredictable ways as you drill into a problem or opportunity and interact with the data. For example, you might answer one question but come up with another and therefore want to dig more deeply. Microsoft Dynamics CRM provides several tools for interacting with the data; two of the simplest are filters and charts.

In this chapter, you will learn how to drill into your data by using the filter and chart tools.

Practice Files There are no practice files for this chapter.

Important The images used in this book reflect the default form and field names in Microsoft Dynamics CRM. Because the software offers extensive customization capabilities, it's possible that some of the record types or fields have been relabeled in your Microsoft Dynamics CRM environment. If you cannot find the forms, fields, or security roles referred to in this book, contact your system administrator for assistance.

Important You must know the location of your Microsoft Dynamics CRM website to work the exercises in this book. Check with your system administrator to verify the web address if you don't know it.

Applying Filters to Your Data and Saving Filtered Views

In Chapter 17, "Reporting with Excel," you will learn how to use Microsoft Excel as a reporting tool for Microsoft Dynamics CRM data. In addition to using Excel for reporting, it is common for users of business applications to export data to Excel to filter the data and scrutinize a subset of the records. With Microsoft Dynamics CRM, you can filter your records in real time to zero in on the most important data in your system with a few clicks of the mouse, without leaving the Microsoft Dynamics CRM application.

In this exercise, you will use a filter to view the opportunities that have an estimated close date in the current year and that have a probability associated with them.

 SET UP Use the Windows Internet Explorer web browser to navigate to your Microsoft Dynamics CRM website before beginning this exercise.

1. In the **Sales** area, click **Opportunities**.

   The Opportunity grid view appears.

2. In the view selector, select **Open Opportunities**.

   The list of Open Opportunities is displayed.

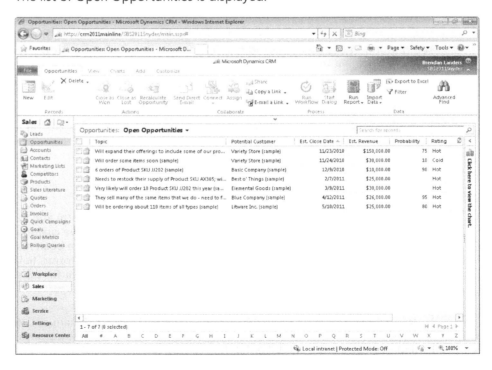

3. On the **Opportunities** tab of the ribbon, in the **Data** group, click the **Filter** button.

Filter arrows appear in the grid column headers.

4. Click the arrow to the right of the **Est. Close Date** field, select **Filter by Year**, and then select the **This Year** check box.

> **Important** If the Est. Close Date field does not exist in your view, choose another field for this example.

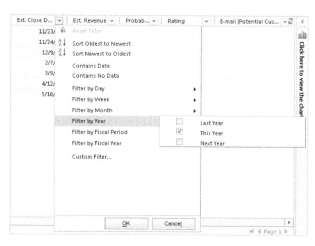

5. Click **OK** on the filter menu.

The updated results will reflect all opportunities that will be closing this year.

6. Click the arrow to the right of the **Probability** field and select **Contains Data**.

This will further filter the data to show opportunities that are closing this year and that have a probability recorded.

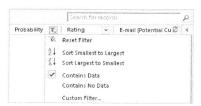

7. On the **View** tab of the ribbon, click the **Save As** button to save your view.

   The View Information dialog box appears.

8. In the **Name** field, enter ***Opportunities Projected to Close This Year***, and then click **OK**.

   The filtered view is saved as a personal view in Microsoft Dynamics CRM.

Setting Additional Filters on a Saved View

Over time, you will undoubtedly create additional views of filtered data to support your changing needs. You might find that the filters you applied to a view need to be refined to meet your needs or to provide a more accurate view of your data. In the example in the previous section, you might have noticed that one of the opportunities in the view has a rating of Cold. Because the probability of the opportunity is very low, you would probably want to remove it from your Opportunities Projected To Close This Year view.

In this exercise, you will set additional filters on a previously saved view.

 SET UP Use the Internet Explorer web browser to navigate to your Microsoft Dynamics CRM website, if necessary, before beginning this exercise. You need the Opportunities Projected To Close This Year view you created and saved in the previous exercise.

1. In the **Sales** area, click **Opportunities**.

   The Opportunity grid view appears.

2. In the view selector, select **Opportunities Projected to Close This Year**.

   The view you saved in the previous exercise is displayed.

3. On the ribbon, click the **Filter** button.

   Filter arrows appear in the grid column headers.

4. Click the arrow to the right of the **Rating** field, and select the **Hot** check box. You may need to scroll to the right to see the **Rating** field.

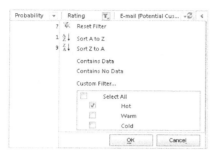

5. Click **OK**. The subset of data is now displayed.

6. On the **View** tab of the ribbon, click the **Save Filters** button.

The additional filter has been applied to your previously saved view.

Using Charts to Analyze Microsoft Dynamics CRM Data

In Chapter 15, "Using the Report Wizard," and Chapter 17, you will learn how to create reports with Microsoft Dynamics CRM data by using the Report Wizard and Excel tools. These tools allow you to create visually appealing reports by using chart controls within the respective tools. These are great options, but they require you to leave the area of the system you are working on and enter a different application. In addition to these options, Microsoft Dynamics CRM allows you to create and view charts within the application.

Consider the following scenarios:

- A sales manager is evaluating sales trends for the current quarter. She filters opportunities to see those owned by a subset of sales representatives. The sales manager wants to quickly get aggregate values for all opportunities for those sales representatives.

- A marketing manager would like to execute a lead generation campaign. He has limited resources and would like to target the campaign to geographies that have the most current customers.

You can easily view this information by using charts in Microsoft Dynamics CRM. You will find that many of your chart needs are covered by the 52 charts that Microsoft Dynamics CRM comes with, shown in the following table.

Entity	Charts	
Account	Accounts By Industry	Accounts By Territories
	Accounts By Owner	New Accounts By Month
Activity	Activities By Month Due	Activities By Priority
	Activities By Owner	Activities By Type
	Activities By Owner and Priority	Activities By Type and Priority
Article	Articles By Status	
Campaign	Campaign Budget vs. Actual Costs (By Fiscal)	Campaign Type Mix
	Campaign Budget vs. Actual Costs (by Month)	
Case	Case Mix (By Business Unit)	Cases By Origin (By Day)
	Case Mix (By Origin)	Cases By Priority (Per Day)
	Case Mix (By Priority)	Cases By Priority (Per Owner)
	Case Mix (By Type)	Resolved Case Satisfaction
	Case Resolution Trend (By Day)	Service Leaderboard
Goal	Percentage Achieved	Today's Target vs. Actuals (Count)
	Goal Progress (Count)	Today's Target vs. Actuals (Money)
	Goal Progress (Money)	
Lead	Incoming Lead Analysis By Month	Leads By Rating
	Lead Generation Rate	Leads By Source
	Leads By Owner	Leads By Source Campaign
Opportunity	Actual Revenue by Fiscal Period	Opportunity By Campaigns
	Actual Revenue by Month	Revenue Generated By Campaign
	Deals Won vs. Deals Lost	Sales Leaderboard
	Deals Won vs. Deals Lost By Fiscal Period	Sales Pipeline
	Deals Won vs. Deals Lost By Owner	Sales Progress By Territory
	Estimated vs. Actual Revenue (By Fiscal)	Top Customers
	Estimated vs. Actual Revenue (by Month)	Top Opportunities
Order	Actual Revenues By Fiscal Period	Actual Revenues By Owner
	Actual Revenues By Month	

In this exercise, you will view charts within Microsoft Dynamics CRM.

 SET UP Use the Internet Explorer web browser to navigate to your Microsoft Dynamics CRM website, if necessary, before beginning this exercise.

1. In the **Sales** area, click **Opportunities**.

   The Opportunities grid view appears.

2. In the view selector, select **Closed Opportunities**.

3. On the ribbon, click the **Charts** tab.

 4. In the **Layout** group, click the **Chart Pane** button, and then select **Right**.

> **Tip** Charts can be displayed either on top of or to the right of the grid.

5. In the chart view list, select **Top Customers**.

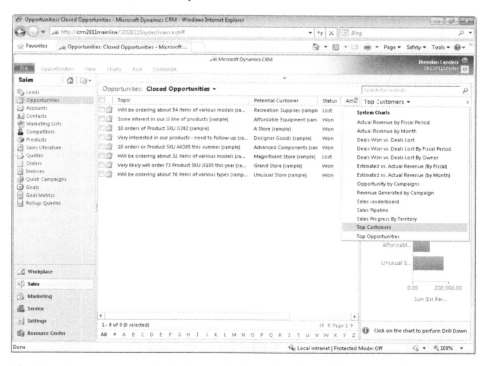

The Top Customers chart displays data from the Closed Opportunities view.

> **Tip** Microsoft Dynamics CRM Charts are contextual, meaning that they will reflect the data from the current grid list of records. As you filter the data or switch views, the charts will update appropriately.

6. In the view selector, select **Open Opportunities**.

The same chart is displayed, but it is updated to show open opportunities.

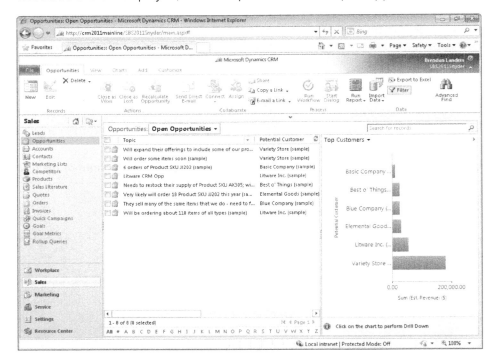

7. In the **Top Customers** chart, click the potential customer **Litware Inc.** bar.

> **Important** If you do not have Litware Inc. as a potential customer for an opportunity, click a different potential customer, preferably one with multiple open opportunities.

The grid list is filtered to show the open opportunities for Litware Inc., and a drill-down menu appears.

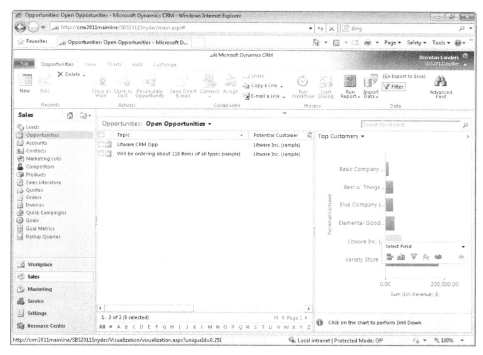

8. In the **Select Field** list on the drilldown menu, select **Owner**.

9. Click the **Pie Chart** icon, and then click the **Results** arrow.

A pie chart appears, showing the estimated revenue of the Litware Inc. opportunities by opportunity owner.

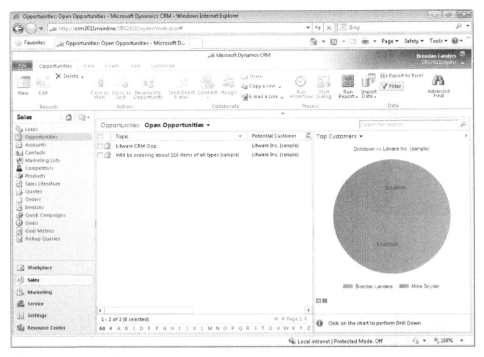

10. Click one of the pie chart sections.

The grid updates with the records specific to the section you clicked.

Creating a New Chart

You now understand the power of the built-in charts that come with Microsoft Dynamics CRM. In addition to the charts provided by the application, you can create your own charts to support your unique needs. You can create charts for custom entities as well as for the entities included with Microsoft Dynamics CRM, as shown in the following list.

Entities Available for Chart Use

Account	Goal	Quick Campaign
Activity	Goal Metric	Quote
Appointment	Invoice	Quote Product
Article	Invoice Product	Recurring Appointment
Campaign	Lead	Report
Campaign Activity	Letter	Rollup Query
Campaign Response	Marketing List	Sales Literature
Case	Opportunity	Service
Competitor	Opportunity Product	Service Activity
Connection	Order	Task
Contact	Order Product	Team
Contract	Phone Call	Territory
E-Mail	Price List	Unit Group
Fax	Product	User
	Queue Item	

In this exercise, you will create a custom chart within Microsoft Dynamics CRM.

SET UP Use the Internet Explorer web browser to navigate to your Microsoft Dynamics CRM website, if necessary, before beginning this exercise.

1. In the **Sales** area, click **Accounts**.

   The Accounts grid view appears.

2. In the view selector, select **Active Accounts**.

3. On the ribbon, click the **Charts** tab, and then click the **New Chart** button.

   The Chart Designer appears to the right of the grid.

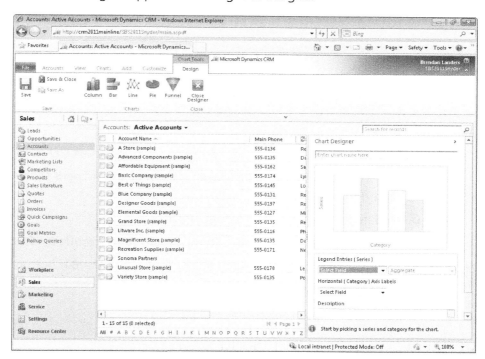

4. In the **Legend Entries (Series)** area, select **Account Name** in the **Select Field** list.

5. In the **Horizontal (Category) Axis Labels** area, select **Address 1: State/Province**.

You will see that the chart has been given a title of *Account Name by Address 1: State/Province.*

6. Update the chart title to ***Accounts by State***.

7. In the **Description** field, enter ***Show a Count of Accounts by State***.

8. On the **Chart Tools Design** tab of the ribbon, click the **Bar** button to change the chart to a bar chart.

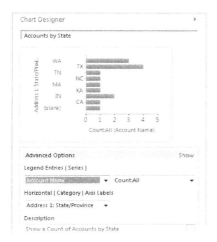

9. On the ribbon, click the **Save** button to save the chart, and then click the **Close Designer** button.

Your chart is now available in the list of available charts.

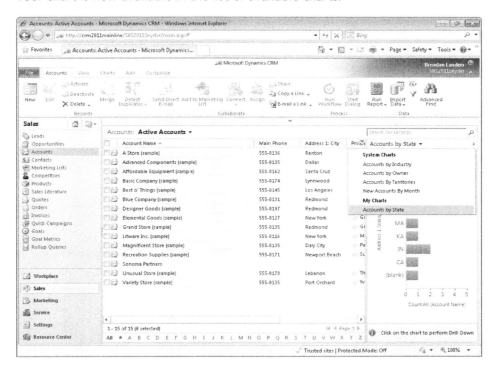

Sharing a Chart

It's likely that the reports and charts you create will also be useful to your colleagues. Rather than trying to articulate the steps it took for you to create a chart, you can share the Chart with other users in Microsoft Dynamics CRM. Typically, a sales manager or other advanced user creates a chart that will be valuable to other team members. These shared charts allow users of all computer skill levels to solve business-critical reporting needs.

In this exercise, you will share a custom chart with another Microsoft Dynamics CRM user.

 SET UP Use the Internet Explorer web browser to navigate to your Microsoft Dynamics CRM website, if necessary, before beginning this exercise. You need the Accounts By State chart you saved in the previous exercise.

1. In the **Sales** area, click **Accounts**.

   The Account grid view appears.

2. On the ribbon, click the **Charts** tab. Then click the **Chart Pane** button and select **Right**.

3. In the **Chart View** list, select **Accounts by State**.

   The Accounts By State chart you created in the previous exercise appears.

 4. On the **Charts** tab of the ribbon, in the **Collaborate** group, click the **Share** button.

   The Who Would You Like To Share The Selected User Chart With? dialog box appears.

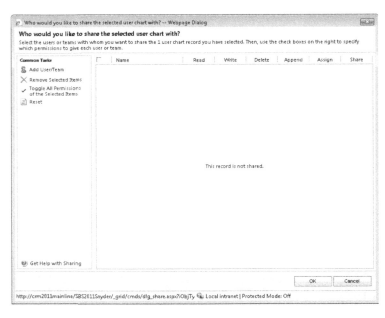

5. Click **Add User/Team**.

The Look Up Records dialog box appears.

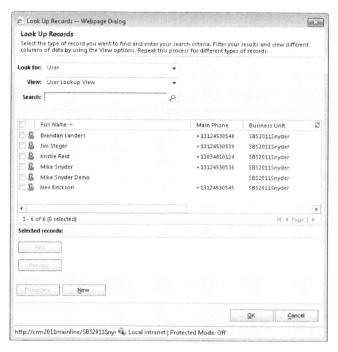

6. In the **Look Up Records** dialog box, select a colleague to share the chart with, click the **Add** button, and then click **OK**.

7. Click **OK** to exit the **Who would you like to share the selected user chart with?** dialog box.

Your chart is now shared with the selected colleague and will appear in his or her chart list.

> **See Also** For more information on record sharing, see Chapter 16, "Using Advanced Find."

Key Points

- You can use filters on any list of records to help analyze your data.

- Charts are available to provide inline real-time reporting.

- You can interact with charts and drill through to obtain the necessary details.

- Charts work in conjunction with lists of records; as you drill into a chart, the list of records will update and, conversely, as you change the view, the chart will update.

- Although Microsoft Dynamics CRM comes with many charts, you can also easily create new charts to support your specific reporting needs.

- You can share charts with your colleagues as needed so that they can benefit from the reports you've built.

Chapter at a Glance

Use a built-in dashboard, **page 298**

Create a new dashboard, **page 303**

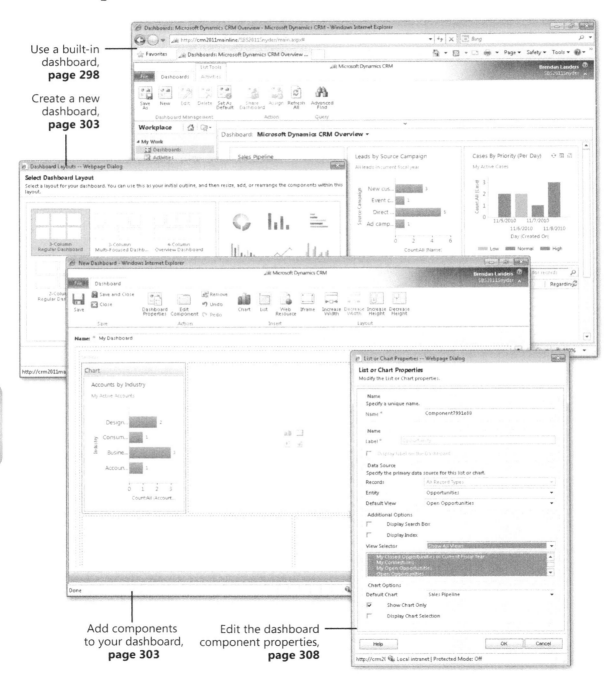

Add components to your dashboard, **page 303**

Edit the dashboard component properties, **page 308**

14 Using Dashboards

In this chapter, you will learn how to

- ✔ Use built-in dashboards.
- ✔ Create additional dashboards.
- ✔ Edit a dashboard.
- ✔ Set a default dashboard.
- ✔ Share a dashboard with a co-worker.

These days, every organization seems to be either using or aspiring to use dashboards. The term *dashboard* often has different connotations for different people, but it is almost always used to describe the presentation of various sets of data in a single screen. The most common types of dashboards are:

- **Strategic** Typically used by managers to understand overall performance. For example, a typical strategic dashboard could include charts showing sales versus goals for a specified time period, along with current pipeline and customer service metrics.

- **Tactical** Typically used by employees to highlight current or recent work. For example, a typical tactical dashboard could include a list of current activities due this week presented along with opportunities expected to close this month.

Knowledge is power. Managers and employees alike want the ability to monitor performance at a glance. Microsoft Dynamics CRM provides you with the flexibility to use the built-in dashboards to monitor performance and create additional dashboards to meet your unique business needs.

In this chapter, you will learn how to use the dashboard features of Microsoft Dynamics CRM.

> **Practice Files** There are no practice files for this chapter.

> **Important** The images used in this book reflect the default form and field names in Microsoft Dynamics CRM. Because the software offers extensive customization capabilities, it's possible that some of the record types or fields have been relabeled in your Microsoft Dynamics CRM environment. If you cannot find the forms, fields, or security roles referred to in this book, contact your system administrator for assistance.

> **Important** You must know the location of your Microsoft Dynamics CRM website to work the exercises in this book. Check with your system administrator to verify the web address if you don't know it.

Using Built-in Dashboards

In Chapter 13, "Working with Filters and Charts," you learned how to view, analyze, and drill down into your application data. You focused on specific areas of the application in each exercise. Dashboards allow you to pull the charts and views available in other parts of the application into a single view. Microsoft Dynamics CRM provides several built-in dashboards that are ready for your organization to use. These are listed in the following table.

Name	Type	Charts Included	Views Included
Customer Service Operations Dashboard	3-Column Multi-Focused Dashboard	Activities By Owner and Priority Service Leaderboard Articles By Status Cases By Origin (Per Day) Cases By Priority (Per Day)	
Customer Service Performance Dashboard	2-Column Regular Dashboard	Service Leaderboard Case Resolution Trend (By Day) Goal Progress (Count) Articles By Status	
Customer Service Representative Dashboard	2-Column Regular Dashboard	Case Mix (By Origin) Cases By Priority (Per Day) Case Resolution Trend (By Day) Goal Progress (Count)	My Activities

Name	Type	Charts Included	Views Included
Marketing Dashboard	2-Column Regular Dashboard	Campaign Type Mix	My Activities
		Campaign Budget vs. Actual Costs (By Fiscal)	
		Leads by Source Campaign	My Campaigns
		Revenue Generated by Campaign	
Microsoft Dynamics CRM Overview	3-Column Focused Dashboard	Sales Pipeline	My Activities
		Leads By Source Campaign	
		Cases By Priority (Per Day)	
Sales Activity Dashboard	3-Column Focused Dashboard	Sales Pipeline	My Activities
		Percentage Achieved	
		Leads By Source	
		Top Opportunities	
		Top Customers	
Sales Performance Dashboard	3-Column Focused Dashboard	Sales Pipeline	
		Goal Progress (Money) - My Goals	
		Goal Progress (Money) - My Group's Goals	
		Percentage Achieved	
		Sales Leaderboard	
		Deals Won vs. Deals Lost By Owner	

In this exercise, you will use the built-in dashboard features of Microsoft Dynamics CRM. You will also interact with the dashboard elements.

SET UP Use the Windows Internet Explorer web browser to navigate to your Microsoft Dynamics CRM website before beginning this exercise.

1. In the **Workplace** area, click **Dashboards**.

   The dashboard view appears.

2. In the view selector, select **Microsoft Dynamics CRM Overview**.

   The screen changes to show the dashboard elements as described in the table shown earlier in this section.

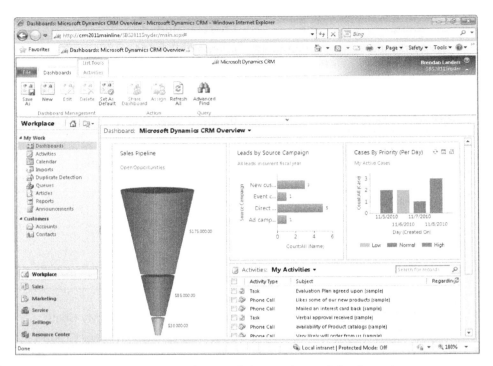

3. In the **Sales Pipeline** chart, click one of the sections of the funnel.

4. In the **Select Field** box on the shortcut menu, select **Probability**, and then click the arrow to submit the field.

The drilldown data appears in a bar chart format.

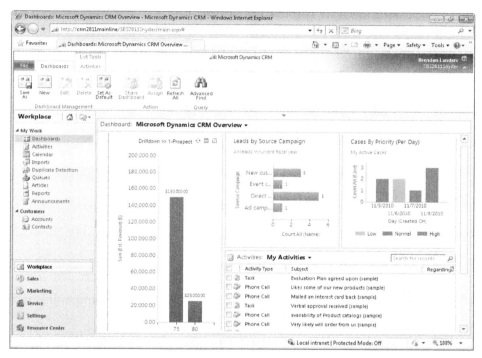

5. Drill into one of the chart bars by clicking it. Choose **Est. Close Date** in the **Select Field** box, and then click the arrow to submit.

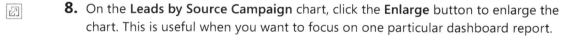

6. In the lower-left corner of the chart, click the **Back** button.

You are returned to the previous view.

7. In the lower-left corner of the chart, click the **Home** button.

You return to the original Sales Pipeline chart.

8. On the **Leads by Source Campaign** chart, click the **Enlarge** button to enlarge the chart. This is useful when you want to focus on one particular dashboard report.

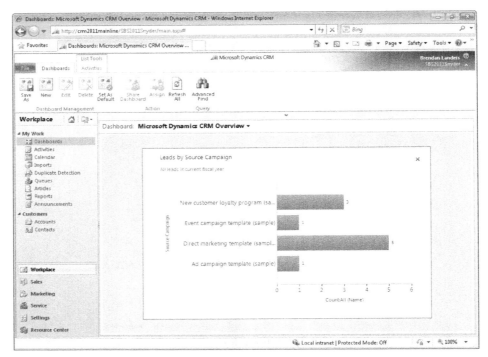

9. In the upper-right corner of the **Leads by Source Campaign** chart, click the **Close** button.

You return to the Microsoft Dynamics CRM Overview dashboard.

10. In the upper-right corner of the **Leads by Source Campaign** chart, click the **View Records** button.

A list of the records that are included in the chart is displayed alongside the chart in a new window.

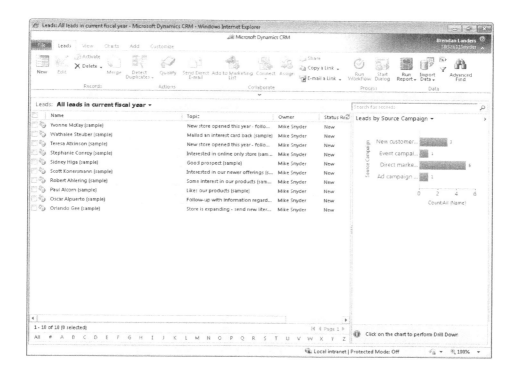

Creating Additional Dashboards

You might find that the seven built-in dashboards satisfy a majority of your needs, but they will probably not provide all the visibility you'd like. With more than 50 charts and hundreds of lists, the possible dashboard combinations seem endless. Microsoft Dynamics CRM allows you to create your own dashboards by using the built-in charts and lists or custom charts and lists that your company creates in the system.

> **See Also** For more information about creating custom charts and lists, see Chapter 13.

> **See Also** Dashboards can contain web resources and iFrames in addition to charts and lists. Web resources and iFrames are beyond the scope of this book, but you can learn more about creating them in Working with Microsoft Dynamics CRM 2011 by Mike Snyder and Jim Steger (Microsoft Press, 2011).

In this exercise, you will create a sample sales representative dashboard in Microsoft Dynamics CRM.

 SET UP Use the Internet Explorer web browser to navigate to your Microsoft Dynamics CRM website, if necessary, before beginning this exercise.

1. In the **Workplace** area, click **Dashboards**.

   The dashboard view appears.

 2. On the ribbon, in the **Dashboard Management** group, click the **New** button.

   The Select Dashboard Layout dialog box appears.

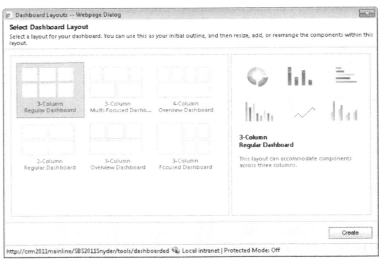

3. Select the **3-Column Multi-Focused Dashboard**, and then click **Create**.

   The dashboard layout screen appears.

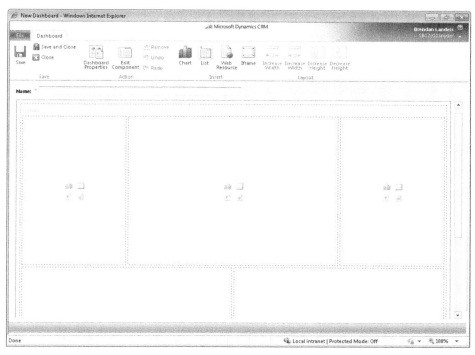

4. In the **Name** field, type *My Dashboard*.

5. As you might have noticed, each available section on the dashboard layout screen contains four buttons. In the upper-left section, click the **Chart** button.

The Component Designer dialog box appears.

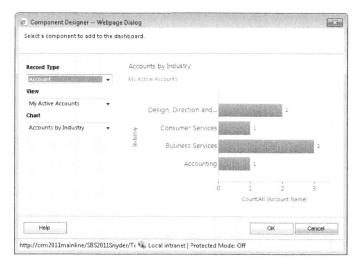

6. In the **Record Type** field, leave **Account** selected.

7. In the **View** field, leave **My Active Accounts** selected.

8. In the **Chart** field, leave **Accounts by Industry** selected, and click **OK**.

This adds the Accounts By Industry chart to the dashboard.

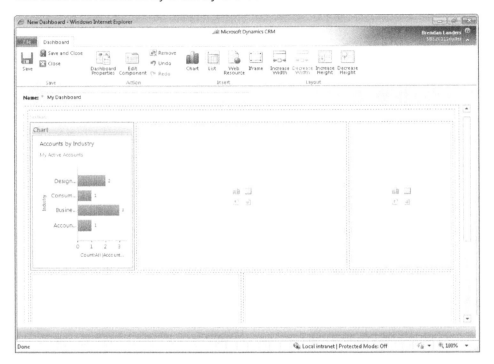

9. In the upper-middle section of the dashboard, click the **Chart** button.

10. In the **Component Designer** dialog box, in the **Record Type** list, select **Opportunity**.

11. Leave **My Open Opportunities** selected in the **View** list, and select **Sales Pipeline** in the **Chart** selection box. Click **OK**.

This adds the Sales Pipeline chart to the dashboard.

12. In the upper-right section of the dashboard, click the **Chart** button.

13. In the **Record Type** list in the **Component Designer** dialog box, select **Lead**.

14. Leave **My Open Leads** selected in the **View** list, select **Leads by Rating** in the **Chart** list, and then click **OK**.

This adds the Leads By Rating chart to the dashboard.

15. In the lower-left section of the dashboard, click the **List** button.

16. In the **Record Type** list, select **Activities**.

17. In the **View** list, leave **My Activities** selected, and click **OK**.

This adds the My Activities list to the dashboard.

18. In the lower-right section of the dashboard, click the **List** button.

19. In the **Record Type** list, select **Leads**.

20. In the **View** list, leave **My Open Leads** selected, and click **OK**.

This adds the My Open Leads list to the dashboard.

Save and Close **21.** Click **Save and Close** to save the dashboard and return to the dashboard view.

The newly created dashboard is displayed.

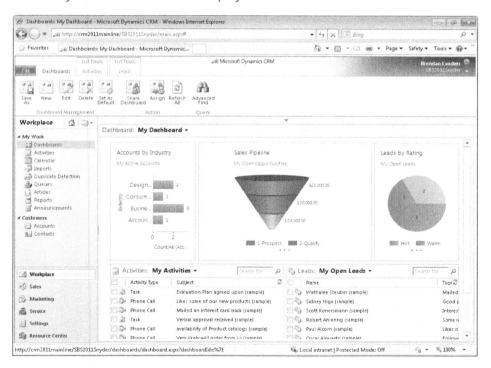

Editing Dashboards

In the previous exercise, you were able to create a robust dashboard in just a few minutes by using the Dashboard designer. As your needs change, you might want to modify your dashboards accordingly. For example, you might want to add, remove, or replace a chart or list. Similarly, you might want to modify the size of a particular dashboard component. By using the same designer, you can accomplish these goals and more.

In this exercise, you will edit a dashboard in Microsoft Dynamics CRM.

 SET UP Use the Internet Explorer web browser to navigate to your Microsoft Dynamics CRM website, if necessary, before beginning this exercise. You need the My Dashboard dashboard you created in the previous exercise.

1. In the **Workplace** area, click **Dashboards**.

2. In the view selector, select **My Dashboard**.

   The dashboard created in the previous exercise appears.

Edit

3. On the ribbon, in the **Dashboard Management** group, click the **Edit** button to edit the dashboard.

   The dashboard layout screen is displayed.

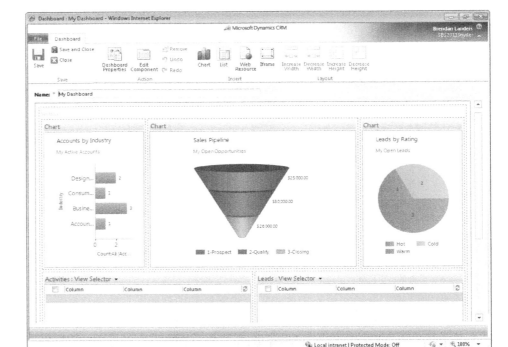

4. Select the **Sales Pipeline** chart by clicking it.

5. In the **Layout** group on the ribbon, click the **Decrease Width** button.

The chart width decreases in the designer.

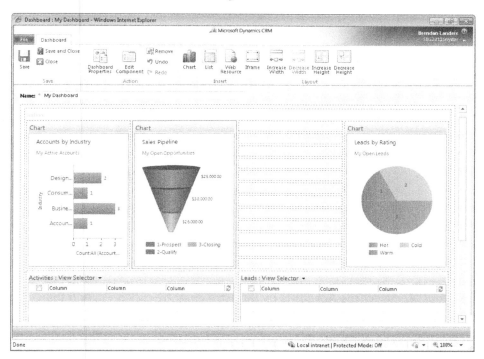

6. Drag the **Sales Pipeline** chart to the right so that it is next to the **Leads by Rating** chart.

> **Tip** Dragging chart objects in the designer is a little challenging at first. When you have dragged the chart to an acceptable place, you will see a red line appear in the designer.

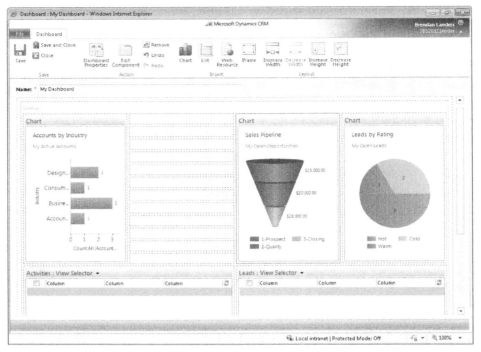

7. Select the **Accounts by Industry** chart by clicking it, and then click the **Increase Width** button on the ribbon.

The Accounts By Industry chart is expanded.

8. Select the **Leads by Rating** chart, and then click **Edit Component** in the **Action** group on the ribbon.

The List Or Chart Properties dialog box appears.

9. At the bottom of the dialog box, select the **Display Chart Selection** check box, and then click **OK**.

   This allows you to change the chart to any of the other lead-based charts on the dashboard.

10. Select the **Sales Pipeline** chart, and click **Edit Component** on the ribbon.

11. In the **Data Source** area of the **List or Chart Properties** dialog box, in the **Default View** field, select **Open Opportunities.**

12. In the **View Selector** field, select **Show All Views**.

    This allows you to change the view behind the chart on the dashboard.

13. Click **OK** to return to the dashboard layout screen.

14. Click **Save and Close** to view the modified dashboard.

The view and chart selectors are now present on the dashboard.

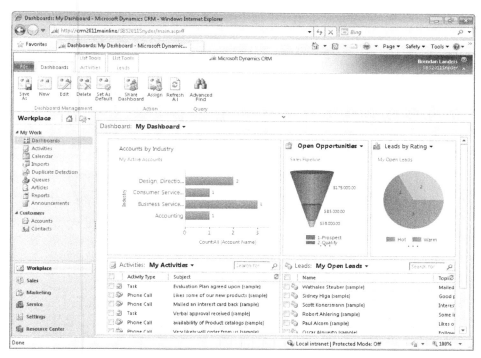

15. In the view selector on the **Sales Pipeline** chart, change the view to **Opportunities Closing Next Month**.

The chart is now updated to show the subset of opportunities.

16. In the chart selector on the **Leads by Rating** chart, change the chart to **Leads by Source**.

The dashboard is updated to display the Leads By Source chart.

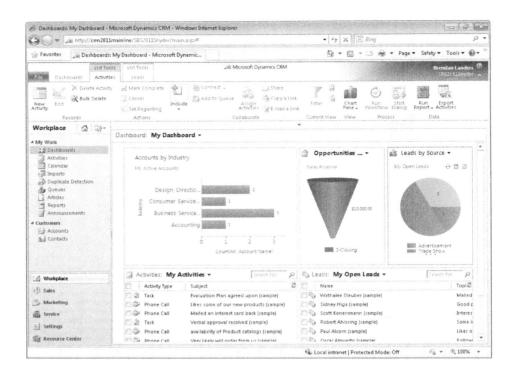

Setting a Default Dashboard

Now that you are able to create and modify dashboards, you will probably find that you are using one particular dashboard more often than others. You might find it inconvenient to continually change the dashboard to your favorite each time you return to the dashboard screen. Microsoft Dynamics CRM allows you to set up a default dashboard to provide a convenient way to access your most heavily used dashboard.

In this exercise, you will set a default dashboard in Microsoft Dynamics CRM.

 SET UP Use the Internet Explorer web browser to navigate to your Microsoft Dynamics CRM website, if necessary, before beginning this exercise. You need the My Dashboard dashboard you created earlier in this chapter.

1. In the **Workplace** area, click **Dashboards**.

2. In the view selector, select **My Dashboard**.

   The dashboard created in the earlier exercise appears.

 3. In the **Dashboard Management** group on the ribbon, select the **Set As Default** button.

   The My Dashboard dashboard is now set as the default.

4. In the **Workplace** area, click **Activities**

5. In the **Workplace** area, click **Dashboards**.

My Dashboard now appears as the default dashboard.

Sharing a Dashboard

In Chapter 13, you learned how to share custom charts with your colleagues. As with charts, it's likely that your dashboards will also be useful to your colleagues. You can share a dashboard with other users in Microsoft Dynamics CRM.

In this exercise, you will share a custom dashboard with another Microsoft Dynamics CRM user.

 SET UP Use the Internet Explorer web browser to navigate to your Microsoft Dynamics CRM website, if necessary, before beginning this exercise. You need the My Dashboard dashboard you created earlier in this chapter.

1. In the **Workplace** area, click **Dashboards**.

The dashboard view appears.

2. In the view selector, select **My Dashboard,** if necessary.

 3. In the **Action** group on the ribbon, click **Share Dashboard**.

The Who Would You Like To Share The Selected User Dashboard With? dialog box appears.

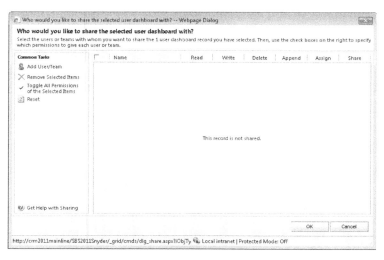

4. Click **Add User/Team**.

The Look Up Records dialog box appears.

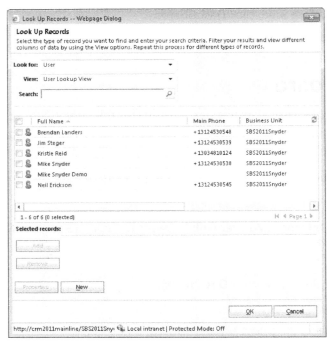

5. In the **Look Up Records** dialog box, select a colleague to share the dashboard with, click the **Add** button, and then click **OK**.

6. Click **OK** to exit the previous dialog box.

   Your dashboard is now shared with the selected colleague and will appear in his or her dashboard list.

> **See Also** For more information on record sharing, see Chapter 16, "Using Advanced Find."

Key Points

- Several dashboards are built into Microsoft Dynamics CRM for immediate use.
- You can easily create additional dashboards to satisfy your unique business requirements.
- After your dashboard has been created, you can modify them as your needs evolve.
- You can set up your own default dashboard.
- You can share dashboards with your colleagues so they can benefit from the dashboards you've built.

Chapter at a Glance

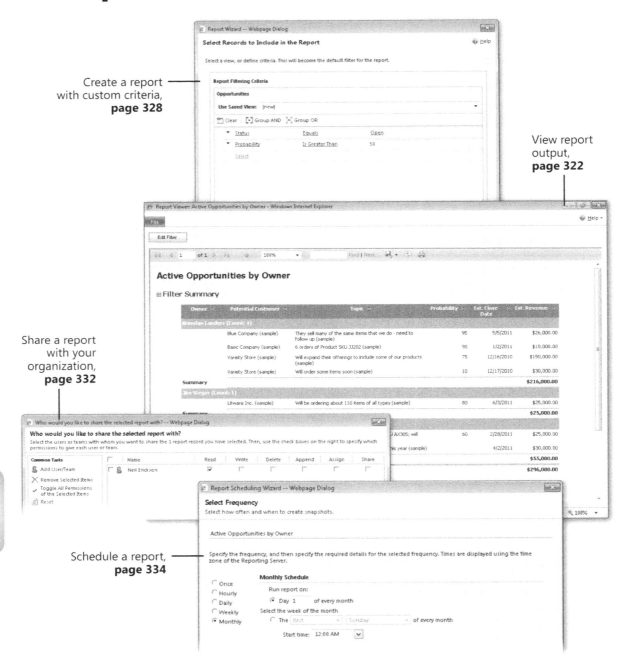

Create a report with custom criteria, **page 328**

View report output, **page 322**

Share a report with your organization, **page 332**

Schedule a report, **page 334**

15 Using the Report Wizard

In this chapter, you will learn how to

✔ Create a report with the Report Wizard.

✔ Modify a report.

✔ Share a report.

✔ Schedule a report.

✔ Categorize a report.

In Chapter 13, "Working with Filters and Charts," and Chapter 14, "Using Dashboards," you learned how to use the chart and dashboard tools to create real-time visualizations to enhance the user experience and allow for more efficient decision making. Although those options are powerful and will meet many of your reporting needs, Microsoft Dynamics CRM also uses Microsoft SQL Server Reporting Services for advanced reporting solutions. Programmers can create advanced reports by working directly within SQL Server Reporting Services, but Microsoft Dynamics CRM also includes a Report Wizard that provides users of all skill levels with a tool to create SQL Server Reporting Services reports. The following table compares the features of charts and dashboards with those of the SQL Server Reporting Services Report Wizard.

	Charts and Dashboards	SQL Server Reporting Services Report Wizard
Report output	Inline visualizations presented within Microsoft Dynamics CRM grids and forms	Web-based reports that can be exported to additional formats, such as Microsoft Excel, PDF, and CSV
Skill level required to create or modify reports	Beginner	Beginner
Ability to schedule reports for email delivery	No	Yes

(continued)

	Charts and Dashboards	SQL Server Reporting Services Report Wizard
Support for charts and graphs	Yes	Yes
Ability to include data from multiple record types in results	No	Yes
Ability to include data from multiple record types in the report query	Yes	Yes
Ability to prompt users to enter parameters before running reports	No	Yes
Ability to restrict access for some users	Yes	Yes
Respect for Microsoft Dynamics CRM record-level security settings by default	Yes	Yes

Microsoft Dynamics CRM includes 25 standard SQL Server Reporting Services reports in the base product. You can find these reports by navigating to the Workplace area and clicking the Reports link.

You will find that these reports solve some of your reporting needs and will probably serve as a solid starting point for your organization. The reports also give you a high-level understanding of the possibilities that exist with SQL Server Reporting Services. The following table summarizes the reports and their applicability within the Marketing, Sales, Service, and Administrative areas of Microsoft Dynamics CRM.

Report Name	Marketing	Sales	Service	Other
Account Distribution	X	X	X	
Account Overview	X	X	X	
Account Summary	X	X	X	
Activities				X
Campaign Activity Status	X			
Campaign Comparison	X			
Campaign Performance	X			
Case Summary Table			X	

Report Name	Marketing	Sales	Service	Other
Competitor Win Loss		X		
Invoice		X		
Invoice Status		X		
Lead Source Effectiveness	X	X		
Neglected Accounts		X		
Neglected Cases			X	
Neglected Leads		X		
Order		X		
Products By Account		X		
Products By Contact		X		
Progress Against Goals		X		
Quote		X		
Sales History		X		
Sales Pipeline		X		
Service Activity Volume			X	
Top Knowledge Base Articles			X	
User Summary				X

In this chapter, you will learn how to create, modify, and format reports by using the Microsoft Dynamics CRM Report Wizard. You will also learn how to share a report with other users, schedule delivery of a report, and categorize a report.

Practice Files There are no practice files for this chapter.

Important The images used in this book reflect the default form and field names in Microsoft Dynamics CRM. Because the software offers extensive customization capabilities, it's possible that some of the record types or fields have been relabeled in your Microsoft Dynamics CRM environment. If you cannot find the forms, fields, or security roles referred to in this book, contact your system administrator for assistance.

Important You must know the location of your Microsoft Dynamics CRM website to work the exercises in this book. Check with your system administrator to verify the web address if you don't know it.

Creating a Report with the Report Wizard

The Report Wizard allows you to create sophisticated reports within the Microsoft Dynamics CRM interface by guiding you through a step-by-step process that is easy to understand. It allows you to produce grouped, summary-level data in addition to record-level data. Consider the following scenarios:

- You need to create an Opportunity Pipeline report that shows all opportunities by owner and includes the sum of all estimated revenue across those opportunities.

- You need to compare the number of accounts assigned to each user to determine account distribution levels.

With the Report Wizard, you can get the aggregated summary numbers for these types of reports.

In this exercise, you will use the Report Wizard to create a report that shows active opportunities by owner.

 SET UP Use your own Microsoft Dynamics CRM installation in place of the site shown in this exercise. Use the Windows Internet Explorer web browser to navigate to your Microsoft Dynamics CRM website before beginning this exercise. You need a user account that has privileges to create reports.

1. In the **Workplace** area, click **Reports**.

 2. In the **Records** group on the ribbon, click the **New** button to launch the **New Report** form.

3. In the **Source** section of the form, click the **Report Wizard** button.

    The Report Wizard Get Started page displays.

4. In the **Report Wizard**, leave **Start a new report** selected, and click **Next** to move on to the **Report Properties** page.

5. In the **Report name** field, enter **_Active Opportunities by Owner_**, and in the **Report description** field, enter **_List of opportunities grouped by owner_**.

6. In the **Primary record type** field, select **Opportunities**.

7. Click **Next** to move on to the **Select Records to Include in the Report** page.

8. In the **Report Filtering Criteria** section, replace the default **Modified On** search parameter by choosing **Status** instead of **Modified On** in the **Select** list.

9. Leave **Equals** in the operator field, and in the **Enter Value** field, select **Open**.

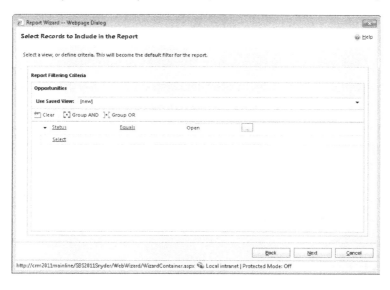

10. Click **Next** to move on to the **Lay Out Fields** page.

11. Click in the **Click here to add a grouping** field.

The Add Grouping dialog box appears.

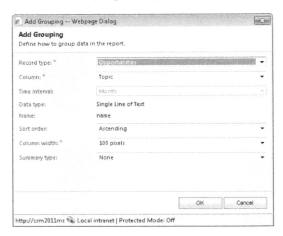

12. In the **Column** list, select **Owner**.

13. In the **Summary Type** field, select **Count**, and then click **OK** to add this grouping to your report.

This summary type will allow you to see how many active opportunities exist for each owner.

14. Click **Click here to add a column**. The **Add Column** dialog box appears.

15. In the **Column** field, select **Potential Customer**. Set the column width to 150 pixels, and click **OK** to add the column to your report.

16. To the right of **Potential Customer**, click in the **Click here to add a column** field to add another column to your report. Continue this process to add the following fields and related information:

Column	Column Width	Summary Type
Topic	300 pixels	None
Probability	75 pixels	None
Est. Close Date	100 pixels	None
Est. Revenue	100 pixels	Sum

Your additions are reflected on the Lay Out Fields page of the wizard.

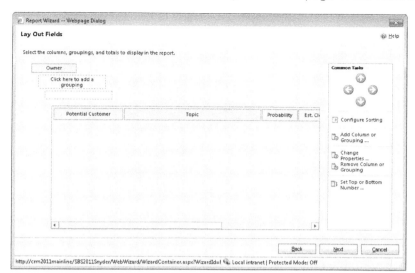

17. In the **Common Tasks** pane, click **Configure Sorting**.

The Configure Sort Order dialog box appears.

18. In the **Sort By** field, select **Probability**. Then select **Descending Order**.

19. Click **OK**, and then click **Next** to move on to the **Format Report** page.

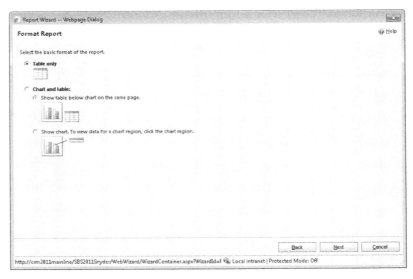

20. Leave **Table only** selected for your report format, and then click **Next**.

    The Report Summary screen displays your report selections.

21. Review the report details, and then click **Next**.

    The Report Successfully Created confirmation page appears, indicating that you have successfully created a report.

22. On the confirmation page, click **Finish** to exit the **Report Wizard**.

    The Report Wizard closes and you are returned to the New Report form, which automatically updates to reflect the details of your report. To see the results, you will have to run the report.

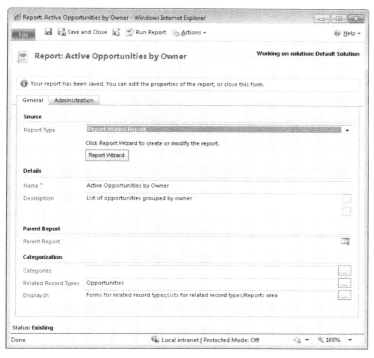

 23. On the form toolbar, click the **Run Report** button.

Your report displays within SQL Server Reporting Services. The resulting report provides insight into how many open opportunities exist for each owner.

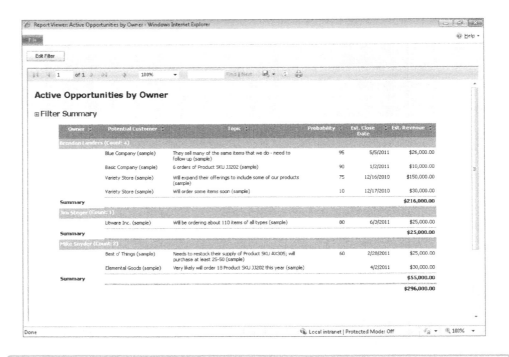

Tip After running the report, you can modify the filter to refine your report output, export to other formats (usually PDF, Excel, or Microsoft Word), or view an opportunity record by clicking the topic in the output.

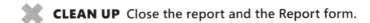 **CLEAN UP** Close the report and the Report form.

Modifying a Report

Now that you have seen the power of the Report Wizard, you can use it to create reports that are relevant to your business needs. Business needs change over time, and your reports will need to change accordingly. Additionally, you will often want to make small tweaks to the reports you have already built. For example, you might want to add a column or a grouping level, or you might want to modify the sort order. You can use the same interface in the Report Wizard to modify existing reports without having to start over.

In this exercise, you will modify the Active Opportunities By Owner report you created in the previous exercise. Specifically, you will modify the filter to include only those opportunities with a closing probability greater than 50 and group results by manager in addition to record owner.

SET UP Use your own Microsoft Dynamics CRM installation in place of the site shown in this exercise. Use the Internet Explorer web browser to navigate to your Microsoft Dynamics CRM website, if necessary, before beginning this exercise. You need the Active Opportunities By Owner report you created in the previous exercise, and you need a user account that has privileges to create and update reports.

1. In the **Workplace** area, click **Reports**.

2. Select **Active Opportunities by Owner** without opening it. In the **Records** group on the ribbon, click the **Edit** button.

   The Report form appears.

3. In the **Report** form, click **Report Wizard** to launch the **Report Wizard**.

4. On the **Get Started** page of the **Report Wizard**, leave the default selections to work from your existing report so that your changes will overwrite the original settings. Click **Next** to proceed to the next step.

5. On the **Report Properties** page, leave the current settings intact and click **Next** to proceed to the next step.

   The Select Records To Include In The Report page appears, displaying the Status report parameter you configured in the previous exercise.

6. Add a new row by clicking **Select** and then choosing **Probability**.

7. Select **Is Greater Than** as the operator.

8. In the **Enter Value** field, enter **50**.

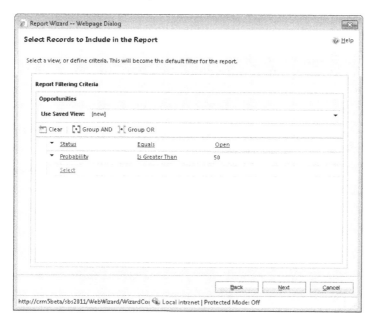

9. Click **Next** to proceed to the next step of the **Report Wizard**.

   This selection refines your results to include only records with a probability value greater than 50.

10. On the **Lay Out Fields** page, revise the report format by clicking in the **Click here to add a grouping** field.

    The Add Grouping dialog box appears.

11. In the **Record type** field, select **Owning User (User)**.

12. In the **Column** field, choose **Manager**.

13. In the **Summary type** field, select **Count**.

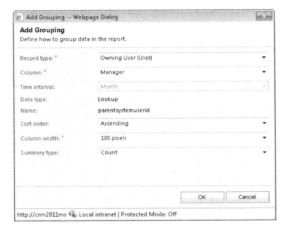

With these selections, you are adding the owner's manager to the report as an additional grouping level.

14. Click **OK** to close the **Add Grouping** dialog box. The new grouping level is added below the existing **Owner** grouping level in the report.

15. In the **Common Tasks** pane, click the up arrow.

    This moves the manager grouping level above the owner, so that the opportunities for each sales owner will be grouped by the sales managers.

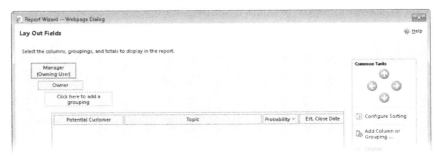

> **Troubleshooting** You might see a warning message showing that the table exceeds the width of one printed page. This is due to the total pixel count of all columns in the report. To keep the report under one page wide for printing purposes, make sure that the sum of your column pixels is less than 960.

16. Click **Next** to proceed to the next step of the **Report Wizard**.

17. On this page and on the Report Summary page that follows, click **Next** to maintain the current selections.

The Report Successfully Created confirmation page appears, indicating that you have successfully updated the report.

18. Click **Finish** to exit the **Report Wizard**.

The Report Wizard closes and you are returned to the Report form. The changes to your report are automatically saved.

19. In the form toolbar, click **Run Report** to view the report with your changes.

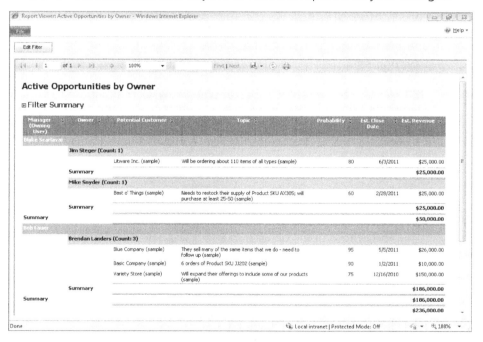

The report now includes an additional grouping level that shows total open opportunities at the manager level as well as at the owner level, and only includes those opportunities with a closing probability greater than 50. You can continue to refine your reports at any time with the Report Wizard.

 CLEAN UP Close the report and the Report form.

Sharing a Report

The report you created in the previous exercise will reside in the Reports view of the Workplace area but will only display for you; most other users will *not* be able to see the report unless they have system administrator or other security rights. By default, Microsoft Dynamics CRM prevents other users from being able to use your report at this point, but it does allow you to share the report with other users as you see fit. This is helpful because:

- Several different users might use the Report Wizard to create many reports. If all reports are immediately available to everyone, the number of reports in the list will grow quickly and might lead to confusion.

- You might need a report for a very specific reason that does not apply to any other users, and therefore there is no reason to share it.

Although reports are not shared immediately, you can share them with other users in just a few steps.

In this exercise, you will share the report you created in the previous section with a specific user and then make it available to all users in your Microsoft Dynamics CRM environment.

 SET UP Use the Internet Explorer web browser to navigate to your Microsoft Dynamics CRM website, if necessary, before beginning this exercise. You need the Active Opportunities By Owner report you created earlier in this chapter, and you need a user account that has a security role with privileges to publish reports.

1. In the **Workplace** area, click **Reports**.

2. Select **Active Opportunities by Owner** without opening the report.

 3. In the **Collaborate** group on the ribbon, click the **Share** button.

   The Who Would You Like To Share The Selected Report With? dialog box appears.

4. In the **Common Tasks** pane, click **Add User/Team**.

   The Look Up Records dialog box appears.

5. Search for system users and select any user. Then add the user to the **Selected Records** area, and click **OK**.

   The selected user displays in the sharing dialog box, with Read rights assigned by default. You can modify the sharing rights to suit your specific needs.

6. Click **OK** to save your sharing settings for the report.

The specified user will now see the report in the Reports view of the Workplace area.

Occasionally you might want to make the report available for every user rather than for specific users. Although you could select all users in the sharing dialog box, users that join your organization at a later time will not automatically have access to the report. In the next steps, you will make a report available to the entire organization so that even users who are added later are still able to access your report.

7. In the **Reports** view, select the **Active Opportunities by Owner** report without opening it, and on the ribbon, click **Edit**.

The Report form is displayed.

8. On the form toolbar, click **Actions,** and then select **Make Report Available to Organization**.

> **Troubleshooting** If the Make Report Available To Organization option does not appear in the Actions menu, you do not have rights to publish reports. Contact your system administrator about adding the Publish Reports privilege to your security role.

Your report is now available to the entire organization. You can also make the report a personal report again by following steps 7 and 8 above and selecting Revert To Personal Report.

 CLEAN UP Close the Report form.

Scheduling a Report

When you run a report by using SQL Server Reporting Services in Microsoft Dynamics CRM, the report runs in real time and reflects the current data in the application. This works well for most of your reporting needs, but it can also pose challenges. For instance:

- Users who run the report at different times can communicate conflicting information, which leads to confusion and data integrity concerns.
- Real-time reports provide no historical perspective for comparison or trending purposes.

For example, you might want to run a monthly pipeline report to understand how the pipeline looks at the beginning of each month and to compare to previous months.

Microsoft Dynamics CRM provides a Report Scheduling Wizard to address this need. The wizard allows you to generate report snapshots either on demand or at a regularly scheduled time.

> **Important** The Report Scheduling Wizard is not available in Microsoft Dynamics CRM Online.

In this exercise, you will schedule a report to run once a month at midnight.

 SET UP Use the Internet Explorer web browser to navigate to your Microsoft Dynamics CRM website, if necessary, before beginning this exercise. You need the Active Opportunities By Owner report you created earlier in this chapter, and you need a user account that has a security role with privileges to add Reporting Services reports.

1. In the **Workplace** area, click **Reports**.
2. Select **Active Opportunities by Owner** without opening the report.
3. In the **Actions** group of the ribbon, click **Schedule Report**.

Schedule Report

> **Troubleshooting** If the Schedule Report button is not available on the ribbon, you do not have rights to schedule reports. Contact your system administrator about adding the Add Reporting Services Reports privilege to your security role.

The Report Scheduling Wizard appears. Here you can specify when a snapshot should occur.

4. Select **On a Schedule**, and then click **Next** to proceed to the **Select Frequency** page.

5. On the **Select Frequency** page, select **Monthly** and leave the default settings for the monthly schedule.

The default settings schedule the report for the first day of the month at midnight.

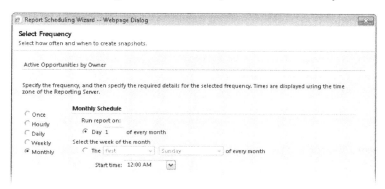

6. Click **Next** to proceed to the next step of the **Report Scheduling Wizard**.

7. On the **Select Start and End Dates** page, leave the current date as the default start date, and leave **No end date** selected.

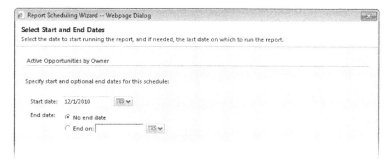

8. Click **Next** to proceed to the next step.

The Define Report Parameters page is displayed, indicating that there are no parameters for the selected report.

9. Click **Next** to proceed to the next step of the **Report Scheduling Wizard**.

The Review Snapshot Definition page is displayed.

10. Verify that the settings are correct, and then click **Create** to schedule your report.

A Completing The Report Scheduling Wizard confirmation page displays when the scheduling process is complete.

11. On the confirmation page, click **Finish** to exit the **Report Scheduling Wizard**.

You have successfully scheduled the report. On the first day of the next month, the report snapshot will be taken and will be available for all users who have access to the report. When the report is run, an additional report will appear in the list with a name similar to the original report that includes a timestamp of the report's run date.

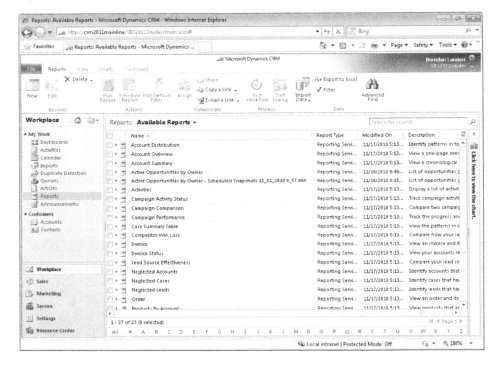

Important The report will not display any results until the first snapshot is generated, according to the schedule you specify in the Report Scheduling Wizard. Only the eight most recent report snapshots will be stored. When the ninth report is created, the oldest report will be deleted.

 CLEAN UP Close the Report form.

Categorizing a Report

You now know how to create, modify, share, and schedule reports. As you begin creating additional reports, you'll find proper categorization very helpful for organizing different types of reports into logical groupings. By default, the following categories are available for reports in Microsoft Dynamics CRM:

- Administrative Reports
- Marketing Reports
- Sales Reports
- Service Reports

> **Tip** Users with elevated security rights can modify and add report categories to match their business needs. This option is available on the Reporting tab of the System Settings dialog box, which is accessible in the Settings area. Contact your system administrator if you do not have access to this area.

In addition to providing local groupings for reports, the categorization feature provides other options, as described in the following table.

Categorization Field	Description
Related Record Types	This specifies the types of records relevant to the report. By default, this is set to the primary record type. In the Active Opportunities By Owner report example in this chapter, the Related Record Type is set to Opportunities.
Display In	This specifies where the report can be accessed within Microsoft Dynamics CRM. The available options are: • Forms For Related Record Types • Lists For Related Record Types • Reports Area

Reports can be configured so that users can access them from grid and form toolbars as well as from the Reports view in the Workplace area. The Display In option of each report allows you to designate where the report can be accessed. The Reports Area option is set by default and makes the report available under the Reports list in the Workplace area. The other options are:

- **Forms For Related Record Types** This option is selected by default and allows a report to be run from within a record. For example, the Account Overview report can be run from within an account record.

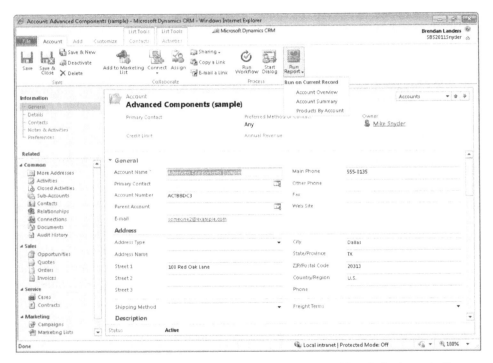

- **Lists For Related Record Types** This option is selected by default and allows a report to be run from the grid toolbar. Again, the native Account Overview report can be run from account grids. You can select multiple records to include in the report, or run it for a single record.

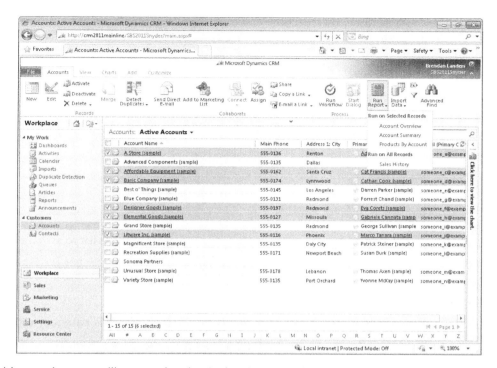

In this exercise, you will categorize the Active Opportunities By Owner report you created earlier in this chapter.

SET UP Use the Internet Explorer web browser to navigate to your Microsoft Dynamics CRM website, if necessary, before beginning this exercise. You need the Active Opportunities By Owner report you created earlier in this chapter.

1. In the **Workplace** area, click **Reports**.

2. Select the **Active Opportunities by Owner** report without opening it, and on the ribbon, click the **Edit** button.

   The Report form displays.

3. In the **Categorization** section, in the **Categories** field, click the ellipsis button.

   The Select Values dialog box appears.

4. In the **Available Values** section, click **Sales Reports**, and then click the right arrow button to select the value.

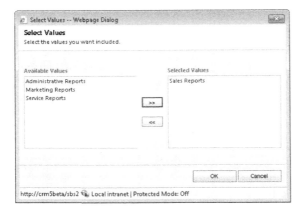

Tip You can add multiple values to the Selected Values list to assign the report to multiple categories.

---

5. Click **OK** to close the dialog box.

 6. On the **Report** form, click **Save and Close** to save the category selection.

7. In the **Reports** grid, in the view selector, select **Sales Reports**.

The Active Opportunities By Owner report now appears in the sales grouping.

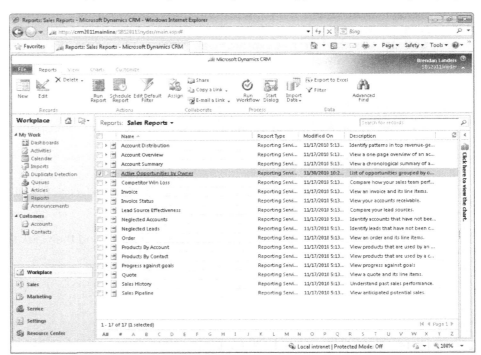

Key Points

- The Report Wizard allows you to create SQL Server Reporting Services reports through an easy interface by using a step-by-step process.

- You can aggregate data by grouping fields with the Report Wizard. Additionally, you can specify which columns to include in the output of the report.

- Several report formatting options are available, including column width definition, column ordering, and sorting.

- You can modify Report Wizard reports by using the same wizard you use to create reports.

- You can share reports you create with other users or make them available to all users in your organization.

- Report scheduling allows you to record point-in-time snapshots of a report automatically by specifying a single or recurring time. You can also record a report snapshot on demand.

- Microsoft Dynamics CRM provides several report categorization options to enable you to specify how a report is grouped and where the report is available to be run within the application.

Chapter at a Glance

Build an
Advanced Find
query, **page 344**

Format the results
of an Advanced Find
query, **page 349**

Share a saved
view, **page 353**

Update records with
the edit multiple records
tool, **page 358**

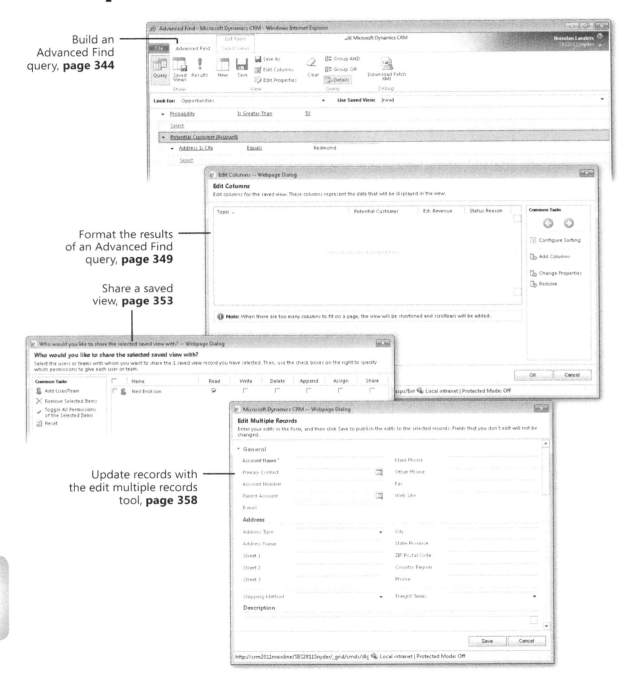

16 Using Advanced Find

In this chapter, you will learn how to

✔ Perform ad hoc queries by using Advanced Find.

✔ Organize and format Advanced Find results.

✔ Create a saved view.

✔ Share your saved views with other users.

✔ Build a complex query to search data.

✔ Use the edit multiple records and assign multiple record tools to take action on query results.

An important benefit of CRM systems is the central repository of customer data that builds as sales, marketing, and customer service teams track their interactions with customers. As this store of data grows, managers face the need to report on and analyze the data to understand trends and identify areas for improvement. Microsoft Dynamics CRM provides a variety of tools for extracting data and presenting it in a simple and easy-to-use format. This chapter focuses on the best tool for this task: Advanced Find. The Advanced Find tool lets you create your own queries by using a simple interface. When end users are empowered to create reports and filter the results to return only the records they want, they can perform their jobs, and the organization's IT resources can stay focused on more complex business requirements.

In this chapter, you will learn how to harness the power of the Advanced Find tool by creating a query, saving it as a system view that can be shared with others, and updating multiple records in the results set.

> **Tip** Advanced Find respects the security settings of the end user. As a rule of thumb, you can assume that if a user can see the record elsewhere in the application, that user will be able to gain access to it within Advanced Find.

> **Practice Files** There are no practice files for this chapter.

> **Important** The images used in this book reflect the default form and field names in Microsoft Dynamics CRM. Because the software offers extensive customization capabilities, it's possible that some of the record types or fields have been relabeled in your Microsoft Dynamics CRM environment. If you cannot find the forms, fields, or security roles referred to in this book, contact your system administrator for assistance.

> **Important** You must know the location of your Microsoft Dynamics CRM website to work the exercises in this book. Check with your system administrator to verify the web address if you don't know it.

Performing Advanced Find Queries

Business needs can change frequently over the course of a project and, as a result, reporting needs also change. Ad hoc reporting has become a standard feature within most business applications, but expecting end users to define all of their reporting needs before a system is implemented is unrealistic. The Advanced Find tool within Microsoft Dynamics CRM provides a flexible interface that allows end users to query, view, analyze, and update data on an ongoing basis. With Advanced Find, predefined queries can be saved as the system is implemented and new queries can be created as the reporting needs of a business change. Examples of how Advanced Find is commonly employed by end users include:

- Configuring a customized to-do list to follow up on open opportunities.
- Determining leads that fall into a specific geographical region for distribution and assignment.
- Finding all activities due on the current date for a specific customer service representative who has called in sick, so that the activities can be reassigned to a different representative.
- Obtaining a list of contacts that have not been modified in more than two years, so that they can be considered for deactivation.

Advanced Find queries rely on an intuitive set of operators that you select when building a query. The data fields you select in your query determine the operators that will be available for filtering. The following table highlights the operators available for the different types of data fields.

Data Type	Operators	
User (Owner)	Equals Current User	Contains
	Does Not Equal Current User	Does Not Contain
	Equals Current User's Teams	Begins With
	Equals	Does Not Begin With
	Does Not Equal	Ends With
	Contains Data	Does Not End With
	Does Not Contain Data	
Text	Equals	Does Not Begin With
	Does Not Equal	Ends With
	Contains	Does Not End With
	Does Not Contain	Contains Data
	Begins With	Does Not Contain Data
Numeric	Equals	Is Less Than
	Does Not Equal	Is Less Than or Equal To
	Is Greater Than	Contains Data
	Is Greater Than or Equal To	Does Not Contain Data
Lookup	Equals	Does Not Contain
	Does Not Equal	Begins With
	Contains Data	Does Not Begin With
	Does Not Contain Data	Ends With
	Contains	Does Not End With
Bit	Equals	Does Not Contain
	Does Not Equal	Begins With
	Contains Data	Does Not Begin With
	Does Not Contain Data	Ends With
	Contains	Does Not End With

(continued)

Data Type	Operators	
Date	On	Last X Months
	On or After	Next X Months
	On or Before	Last X Years
	Yesterday	Next X Years
	Today	Any Time
	Tomorrow	Older Than X Months
	Next 7 Days	Contains Data
	Last 7 Days	Does Not Contain Data
	Next Week	In Fiscal Year
	Last Week	In Fiscal Period
	This Week	In Fiscal Period and Year
	Next Month	In or After Fiscal Period
	Last Month	In or Before Fiscal Period
	This Month	Last Fiscal Year
	Next Year	This Fiscal Year
	Last Year	Next Fiscal Year
	This Year	Last X Fiscal Years
	Last X Hours	Next X Fiscal Years
	Next X Hours	Last Fiscal Period
	Last X Days	This Fiscal Period
	Next X Days	Next Fiscal Period
	Last X Weeks	Last X Fiscal Periods
	Next X Weeks	Next X Fiscal Periods

For each query, you can specify as many search criteria as you need. You must designate the primary record type you want to have returned in the results, but you can also include data fields from related records in your query. For example, you might search for top sales opportunities that are assigned to sales representatives in a particular geographic region. Your search could include the data fields that the sales team uses to rate opportunities as well as the sales region field for the user records to which opportunities are assigned.

In this exercise, you will create an Advanced Find query to view the opportunities that have a probability value greater than 50 for accounts in the city of Redmond.

 SET UP Use your own Microsoft Dynamics CRM installation in place of the site shown in this exercise. Use the Windows Internet Explorer web browser to navigate to your Microsoft Dynamics CRM website before beginning this exercise.

1. In the **Data** group on the ribbon, click the **Advanced Find** button.

   The Advanced Find window appears.

2. In the **Look for** list, select **Opportunities**.

   This specifies the primary entity for which you will be executing the query.

3. In the **Select** field, choose **Probability** to set the search criteria for the opportunity's **Probability** field.

   A list of operators displays to the right of the Select field.

   > **Tip** The Select field shows all searchable fields for the specified entity. System administrators can modify the selection of fields that are searchable in the database.

4. In the **Operator** field, select **Is Greater Than**, and then enter *50* in the **Enter Value** field.

   > **Tip** The Select field turns into a list when you click it, and a new row automatically appears below each row you add to your query, so you can add as many rows as needed in your search criteria.

5. In the second row of the Advanced Find query, in the **Select** field, scroll to the bottom of the list to the **Related** section and select **Potential Customer (Account)** to add a data field from the account record type to your search. This allows you to filter on attributes of the accounts related to the opportunities.

6. In the **Select** field, choose **Address 1: City**.

7. Leave **Equals** selected in the **Operator** field, and in the **Enter Value** field, enter **Redmond**.

8. Click the **Results** button in the **Show** group on the **Advanced Find** tab of the ribbon.

The results of your search are displayed.

Tip If you want to modify an existing system view, navigate to the view in the Saved View list before clicking the Advanced Find button. This will open the Advanced Find screen with the criteria from the system view already set. This also allows you to easily understand the criteria used in the system views.

Organizing and Formatting Advanced Find Results

As you can see, Microsoft Dynamics CRM gives you the power to create a report that contains a set of records based on specific, user-defined criteria and yet that is simple to put together. In addition to building your own search query, you can also format Advanced Find results to include additional data columns, and you can sort, order, and size the results columns to meet your reporting needs. You can do the following tasks:

- Add any column you want to the results.
- Adjust the order of the columns.
- Modify the size of each column.
- Define the sort order of the output.

For example, you might want to create a list of contacts that includes the contact name and primary address fields in a specific order. This can be accomplished with ease in Microsoft Dynamics CRM.

In this exercise, you will use the search query you created in the previous exercise, modifying the columns that appear in the output to include the Probability field for each opportunity as well as the Industry field for the customer account. In addition, you will sort and format your results.

 SET UP Use your own Microsoft Dynamics CRM installation in place of the site shown in this exercise. Use the Internet Explorer web browser to navigate to your Microsoft Dynamics CRM website, if necessary, before beginning this exercise.

1. On the ribbon, click the **Advanced Find** button.

The Advanced Find screen appears.

 2. In the **Look for** list, select **Opportunities**, and then click the **Edit Columns** button in the **View** group on the ribbon.

The Edit Columns dialog box appears. Here you can modify the column order, set the column width, add or remove columns, and configure sorting.

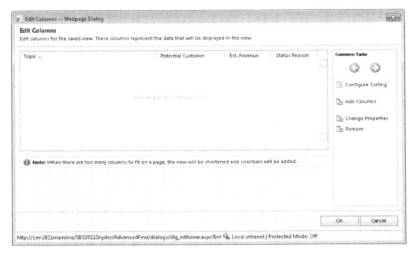

3. In the **Common Tasks** area, click **Add Columns**.

The Add Columns dialog box appears.

4. Locate the **Probability** field and select the check box next to it to add the field to your results.

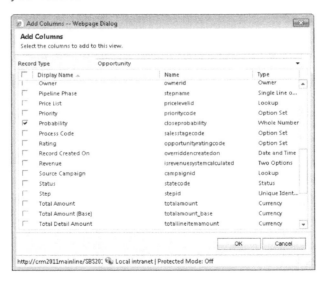

5. In the **Record Type** list at the top of the form, change the record type to **Potential Customer (Account)**.

Notice that you can add columns from related record types in addition to those from the primary record type.

6. Select the **Industry** check box, and click **OK**.

The newly added columns appear to the right of the original columns.

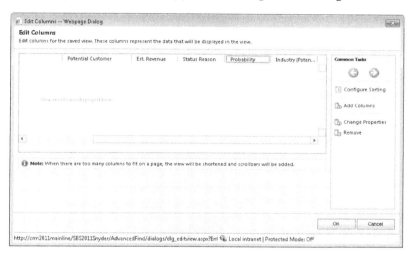

> **Important** For each record type in Microsoft Dynamics CRM, system administrators can configure the default columns that appear in each Advanced Find results set. The images in this chapter show the default view for opportunities in Microsoft Dynamics CRM. It's possible that your results will include different columns. If there is a column you frequently add to your searches, ask your system administrator about adding it to the default Advanced Find view.

7. In the **Edit Columns** dialog box, select (don't double-click) the **Industry** column heading.

The border color changes to green.

8. In the **Common Tasks** area, click the left arrow until the **Industry** column is the first column in the results grid.

9. Double-click the **Industry** column.

The Change Column Properties dialog box appears.

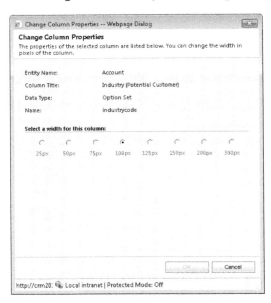

10. Change the column width to 200 pixels by selecting **200px**, and click **OK**.

This setting doubles the column width from the 100-pixel default.

11. In the **Edit Columns** dialog box, in the **Common Tasks** pane, click **Configure Sorting**.

The Configure Sort Order dialog box appears.

12. In the **Sort By** field, select **Probability**, and then select **Descending Order**.

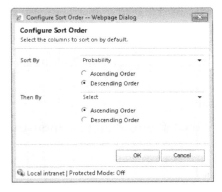

13. Click **OK**. This sorts the results so that the opportunities with the highest closing probability appear at the top of the report.

> **Tip** Notice that you can also sort by a secondary column.

14. In the **Edit Columns** dialog box, click **OK** to close the dialog box.

15. On the **Advanced Find** tab of the ribbon, in the **Show** group, click the **Results** button. The search results are displayed with the new columns you added.

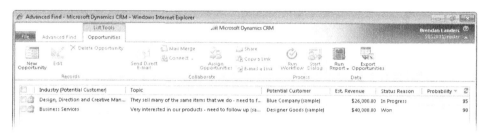

Creating and Sharing a Saved View

What if, sometime in the future, you want to run the same Advanced Find query for which you have already defined the criteria, specified the output format, and defined the sort order to address your needs? You would find it frustrating if you had to go through all of these steps each time you wanted to produce the report. Fortunately, Microsoft Dynamics CRM allows you to create saved views to save your Advanced Find queries for future use. Saved views can be run or modified at a later date, sparing you from recreating reports you run on a regular schedule.

> **Tip** Although saved views store the specified criteria and formatting settings, results are dynamic and reflect the records that match your search criteria at the time the saved view is accessed. Saved views are not point-in-time data snapshots.

In earlier chapters, you learned how to share charts, dashboards, and reports with your co-workers. In addition to sharing these items, you can also share saved views with your colleagues so they too can benefit from your reports.

Saved views can be shared with other users or with teams (groups of users that share access privileges to certain records). By default, each user or team is granted Read access when you share a saved view. This allows the user or team to access the saved view, but not modify it. Additional permissions can be assigned when you share a saved view. The following table outlines the security privileges available when sharing a view.

Privilege	Description
Read	Users can access the view but cannot modify it.
Write	Users can modify the view to include additional criteria, results fields, or other formatting.
Delete	Users can delete the view from the Microsoft Dynamics CRM database.
Append	Users can associate other records with the view.
Assign	Users can assign the view to a new system user.
Share	Users can share the view with additional users or teams while maintaining their own access to the view.

In this exercise, you will save the view you created in the previous section so you can access it in the future. You will also share the view with another user.

SET UP Use your own Microsoft Dynamics CRM installation in place of the site shown in this exercise. Use the Internet Explorer web browser to navigate to your Microsoft Dynamics CRM website, if necessary, before beginning this exercise.

1. In the **Advanced Find** window that displays the query you created in the previous section, click the **Save As** button.

   The Query Properties dialog box appears.

2. In the **Name** field, enter **Hot Opportunities in Redmond Market**.

3. In the **Description** field, enter **Opportunities in Redmond with a probability greater than 50**.

4. Click **OK**. Then, in the **Advanced Find** window, in the **Show** group of the ribbon, click the **Saved Views** button to see the newly created saved view.

In addition to being accessible from the Saved View list, the saved view will appear in the View list on the Opportunities grid.

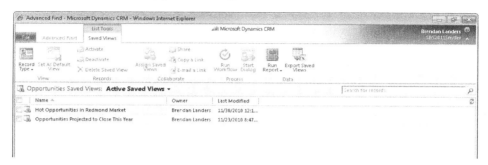

5. Select the newly created view, and then click **Share** in the **Collaborate** group on the **Saved Views** tab of the ribbon.

The Who Would You Like To Share The Selected Saved View With? dialog box appears.

6. In the **Common Tasks** pane, click **Add User/Team**.

The Look Up Records dialog box appears.

7. Enter the name of another system user in the **Search** field, and then press Enter.

8. Select a user record and click the **Add** button to move the record from the **Results** box to the **Selected Records** box. Then click **OK**.

The selected user is returned to the shared user screen. By default, the user receives Read rights to your view. In addition to Read rights, you can empower the user to write, delete, append, assign, and share your view with others.

9. In the **Who would you like to share the selected saved view with?** dialog box, click **OK**.

   With just a few clicks, you have now allowed your colleagues to benefit from the reports you created.

Using Advanced Filter Criteria

By default, Microsoft Dynamics CRM applies AND logic to queries that include two or more search criteria. This means that results are limited to those records that meet all search criteria in the query. However, you also might be required to produce a report with records that match only one of several criteria. In this instance, you could use OR logic in Advanced Find to search multiple fields to find records that have matching data in only one of the fields.

In this exercise, you will use the Group AND and Group OR functionality of the Advanced Find tool. As you saw earlier, the original criteria we applied to the Hot Opportunities In Redmond Market saved view included all opportunities that met the following criteria:

- The opportunity probability is greater than 50.
- The accounts are in the city of Redmond.

Now you will expand the criteria to include opportunities in Chicago in addition to those in Redmond.

SET UP Use your own Microsoft Dynamics CRM installation in place of the site shown in this exercise. Use the Internet Explorer web browser to navigate to your Microsoft Dynamics CRM website, if necessary, before beginning this exercise.

1. Launch **Advanced Find** if it is not open already.

2. In the **Advanced Find** query window, in the **Look for** field, select **Opportunities**, and then select **Hot Opportunities in Redmond Market** in the **Use Saved View** list.

   The criteria for the saved query display.

3. On the **Advanced Find** tab of the ribbon, in the **Query** group, click the **Details** button.

> **Tip** By default, the Advanced Find mode is set to Simple, which means that the details of the query are not shown until you click the Details button. You can change this setting on the General tab in the Set Personal Options area, which is accessible from the Options menu on the File tab of the ribbon.

4. In the **Potential Customer (Account)** section, click the **Select** field underneath the row that specifies the city as **Redmond**.

5. In the **Select** field, choose **Address 1: City**.

6. In the **Enter Value** field, enter *Chicago*.

   Because Microsoft Dynamics CRM uses AND logic by default, if you click **Find** at this point, your search will not return any results, because no single account record can have a primary address in both Redmond and in Chicago.

7. Click the arrow to the left of the first **Address 1: City** field, and then click **Select Row**.

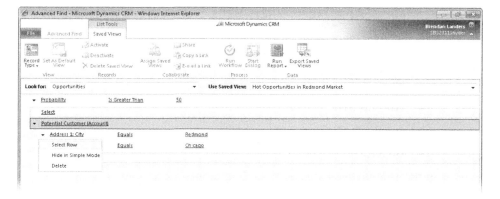

8. Click the arrow to the left of the second **Address 1: City** field, and then click **Select Row**.

9. On the **Advanced Find** tab of the ribbon, in the **Query** group, click the **Group OR** button.

This selection updates the logic so that records that have a primary address in the city of Redmond or Chicago will be returned in the results.

10. Click the **Results** button in the **Show** group to see the results matching your new query.

Using Edit Multiple Records and Assign Multiple Records from Advanced Find

It is certainly powerful and exciting to have the ability to create a list of records that match your specific criteria. The ability to take action on those records to strengthen your Microsoft Dynamics CRM database and adapt it to your business as it evolves is equally important. With Microsoft Dynamics CRM, you can take many actions on the results of an Advanced Find query. For example, you can:

- Export the data to Microsoft Excel.
- Edit multiple records.
- Assign multiple records.
- Deactivate the records.

In this section, we focus on the edit multiple records and assign multiple records functionalities. With the Microsoft Dynamics CRM edit multiple records functionality, you can make a change to many records at one time from any grid. For example, you might use edit multiple records or assign multiple records if:

- You realize that data has been entered incorrectly for several records.
- You add a new attribute that you would like to populate for all records.
- An employee decides to leave your company, and you need to distribute the records that the employee owns to other team members.

> **Important** Multiple record edit rights might not be available for every user. The user's ability to use edit multiple records is configured by system administrators in the user's security role.

In this exercise, you will edit the Address 1: City field of multiple records by using the edit multiple records tool. In addition, you will use the assign multiple records functionality to assign ownership of multiple records.

 SET UP Use your own Microsoft Dynamics CRM installation in place of the site shown in the exercise. Use the Internet Explorer web browser to navigate to your Microsoft Dynamics CRM website, if necessary, before beginning this exercise.

1. In the **Workplace** area, click **Accounts**.

   The default view appears in the grid.

   > **Troubleshooting** You will see My Active Accounts as the default view. This view includes the Account Name, Main Phone, Address 1: City, Primary Contact, and E-mail (Primary Contact) fields for the accounts you own. The default view can be modified and therefore might be different in your environment.

2. In the **Data** group on the **Accounts** tab of the ribbon, click the **Advanced Find** button.

   The criteria from the current view populate the Details section.

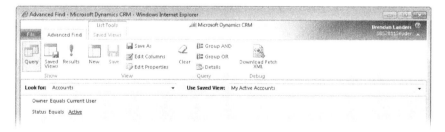

3. Click the **Details** button in the **Query** group to view the details of the query, and then add a new search field by choosing **Address 1: City** in the **Select** field.

4. Leave the operator as **Equals**, and enter *NY* in the **Enter Value** field.

5. Click the **Results** button in the **Show** group.

   All active accounts that you own with a city value of *NY* are displayed. Next, you will update that value to *New York* by using the edit multiple records tool.

> **Important** If your search did not return at least two results, modify the query before continuing with this exercise.

Edit

6. Select several records. In the **Records** group on the **Accounts** tab of the ribbon, select **Edit**.

The Edit Multiple Records dialog box appears. It resembles a blank Account form.

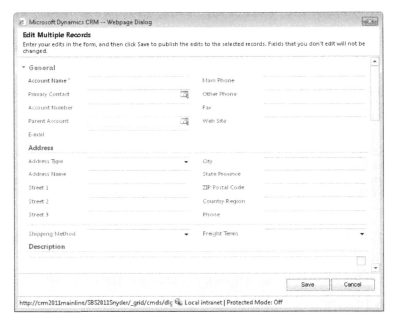

7. Enter *New York* in the **City** field, and then click **Save**.

> **Important** This action cannot be undone.

After you have clicked Save, the underlying records will be updated.

> **Tip** If your query results return multiple pages, you will need to edit records one page at a time. The number of records returned on a page can be modified in the Personal Options area to a maximum of 250.

8. In the results grid, select at least two additional records by pressing the Ctrl key while clicking them.

9. In the **Collaborate** group on the **Accounts** tab of the ribbon, click the **Assign Accounts** button. The Assign Accounts dialog box appears.

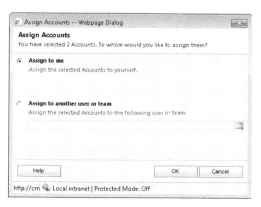

10. In the dialog box, select **Assign to me** to assign the selected records to yourself.

Key Points

- The Advanced Find tool in Microsoft Dynamics CRM allows you to search data in your system. You can filter results and display columns from the primary record type you are searching as well as from related record types.

- You can format and sort the output of your query to meet your specific needs.

- You can save your Advanced Find views for later use.

- With sharing, you can distribute your saved views to other users.

- You can create complex queries by using Group AND and Group OR logic.

- You can take action on the results of an Advanced Find query by using the edit multiple records and assign multiple records functionalities to update multiple records at a time and assign them to other users.

Chapter at a Glance

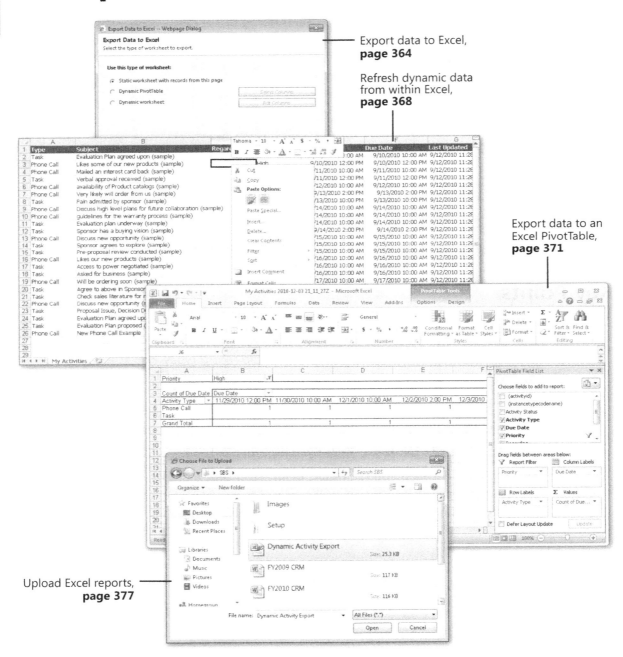

Export data to Excel,
page 364

Refresh dynamic data
from within Excel,
page 368

Export data to an
Excel PivotTable,
page 371

Upload Excel reports,
page 377

17 Reporting with Excel

In this chapter, you will learn how to

✔ Export static data to Excel worksheets.

✔ Export dynamic data to Excel worksheets.

✔ Export dynamic data to Excel PivotTables.

✔ Upload Excel reports to the Reports list in Microsoft Dynamics CRM.

Microsoft Dynamics CRM provides several options for data reporting. The combination of Advanced Find views and the Microsoft SQL Server Reporting Services Report Wizard makes for a powerful suite of reporting tools. Microsoft Dynamics CRM provides an additional reporting option that many users like to use: you can export data to Microsoft Excel. The ability to export your Microsoft Dynamics CRM data to Excel within the Microsoft Dynamics CRM interface allows you to export data into a static worksheet, a dynamic worksheet, or a dynamic PivotTable for further analysis and reporting. By choosing a dynamic export option, you can ensure that the Excel file maintains a live connection to the Microsoft Dynamics CRM database that allows you to refresh the data from within Excel. Consider how useful this functionality would be in the following scenarios:

- You have an Advanced Find view that you export weekly to print for a meeting. You can export to a dynamic file one time, format the report to your liking, and open it up from a saved location to get the most recent data.

- You have a PivotTable report that you use to view aggregated data. You can set up the PivotTable one time and reuse it as needed.

When you export data to Excel, Microsoft Dynamics CRM security settings apply, so that you can only export those records to which you have access in Microsoft Dynamics CRM.

In this chapter, you will learn how to create static and dynamic Excel reports. You will also learn how to create PivotTable reports that use data from Microsoft Dynamics CRM. Finally, you will learn how to upload an Excel report into the Reports area of Microsoft Dynamics CRM to share your Excel report with other users.

> **Practice Files** There are no practice files for this chapter.

> **Important** The images used in this book reflect the default form and field names in Microsoft Dynamics CRM. Because the software offers extensive customization capabilities, it's possible that some of the record types or fields have been relabeled in your Microsoft Dynamics CRM environment. If you cannot find the forms, fields, or security roles referred to in this book, contact your system administrator for assistance.

> **Important** You must know the location of your Microsoft Dynamics CRM website to work the exercises in this book. Check with your system administrator to verify the web address if you don't know it.

> **Important** The ability to export data to Excel is configurable at the user level. If you cannot see the export buttons and options referred to in this chapter, contact your system administrator for assistance.

Exporting Static Data to Excel Worksheets

Excel is a tool that most people in traditional business environments are familiar with and use in some capacity. With Excel, you can organize, format, and analyze data. Many business applications give the end user the ability to export or download record-level data into Excel, and Microsoft Dynamics CRM is no exception.

It is very easy to export a list of records into Excel. If you have been using Microsoft Dynamics CRM for a while, you have probably already used this feature to export data to Excel.

For a simple, one-time report, you can export data from any grid in Microsoft Dynamics CRM in a static worksheet. The worksheet is described as static because the data will not be updated in Excel if it is changed in Microsoft Dynamics CRM after it is exported. A static data export reflects a point-in-time snapshot of a set of records in Microsoft Dynamics CRM.

When you export static data into Excel, the data is exported exactly as it appears in the Microsoft Dynamics CRM grid, so that the exported worksheet includes the fields that are displayed in the grid and uses the same field order, sorting, and field widths. You can export most data grids into Excel, including the results of an Advanced Find.

Later in this chapter, you will learn how to establish a live link with your Microsoft Dynamics CRM application by exporting dynamic data, which allows you to continually analyze your business data within Excel.

In this exercise, you will export a static Microsoft Dynamics CRM data view into Excel.

 SET UP Use your own Microsoft Dynamics CRM installation in place of the site shown in this exercise. Use the Windows Internet Explorer web browser to navigate to your Microsoft Dynamics CRM website before beginning this exercise.

1. In the **Workplace** area, click **Accounts**.

2. In the view selector, select **Active Accounts**.

   The data grid updates to display a list of active accounts.

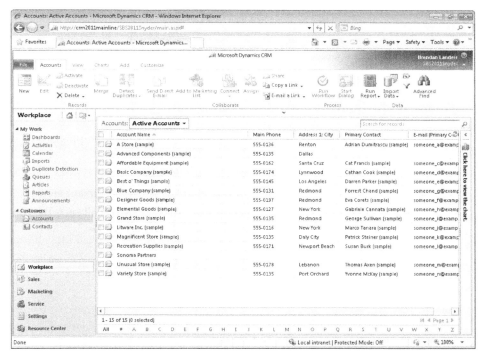

3. On the ribbon, in the **Data** group of the **Accounts** tab, click the **Export to Excel** button.

   > **Tip** The Export To Excel button is available on most grids within Microsoft Dynamics CRM. You can export system-related information such as lists of reports or data imports in addition to lists of core records such as accounts, contacts, and opportunities.

The Export Data To Excel dialog box appears.

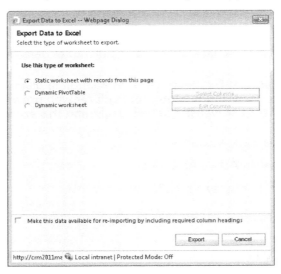

4. Leave **Static worksheet with records from this page** selected, and click the **Export** button.

> **Tip** If the records in the Active Accounts view span multiple pages, you will be presented with two options in step 4:
>
> *Static worksheet with records from this page*
>
> *Static worksheet with records from all pages in the current view*
>
> These options allow you to choose whether to return all records from the view or just the records on the first page of the view results.

The File Download dialog box appears.

5. Click **Open** to launch Excel and open the export file. Alternatively, you can also select **Save** if you want to save the Excel file to your computer.

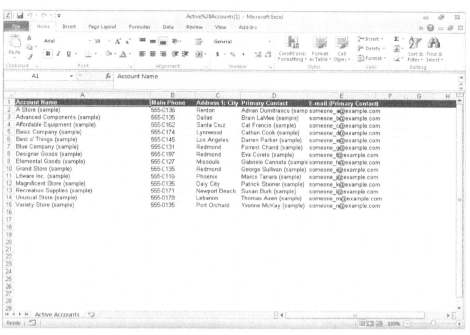

The active account records have now been downloaded to Excel. You can format, modify, and analyze the data in Excel to meet your needs without affecting your Microsoft Dynamics CRM database.

> **Important** If you do not have Excel installed on your computer, the file will not open. Contact your system administrator if you do not have Excel. Alternatively, Microsoft provides a tool called Excel Viewer, which allows you to open Excel files for viewing. Excel Viewer can be found on the Microsoft Download Center site at http://www.microsoft.com/downloads.

Exporting Dynamic Data to Excel Worksheets

If you are using Microsoft Dynamics CRM as it is intended, your data changes regularly. The number of records in your database on a particular day will probably be different the next day, and the data captured within those records will be updated frequently. Consequently, the static data you exported to Excel in the past will probably be out of date after a day or two. You can easily export the static data again, but you will lose any formatting or additions you made to the Excel file. Fortunately, Microsoft Dynamics CRM lets you export dynamic data to Excel so that you can create your desired output once and refresh your data from within Excel. When you tap the power of dynamic worksheets, you can set up your file one time and simply open it when needed. You don't need to have Microsoft Dynamics CRM open to benefit from the data within the application.

Additionally, when you place the dynamic file on a shared network drive, other users can benefit from your report by seeing their data in the format you created. For example, in the exercise in this section, you will create a dynamic file from the My Activities view, which shows only those activities assigned to you. When another user opens the file from his or her workstation, only that user's activities will appear.

In this exercise, you will export data to a dynamic Excel file. You will then update your Microsoft Dynamics CRM application and refresh your data from within Excel to see the power of the dynamic file in action.

 SET UP **Use your own Microsoft Dynamics CRM installation in place of the site shown in this exercise. Use the Internet Explorer web browser to navigate to your Microsoft Dynamics CRM website, if necessary, before beginning this exercise.**

1. In the **Workplace** area, click **Activities**.

   The default activities view, My Activities, appears. If there are no activities in the default activities view, create a new activity for this exercise.

   > **See Also** For more information about creating activities, see Chapter 4, "Working with Activities and Notes."

2. Click the **Export to Excel** button.

   The Export Data To Excel dialog box appears.

3. Select **Dynamic worksheet**. The Edit Columns button becomes active.

   This button allows you to modify the columns in the output of your dynamic worksheet, in case you want to add columns or reorder the fields in the data grid.

4. Click the **Edit Columns** button to launch the **Edit Columns** dialog box.

> **See Also** The Edit Columns screen functionality was reviewed earlier in this book. If you need a refresher on editing columns, see "Organizing and Formatting Advanced Find Results" in Chapter 16, "Using Advanced Find."

5. In the **Common Tasks** pane, click **Add Columns**.

The Add Columns dialog box appears.

6. Select the check box next to the **Last Updated** field to add the modified date to your export, and then click **OK**.

The Last Updated field is added to the grid preview in the Edit Columns dialog box.

7. Click **OK** to save your changes and return to the **Export Data to Excel** dialog box.

8. Click **Export** to export the dynamic data to Excel.

The File Download dialog box appears.

9. Click **Save** and save the file to a familiar location, using the file name *Dynamic Activity Export*.

The Download Complete dialog box displays when the file has been saved.

10. Click the **Open** button in the **Download Complete** dialog box to view the **Dynamic Activity Export** file.

The file includes the records from the My Activities view.

> **Important** You might get a security alert beneath the ribbon in Excel showing that data connections have been disabled. You can enable the content by clicking the Options button and selecting Enable This Content.

11. In the Excel file, rename the **Activity Type** column header to *Type*.

12. On the keyboard, press Ctrl+A to select all of the rows in the Excel worksheet. In the **Font Type** field, select **Tahoma**.

13. Save the Excel file, and then close Excel.

14. Navigate back to the **My Activities** view within Microsoft Dynamics CRM.

15. On the **Activities** tab of the ribbon, click the **New** button to add a new activity.

The New Activity menu appears.

16. Click the **Phone Call** button.

The New Phone Call form appears.

17. Enter a subject, a Regarding value, and a due date.

18. Click the **Save and Close** button.

The new activity now appears in the My Activities view.

> **See Also** Working with activities was discussed earlier in this book. If you need a refresher on this subject, see Chapter 4.

19. Open the **Dynamic Activity Export** file from within Excel or Windows Explorer.

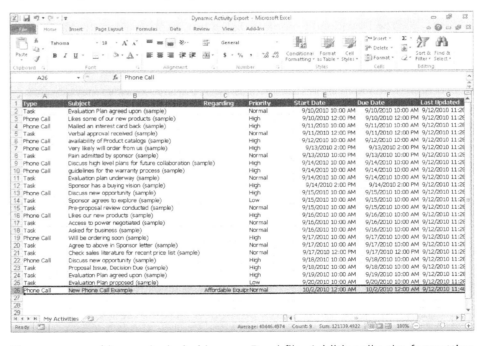

The new record is now included in your Excel file. Additionally, the formatting changes you made remain intact. Any time you open the file from now on, it will automatically refresh.

If you want to refresh the file without closing and reopening it, you can simply right-click within the resulting rows and select Refresh.

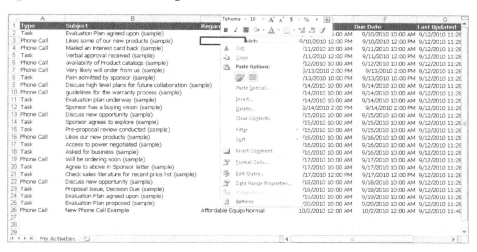

Exporting Dynamic Data to Excel PivotTables

In addition to letting you export data to dynamic Excel worksheets, Microsoft Dynamics CRM lets you export data to Excel PivotTables. Excel PivotTables give you the ability to cross-tabulate data to produce summarized reports.

Some people initially struggle with the concept of PivotTables. Consider the following example, in which you have this table of activities:

Activity Type	Owner	Due Date
Phone Call	Mike Snyder	8/15/2010
Task	Jim Steger	8/15/2010
Appointment	Jim Steger	8/12/2010
Phone Call	Jen Ford	8/19/2010
Phone Call	Jim Steger	9/1/2010
Task	Jen Ford	9/5/2010
E-mail	Mike Snyder	9/5/2010
Appointment	Jen Ford	9/7/2010
Task	Jen Ford	9/7/2010
Phone Call	Jim Steger	9/7/2010

This table consists of flat data in columns and rows. Flat data generally serves as the basis for a PivotTable. With a data set of this size, you can easily count the records to summarize the data in a variety of ways. For example:

- Four of the activities are phone calls.
- Mike Snyder is the owner of two activities.
- Three activities have a due date of 9/7/2010.

However, as your data set grows, summarizing the data at a glance becomes impossible. With a PivotTable, you can eliminate the manual calculation and *pivot* the data to get the answers. The following table is an example of a PivotTable on the flat data sample.

	Jim Steger	Jen Ford	Mike Snyder	Grand Total
Appointment	1	1		2
E-mail			1	1
Phone Call	2	1	1	4
Task	1	2		3
Grand Total	4	4	2	10

With the PivotTable, you can easily see how many activities exist for each owner by type and in total. It also becomes clear how many total activities exist by type. You could have pivoted the data by due date rather than by owner or activity type to see aggregates by due date.

> **Important** This chapter is not intended to teach you the full capabilities of PivotTables; it's meant to provide insight into basic PivotTable capability as it relates to your Microsoft Dynamics CRM data. For more information about PivotTables, see Microsoft Excel 2010 Step by Step, by Curtis Frye (Microsoft Press, 2010).

Although the concept of PivotTables might be intimidating at first, when you have gained familiarity with the process, you will be able to create powerful reports very efficiently. Similar to a dynamic worksheet, a dynamic PivotTable establishes a live link with your Microsoft Dynamics CRM database. Report setup is a one-time investment that you can benefit from continually. And learning how to use Excel PivotTables can help you solve reporting needs from other business-critical applications as well.

In this exercise, you will export data to a dynamic PivotTable to organize and summarize your Microsoft Dynamics CRM data.

SET UP Use your own Microsoft Dynamics CRM installation in place of the site shown in this exercise. Use the Internet Explorer web browser to navigate to your Microsoft Dynamics CRM website, if necessary, before beginning this exercise.

1. In the **Workplace** area, click **Activities**.

The default activities view, My Activities, appears.

2. Click the **Export to Excel** button.

The Export Data To Excel dialog box appears.

3. Select **Dynamic PivotTable**. Notice that the **Select Columns** button becomes active.

4. Click the **Select Columns** button.

The Select PivotTable Columns dialog box appears. The columns that appear in the My Activities grid are selected by default.

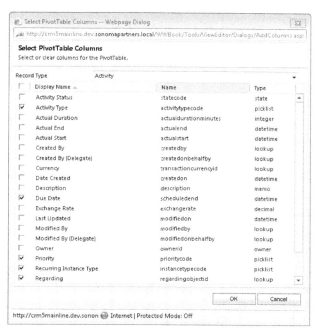

5. Select the check box for the **Activity Status** field, and click **OK**.

This selection will make the Activity Status field available in the PivotTable.

6. Back in the **Export Data to Excel** dialog box, click **Export**.

The File Download dialog box appears.

7. Click **Open**.

This opens Excel and displays an empty PivotTable.

> **Important** You might get a security alert beneath the ribbon in Excel showing that data connections have been disabled. You can enable the content by clicking the Options button and selecting Enable This Content.

8. In the PivotTable field list on the right side of the screen, drag the **Due Date** field to the **Row Labels** section. Then drag the **Due Date** field to the **Values** section.

The PivotTable shows a count of activities by due date.

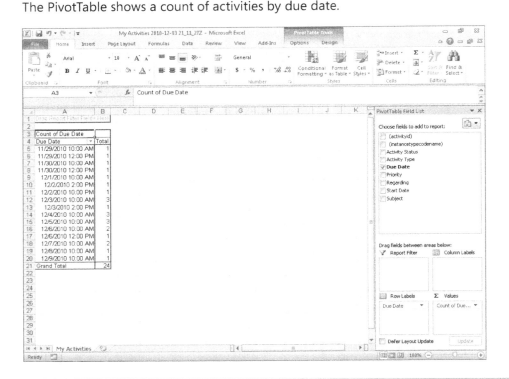

> **Tip** While you are counting records, you can summarize numeric information in a variety of ways by changing the calculation type. To change the calculation type, click the arrow next to the field in the Values section and click Value Field Settings. For example, you can modify the settings to summarize the data by Sum or Average.

9. Drag **Due Date** from the **Row Labels** section to the **Column Labels** section.

The same data is now pivoted in the opposite direction.

10. Drag the **Activity Type** field into the **Row Labels** section.

The count of activities by due date for each activity type is now displayed.

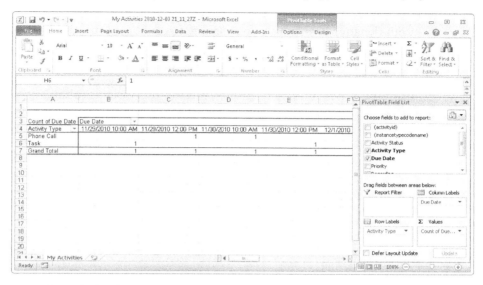

11. Drag the **Priority** field into the **Report Filter** section.

Priority now appears at the top of the PivotTable as a parameter. When you make a selection in the Priority field, the PivotTable results will refresh for records with the selected priority.

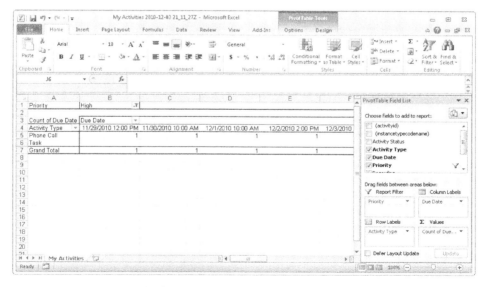

You can continue to add fields into the PivotTable report to refine your analysis.

Advanced PivotTables

With dynamic PivotTables, you can create countless summary-level reports with just a few clicks. To further illustrate the capabilities, here are two examples of dynamic PivotTables created from Microsoft Dynamics CRM data.

Example 1: Revenue by customer, filtered on closing probability

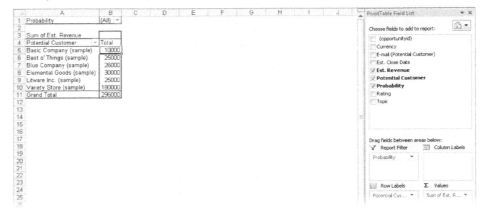

Example 2: Breakdown of customer accounts by city

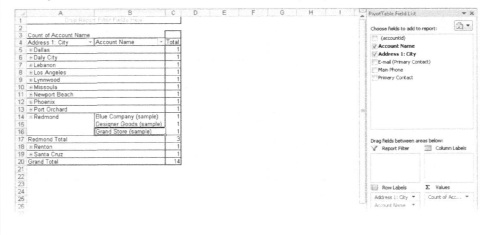

Uploading Excel Reports to the Reports List in Microsoft Dynamics CRM

You are now able to create reports that have value to others in your organization in addition to yourself. Although you learned that you can store dynamic Excel reports in a shared network location, this might be cumbersome and difficult to find. Microsoft Dynamics CRM allows you to also upload reports to the Reports area and share the reports so that users can access all of their reports within the application.

In this exercise, you will upload a report to the Reports area of Microsoft Dynamics CRM.

 SET UP Use the Internet Explorer web browser to navigate to your Microsoft Dynamics CRM website, if necessary, before beginning this exercise. You need the Dynamic Activity Export file you created earlier in this chapter.

1. In the **Workplace** area, click **Reports**.

    The default Report view, Available Reports, appears.

2. Click the **New** button.

    The New Report dialog box appears.

3. In the **Report Type** field, select **Existing File**.

4. In the **Source** section of the dialog box, click the **Browse** button.

    The Choose File To Upload dialog box appears.

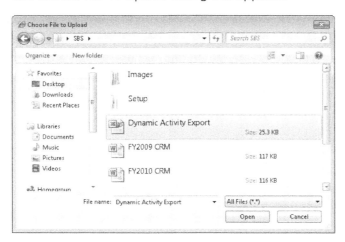

5. Navigate to the **Dynamic Activity Export** file you created earlier in this chapter, and click **Open**.

    The file path now appears in the File Location field of the New Report dialog box.

6. Click the **Save and Close** button to save your report in Microsoft Dynamics CRM. You will now see the report in the available reports list.

7. Double-click the **Dynamic Activity Export** report to run your report. Your report is launched.

   You have successfully uploaded your report to Microsoft Dynamics CRM.

> **See Also** The Reports area, report categorization, and report sharing were discussed earlier in this book. If you need a refresher on this subject, see Chapter 15, "Using the Report Wizard."

Key Points

- You can export data to Excel from most record grids within Microsoft Dynamics CRM by clicking the Export To Excel button.

- When exporting data to Excel, you can choose to export static or dynamic data.

- Static data exports provide a snapshot of data as it exists at the time of export.

- Dynamic data exports establish a live link with the Microsoft Dynamics CRM database and can be refreshed at any time. Any formatting done on a dynamic Excel file is preserved on refresh.

- A dynamic export to an Excel PivotTable provides you with a mechanism to summarize data in a cross-tabbed, or pivoted, table.

- Dynamic exports can be uploaded and shared so that other users can benefit from the reports you create. When another user opens a dynamic report, the data that appears will mirror the data that user can access in Microsoft Dynamics CRM, presented in the format you created.

Part 5
Data Management

18 **Bulk Data Importing** 381

Chapter at a Glance

Map source data, **page 382**

Import records with the
Import Data Wizard,
page 382

Resolve import errors,
page 391

18 Bulk Data Importing

In this chapter, you will learn how to

- ✔ Import records by using the Import Data Wizard.
- ✔ Map data automatically in the Import Data Wizard.
- ✔ View the results of an import.
- ✔ Resolve import errors.
- ✔ Update existing data by using the Data Enrichment feature.

Sales and marketing professionals often need to load bulk data into their Microsoft Dynamics CRM systems. Manually entering these records would be a time-consuming and expensive task. Examples of bulk data that might need to be imported include:

- A list of leads, contacts, or accounts purchased from a third party.
- A list of contacts obtained from a conference recently attended by the sales staff.
- A file full of business contacts brought by an employee who has just joined the company.

Microsoft Dynamics CRM allows users to import data with an easy-to-use Import Data Wizard. With this wizard, you can import hundreds or thousands of records in just a few clicks. In addition to importing core record types such as leads, contacts, and accounts, you can also use the Import Data Wizard to import other record types, including any custom record types created by your system administrator.

In this chapter, you will learn how to import data by using the Import Data Wizard. Additionally, you will learn how to view the results of a data import and how to trouble-shoot import errors. Finally, you will learn how to update existing data quickly by taking advantage of the data enrichment feature.

> **Practice Files** Before you can complete the exercises in this chapter, you need to copy the book's practice files to your computer. The practice file you'll use to complete the exercises in this chapter is in the Chapter18 practice file folder. A complete list of practice files is provided in "Using the Practice Files" at the beginning of this book.

> **Important** The images used in this book reflect the default form and field names in Microsoft Dynamics CRM. Because the software offers extensive customization capabilities, it's possible that some of the record types or fields have been relabeled in your Microsoft Dynamics CRM environment. If you cannot find the forms, fields, or security roles referred to in this book, contact your system administrator for assistance.

> **Important** You must know the location of your Microsoft Dynamics CRM website to work the exercises in this book. Check with your system administrator to verify the web address if you don't know it.

Using the Import Data Wizard

Most data import tools allow users to import simple values into text fields. For more complex data importing—importing into drop-down lists and lookup fields, for example—you usually need to enlist IT resources to write code to map the data. These tasks usually have to go through a prioritization and scheduling process. By the time the data is finally imported, either the need has been met manually or the data is out of date.

The Microsoft Dynamics CRM Import Data Wizard solves most of these challenges. Although the wizard requires the import file to be mapped to the related Microsoft Dynamics CRM attributes, you can accomplish this without enlisting a software development resource. The process of mapping data might sound intimidating; fortunately, the Import Data Wizard does most of the work for you!

Microsoft Dynamics CRM uses data maps as the basis for translating how a source field converts into a related destination field. Consider the following example: suppose you have a file of contacts you would like to import into Microsoft Dynamics CRM. Within your source file, there is a field called *First*, which contains the first name of a contact. In Microsoft Dynamics CRM, the related field is named *First Name*. In order to import the data in the source file, you need to map the First field in the source file to the First Name field in the destination (Microsoft Dynamics CRM).

The Import Data Wizard is a simple and intuitive interface that navigates you through the import process. In just a few steps, you can import your records into Microsoft Dynamics CRM. Most entities are available for data import. By default, the following record types are available for import.

Account	Document Location	Product
Address	E-mail	Queue
Announcement	Facility/Equipment	Queue Item
Appointment	Fax	Price List Item
Article	Goal	Quote
Article Template	Goal Metric	Quote Close
Business Unit	Invoice	Quote Product
Campaign	Invoice Product	Recurring Appointment
Campaign Activity	Lead	Rollup Query
Campaign Response	Letter	Sales Attachment
Case	Marketing List	Sales Literature
Case Resolution	Note	Security Role
Competitor	Opportunity	Service
Connection	Opportunity Close	Service Activity
Contact	Opportunity Product	Sharepoint Site
Contract	Opportunity Relationship	Site
Contract Line	Order	Subject
Contract Template	Order Close	Task
Currency	Order Product	Team
Customer Relationship	Phone Call	Territory
Discount	Price List	Unit
Discount List		User

> **Tip** Custom entities are also available for data import. It is unlikely that the user will know which entities are custom and which are native, so be sure to check the list of record types available in the Import Data Wizard. Contact your system administrator if you would like a list of custom entities.

The Import Data Wizard requires you to input the following information:

- The name and path of the data file to be imported
- Delimiter settings
- Data mappings
- The target record type
- The duplicate detection setting
- The name of the record owner

In this exercise, you will use the Import Data Wizard to import data.

SET UP Use the Windows Internet Explorer web browser to navigate to your Microsoft Dynamics CRM website before beginning this exercise. You need the ContactImport1.csv file located in your Chapter18 practice file folder to complete this exercise.

1. In the **Workplace** area, click **Imports**, and then click the **Import Data** button on the **Imports** tab of the ribbon.

    The Import Data Wizard appears.

2. Click **Browse**, and then locate the **ContactImport1.csv** file.

3. Click **Next** to select the file as the data source for your import.

> **Important** A delimiter is a character or series of characters that indicates a boundary in certain files. In comma-separated files, each value is separated by a comma, which is specified in the Field Delimiter field in the Import Data Wizard. The following line shows a record that has a Data Delimiter value of Quotation Mark (") and a Field Delimiter value of Comma (,).
>
>   *"Jesper","Aaberg","someone@example.com",555-0173*
>
> Depending on the input file, you might need to change the delimiter options.

4. On the **Review File Upload Summary** page, click **Next** to select the data map for your import.

5. In the **System Data Maps** list, select **Default (Automatic Mapping)**.

> **Tip** Microsoft Dynamics CRM comes with several data maps for common import scenarios. For more complex data imports, you can import multiple files in a single import by using a .zip file.

6. Click **Next** to proceed to the next step of the Import Data Wizard.

7. On the **Map Record Types** page, in the **Microsoft Dynamics CRM Record Types** field, select **Contact**, and then click **Next**.

8. On the **Map Fields** page, in the **Source Fields** column, select **Last** in the **Required Fields** list.

This will map the Last column of the source file to the required Last Name field in Microsoft Dynamics CRM.

9. Map the additional fields to match those in the following table:

Source Fields	CRM Fields
City	Address 1: City
E-mail	E-mail
First	First Name
State	Address 1: State/Province
Street	Address 1: Street 1
Type of Address	Address 1: Address Type (Option Set)
Work Num	Business Phone
Zip	Address 1: ZIP/Postal Code

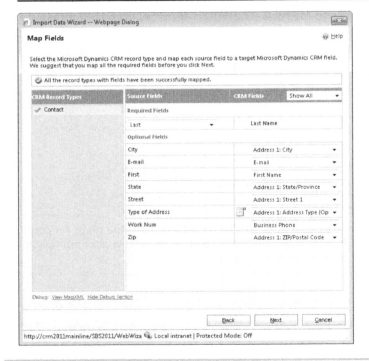

Important When you map the Address1: Address Type field, a dialog box appears so that you can map the picklist values. In this example, the fields map directly, so you can click OK.

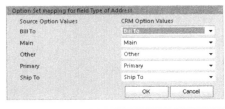

10. Click **Next** to move to the next page. Then, on the **Review Mapping Summary** page, click **Next**.

11. On the **Review Settings and Import Data** page, select **Yes** in the **Allow Duplicates** area.

> **Troubleshooting** The duplicate detection option will be presented only if duplicate detection is turned on for data imports.

12. In the **Select Owner for Imported Records** area, leave the default selection. In the **Data Map Name** area, enter **_Contact Import Example_**.

13. Click **Submit**.

The data will now be imported, and the Contact Import Example data map will be created for future use.

> **Tip** Data imports are processed in the background; therefore, your data might not be available immediately. Allow a few minutes for your data to be imported.

14. Click **Finish** to exit the **Import Data Wizard**.

The Imports grid appears with a new record called ContactImport1.csv {Contact}, indicating that the import has been submitted to the system for processing. The status of the import will update automatically as the import is processed behind the scenes.

Importing Data with Automatic Data Mapping

As the previous exercise demonstrated, stepping through the Import Data Wizard is a straightforward process. The most time-consuming part of the process is mapping the fields, which is a simple task that nevertheless takes patience and an understanding of basic data concepts. To streamline the data import process, Microsoft Dynamics CRM allows you to create files that map automatically. This takes some setup with the Advanced Find tool, but you will find that it saves you valuable time in the long run.

> **See Also** For more information about Advanced Find, see Chapter 16, "Using Advanced Find."

> **Tip** The key to automatic mapping is the column headers in your import file. If the column headers in your import file match the field display names in Microsoft Dynamics CRM, your file will automatically map. You can use Advanced Find or an existing view to create a template for your import file in which the column headers mirror the field values in Microsoft Dynamics CRM, and then perform a copy-and-paste operation to paste the rows of data you would like to import into the template file.

In this exercise, you will create an Advanced Find query that you will export to create an import file that uses automatic mapping.

 SET UP Use your own Microsoft Dynamics CRM installation in place of the site shown in this exercise. Use the Internet Explorer web browser to navigate to your Microsoft Dynamics CRM website, if necessary, before beginning this exercise.

1. On the ribbon, click the **Advanced Find** button.

The Advanced Find window appears.

2. In the **Look For** field, select **Accounts**.

3. In the **Use Saved View** field, select **My Active Accounts**.

> **Important** If you cannot find the view referred to in this step, select one of the available views and continue with the steps.

4. On the ribbon, in the **Show** group, click the **Results** button.

The Results window is displayed with the matching account records.

5. In the **Results** window, click the **Export Accounts** button.

The Export Data To Excel dialog box appears.

6. Select **Static worksheet with records from this page**, and click **Export**.

The File Download dialog box appears.

7. Click **Save**, save the file as *MyAccounts.xls* to a familiar location on your computer, and then close the **Advanced Find** window.

8. Open the **MyAccounts.xls** file in Microsoft Excel, save it as a CSV (comma-separated value) file named *MyAccounts.csv*, and then close Excel.

> **Important** Import files must be in a comma-separated value (CSV) format. To convert an Excel file to a CSV file, open the file in Excel and use the Save As feature. In the Save As Type list, select CSV (Comma Delimited).

9. Back in Microsoft Dynamics CRM, on the **File** menu, click **Tools,** and then click **Import Data** to launch the **Import Data Wizard**.

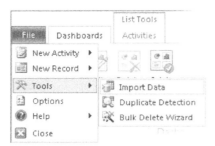

10. Click **Browse** and locate the **MyAccounts.csv** file, then click **Next**.

> **Tip** Make sure you select the file with the .csv extension, not the one with the .xls extension.

11. On the **Review File Upload Summary** page, click **Next**.

12. On the **Select Data Map** page, in the **System Data Maps** list, select **Default (Automatic Mapping)**, and then click **Next**.

13. On the next page, in the **Microsoft Dynamics CRM Record Types** list, select **Account**, and then click **Next**.

    Microsoft Dynamics CRM automatically populates most of the fields. The E-Mail (Primary Contact) field is not mapped because it is from the contact entity, not the account entity.

14. Leave the **E-mail (Primary Contact)** field as **Not Mapped**, and click **Next**. Click **OK** in the warning box regarding the unmapped field.

15. Click **Next** on the **Review Mapping Summary** page.

16. On the **Review Settings and Import Data** page, select **Yes** in the **Allow Duplicates** area and leave the default selection in the **Select Owner for Imported Records** area. Leave the **Data Map Name** blank, and click **Submit**.

> **Tip** Although you might not want to export a file from your Microsoft Dynamics CRM application and import it back into the system, you can easily use the output of the file as a template and paste import data into the file. Your file will automatically map as long as the column headings are not manipulated.

Reviewing the Import Status

The import will run in the background after it has been initiated. You can continue to use Microsoft Dynamics CRM during this time. The process can take a minute to several minutes, depending on the size of the import file.

You will want to review the results of the import to ensure that all records have been imported as expected and, if necessary, troubleshoot import-related errors. Microsoft Dynamics CRM provides a tool that lets you easily obtain this information without leaving the familiar application interface.

After your import is completed, you can view its status in the Imports view, which is available in the Workplace area. Each import is displayed as a separate record in the Imports grid, and if you double-click a record, you can view the details of that import job. Each import record shows important information, such as the name of the user who submitted the import, the date and time the import was submitted, and the import file name and file size. Additionally, you can view the records that were created during the import process and examine the errors for records that failed to import.

The ability to view failures for each import allows you to easily identify issues with your import file so that you can update it and re-import the records that did not get created during the import process. Each error row displays the following information.

Column	Description
Sequence Number	An identifier for the error row
Description	A description of the error for that row
Column Heading	The name of the column in the import file that is causing the error
Column Value	The value that is causing the error
Original Row Number	The number of the row in the import file that is producing the error
Source Row	The full row of text that is failing

Tip Any row that succeeds in the import process (and consequently does not show up in the Failures list) will be imported into Microsoft Dynamics CRM. Do not assume that no records were imported because a single row failed.

Troubleshooting An import file can fail for several reasons. Each specific row in the Failures list can have a different error; therefore, you might need to diagnose more than one issue before attempting to re-import.

In this exercise, you will view the status and troubleshoot related errors for the import you submitted earlier in this chapter. Then you will research the failure so that you can understand the root cause of the issue. Finally, you will correct the error and re-import the error row.

SET UP Use the Internet Explorer web browser to navigate to your Microsoft Dynamics CRM website, if necessary, before beginning this exercise. You need the ContactImport1.csv import you submitted earlier in this chapter.

1. In the **Workplace** area, click **Imports**.

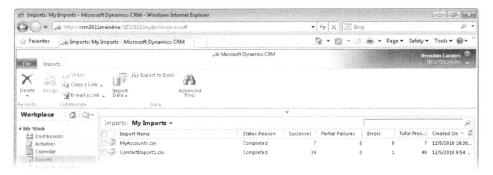

Look for the row that contains the ContactImport1.csv contact import you submitted in the "Using the Import Data Wizard" section earlier in this chapter.

2. Look at the **Status Reason** value for the import.

The Status Reason will be set to either Parsing, Transforming, Importing, or Completed. If the Status Reason is not Completed, return at a later time.

3. Review the **Successes**, **Partial Failures**, **Errors**, and **Total Processed** values.

You should see that 39 rows have completed successfully and one row has errors.

4. Double-click the record to display additional information.

5. In the entity navigation pane, click **Failures**.

The record that failed in the import process is displayed.

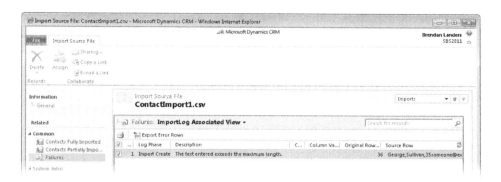

You can attempt to diagnose the error based on the message and data provided in the error row. You know that the issue is related to the 36th row in the import file, and the error description states that the text entered exceeds the maximum length. You can also see that the contact being imported was George Sullivan.

6. Locate and open the import file.

7. Find the text row with **George Sullivan**. Notice that the value in the **Zip** column is erroneous. Update the ZIP Code to *60463*.

8. Delete the other (non-error) rows in the file.

> **Important** Do not delete the first row. The first row contains the column headers from the file.

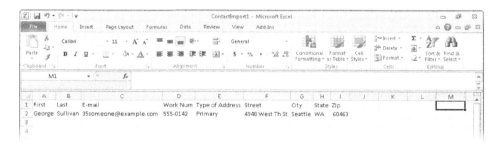

9. Click **Save As**, save the file as *ContactImport1_Update.csv* to a familiar location on your computer, and then close the Excel file.

The next step is to attempt to import the file.

10. In Microsoft Dynamics CRM, on the **File** menu, click **Tools,** and then click **Import Data** to launch the **Import Data Wizard**.

11. Click **Browse**, locate the **ContactImport1_Update.csv** file, and then click **Next**.

12. On the **Review File Upload Summary** page, click **Next**.

13. On the **Select Data Map** page, in the **Customized Data Maps** list, select **Contact Import Example**, and then click **Next**.

> **Important** The Contact Import Example data map was created earlier in this chapter, in the exercise in the "Using the Import Data Wizard" section.

14. On the next page, in the **Microsoft Dynamics CRM Record Types** list, select **Contact**, and then click **Next**.

15. On the **Map Fields** page, click **Next**.

16. Click **Next** on the **Review Mapping Summary** page.

17. Leave the default options on the **Review Settings and Import Data** page, and click **Submit.**

Your error row should now be imported successfully.

Updating Data by Using Data Enrichment

As you can see, Microsoft Dynamics CRM allows users to easily create records in bulk by using a simple, intuitive wizard. In addition to creating data by using this wizard, you might want to update data in bulk through a similar interface. In Chapter 16, you learned how to use the Edit Multiple Records feature to update multiple records in a single action, but this tool only works when you want to make the same updates to all records. Sometimes you might need to update multiple records but make different updates to different records. Consider the following scenarios:

- Your staff has a weekly sales meeting in which salespeople share opportunity status and progress. After this meeting, a designated individual updates Opportunity data to reflect the updates covered at the meeting.

- You add a new field to Microsoft Dynamics CRM to capture an additional pertinent piece of information. You want to update the field for existing records.

Microsoft Dynamics CRM includes a Data Enrichment feature that allows you to export data to Excel, make updates, and then re-import the data. This allows you to make updates in bulk to existing records without having to go record by record.

In this exercise, you will export the list of active opportunities, update the data in Excel, and re-import the data by using the Import Data Wizard.

SET UP Use your own Microsoft Dynamics CRM installation in place of the site shown in this exercise. Use the Internet Explorer web browser to navigate to your Microsoft Dynamics CRM website, if necessary, before beginning this exercise.

1. In the **Sales** area, click **Opportunities**.

2. Select the **Open Opportunities** view.

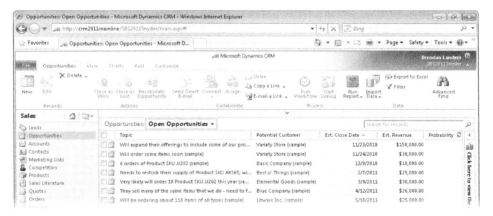

 3. On the **Opportunities** tab of the ribbon, in the **Data** group, click the **Export to Excel** button.

   The Export Data To Excel dialog box appears.

4. Select **Static worksheet with records from this page** as the type of worksheet to export.

5. At the bottom of the dialog box, select the **Make this data available for re-importing by including required column headings** check box.

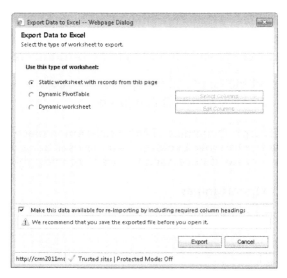

6. Click **Export**. On the **File Download** page, click **Save**, and save the file as *For Re-import - Open Opportunities.xml* to a familiar location on your computer.

7. Open the **For Re-import - OpenOpportunities.xml** file in Excel.

8. Update the **Topic** field and the **Est. Close Date** field for one record, and the **Probability** and **Rating** fields for a different record.

   Notice that the Rating field, which is a picklist in Microsoft Dynamics CRM, offers you a picklist to choose from in Excel.

9. Click **Save**, and close the **OpenOpportunities.xml** file.

10. Back in Microsoft Dynamics CRM, on the **File** menu, click **Tools,** and then click **Import Data** to launch the Import Data Wizard.

    The Import Data Wizard appears.

11. On the first page, click **Browse** and locate the **OpenOpportunities.xml** file. Click **Next**.

12. On the next page, in the **Microsoft Dynamics CRM Record Type** list, select **Opportunity,** and then click **Next**.

13. Click **Next** on the **Map Fields** page and again on the **Review Mapping Summary** page.

14. Leave the default options on the next page, and click **Submit.**

15. On the **Review Settings and Import Data** page, select **Yes** in the **Allow Duplicates** area and leave the default selection in the **Select Owner for Imported Records** area. Click **Submit.**

    The Import Data Wizard updates your records accordingly.

> **Important** Data enrichment is a very powerful capability that is also dangerous. You can create data issues if you are not very careful when you are updating the data in Excel. You should carefully review your data prior to re-importing.

Key Points

- The Import Data Wizard allows Microsoft Dynamics CRM users to import records in bulk by using a straightforward wizard that is available within the familiar application interface.

- Data maps allow users to map data from a field in a source file to its Microsoft Dynamics CRM target field. Data maps are reusable for future data import needs.

- You need to provide a data map only if your column headings do not match the Microsoft Dynamics CRM column headings or if your list values do not match the values in the target mapping column.

- You can view the status of a data import in the Imports view, which is available from the Workplace area. You can do so both while the import is running and after the import process has completed. You can then view successes and failures by opening the related import record.

- You can update existing records by exporting them to Excel and re-importing them by using data enrichment.

Glossary

account A company that might do business with your organization.

activity A general term used to describe an interaction with a customer or potential customer. An activity can be created to remind a user to communicate with a customer or to record a communication that has already occurred. Eight types of activities exist natively: tasks, faxes, phone calls, email messages, letters, appointments, service activities, and campaign responses. Your organization can also create custom activities in addition to these.

allotment type The units of service, such as a case or a range of coverage dates, specified in a service contract to indicate how much access a customer has to customer service.

article Text-based content stored in the knowledge base.

attribute A property of an entity with a specific data type. Attributes are analogous to columns in a database table. When attributes are added to an entity form, they are displayed as fields that correspond to their data type.

campaign activity An activity associated with a specific campaign, such as a letter, fax, or phone call. Campaign activities include campaign-specific information and must be distributed to create the individual activities for users to perform.

campaign response A record of the communication you receive from a potential customer in response to a specific campaign.

case A customer service issue or problem reported by a customer and the activity that a customer service representative uses to resolve it.

child account A record in a hierarchical relationship with a parent account, where a reference to the parent account is stored in the child account record. One parent account record can be related to many child account records, or sub-accounts. Child account records have look-up fields in their forms that allow them to be related to a parent record.

contact A person who represents a customer or potential customer, or an individual related to an account; for example, an individual who purchases products or services for his or her own use, or an employee of an account. A contact might also be a person involved in a business transaction, such as a supplier or a colleague.

contract An agreement to provide support during specified coverage dates or for a specified number of cases or for a specified length of time. When a customer contacts customer service, the level of support the customer receives is determined by his or her contract.

contract line A line item in a contract that describes the service support to be provided. A contract line often includes pricing information and how support will be allotted.

contract template A framework for a contract that is used to ensure consistent layouts and content in similar contracts.

converting a lead Turning a qualified lead into an Account, Contact, and/or Opportunity record.

customer An account or contact with whom business units conduct business transactions.

customer relationship A way of relating a customer record to other customer records. Customer relationships are reciprocal. The relationship defined for one record is also available in the other customer record.

data map A file that contains information about how data from a source system corresponds to data in Microsoft Dynamics CRM.

direct email A mass-mailing of the same message that is sent by using Microsoft Dynamics CRM email templates to multiple email recipients.

distribute To create campaign activities for each account, contact, or lead in a marketing list associated with a campaign, and then to assign the activities to the specified owners, or to perform the activities automatically (such as sending email messages).

dynamic value A value that updates in real time. For example, a dynamic export can be refreshed with the latest data from the Microsoft Dynamics CRM database.

email template A framework for an email message that is used to ensure consistent layouts and content in similar email messages.

field mapping A technique that streamlines data entry when a new record is associated with an existing record. When an entity has an entity relationship with another entity, you can create new related entity records from the associated view that is visible on the primary entity. When the user creates a new record from an associated view, mapped data from the primary entity record is copied to the form for the new related entity record.

going offline The act of disconnecting the Microsoft Dynamics CRM for Outlook with Offline Access client from the Microsoft Dynamics CRM server, which allows you to work with a subset of data while not connected.

going online The act of connecting back to the Microsoft Dynamics CRM server from the offline client for Microsoft Dynamics CRM.

history A list of activities that have been completed or closed. You can access the history for a record in its navigation pane.

knowledge base A repository of an organization's customer service information, such as frequently asked questions, data sheets, solutions to common problems, and user guides. This information is stored as articles and is organized by subject.

lead A potential customer who must be qualified or disqualified as a sales opportunity. If a lead is qualified, it can be converted to an opportunity, account, and/or contact.

lead source A resource through which your company obtains leads.

list member An account, contact, or lead that is included in a marketing list.

local data group A set of filters that determines the data that will be available offline and stored on the local computer.

lookup A field that allows you to choose a value from data stored in a related entity.

marketing campaign A marketing program that uses multiple communication vehicles and is intended to increase awareness of your company, products, or services.

marketing list A list of accounts, contacts, or leads that match a specific set of criteria.

opportunity A potential revenue-generating event or sale to an account that needs to be tracked through a sales process to completion.

parent account An account record that is in a hierarchical relationship with a child record, where a reference to the record is stored in the child record. One parent account record can be related to many child records.

product catalog A compilation of all products that are available for sale.

queue A holding container for activities that need to be completed. Some queues contain cases and activities in the Workplace, and other queues contain articles in the knowledge base.

quick campaign A marketing communication method that creates a single activity for distribution to a group of marketing lists, accounts, contacts, or leads.

Quick Find A mechanism to quickly search for records in the database.

quote A formal offer for products or services, proposed at specific prices and related payment terms, which is sent to an opportunity, account, or contact.

Regarding field Used to link an activity to another record so that you can view the activity from the record. If you create a new activity from a record, this is automatically filled out.

reopen To open a previously closed opportunity for further exploration.

share To allow another user or team to have a specified amount of access to a record, such as a case, account, or contract. For example, you can share an account with a team and specify that its members can read the account record but cannot have write access to it.

static value A value that remains the same and does not update in real time. A static export cannot be refreshed with the latest data from the Microsoft Dynamics CRM database.

sub-account A record in a hierarchical relationship with a parent account, where a reference to the parent account is stored in the sub-account record. One parent account record can be related to many sub-account records, or child accounts. Sub-account records have lookup fields in their forms that allow them to be related to a parent record.

subjects Categories used in a hierarchical list to correlate and organize information. Subjects are used in the subject tree to organize products, sales literature, and knowledge base articles.

track in CRM To create a link between a record in Microsoft Dynamics CRM and a record in Microsoft Outlook. If you change data on a record that is tracked in Microsoft Dynamics CRM, the changes will appear in both Microsoft Dynamics CRM and Outlook.

view A filter applied to a list of records. Users can choose different views that contain all the records or activities of a particular type or that are a subset of that type.

web client The Internet browser–based client for Microsoft Dynamics CRM.

Workplace A pane in the navigation pane that contains the work a user has been assigned, is currently working on, and is available in queues to which the user has access. Users can accept, assign, and delete assignments from here. Users can also use the Workplace to access their calendars and the knowledge base.

Index

A

Account form, 47
Account grid view, 292
accounts. *See also* parent customers
  accessing information on, 47
  attaching files to, 56
  contact relationships, 51-52
  creating, 48-49
  defined, 45, 47, 399
  note creation for, 86
  notes, viewing, 56
  parent, 49
  parent, creating, 50
  primary contact, 53
  red asterisks, 47
  relationships between, 49
  saving, 50
  sharing, 59
  sub-accounts, 49
Activate button, 59
activating
  contracts, 265
  records, 59
active records, 57
Active status for contracts, 264-265
Active status value, 57-58
activities
  attachments, uploading to, 75
  closed, 78, 84, 229
  completing, 78
  converting to opportunities/cases, 78
  creating, 73, 76, 369
  creating, with workflow rules, 68
  custom, 70
  data fields in, 71
  defined, 67, 399
  direction field, 77
  due dates, setting, 80
  filtering, 82-83, 90
  linking to other records, 71-72
  logging, 100
  managing, 88
  marking as completed, 78
  populating automatically, 76
  prioritizing, 89
  Regarding field, 71-73
  related, viewing, 79
  status values for, 78
  tracking, 70, 78-79
  types of, 69
  viewing, 89
Activities area, 89
Activities view, changing, 89
activity rollups, 79, 83
Add A New Section dialog box, 251
Add A Section button, 251
Add Columns dialog box, 324, 350, 369
Add Contacts wizard, 108-109
  color coding in, 110
  importing email messages with, 111
Add Existing Campaign button, 188
Add Existing Marketing List button, 184, 200
Add Existing Product button, 186
Add Existing Sales Literature button, 187
Add From Campaign button, 202
Add Grouping dialog box, 324, 330
Add Members dialog box, 158
Add New Activity button, 76, 182
Add New Campaign Activity button, 197
Add New Campaign Response button, 206
Add New Contact button, 53-54, 107
Add New Contract Line button, 262
Add New Opportunity button, 140
Add Note button, 86
Add To Another Marketing List button, 168
Add To Queue button, 273
Add To Queue dialog box, 273
address books, accessing, with Microsoft Dynamics CRM for Outlook, 114
Advanced Find
  adding fields to, 350
  adding marketing list members with, 157-159
  AND/OR functionality, 356-357
  assigning records, 361
  bulk editing records, 358-361
  column width, changing, 352
  columns, editing, 349
  data mapping with, 388-390
  default column set, 351
  deleting marketing list members with, 159-160
  evaluating marketing list members with, 161-162
  formatting results of, 349, 351, 353
  opening, 347

Advanced Find *(continued)*
 operators for, 345
 overview of, 344
 probability, searching, 347
 query details, viewing, 359
 results, displaying, 348
 saving queries, 353
 search criteria, 356
 searching related records, 346, 348
 searching with, 347-348
 Simple mode, changing, 357
 sorting columns in, 352
 system views, modifying, 348
 uses for, 344
Advanced Find button, 347, 349
aligning charts, 285
allotment type, 399
application areas
 overview of, 21
 specifying options for, 40
application navigation pane, 21
appointments. *See also* activities
 defined, 69
 recurring, 70
 synchronizing, 112
Approve button, 242
approving knowledge base articles, 242, 245
Article Approval Confirmation dialog box, 242
Article Template Properties dialog box, 250
Article Unpublish Confirmation dialog box, 246
articles, 399. *See also* knowledge base articles
Assign Accounts button, 361
Assign Accounts dialog box, 361
Assign button, 62, 223
Assign Queued Items dialog box, 273
Assign To Team Or User dialog box, 223
assigning cases to CSRs, 223
assigning records, 61, 62
Attach File button, 56
attachments
 for activities, uploading, 75
 defined, 56
attributes, 399
authentication, 9. *See also* logging on
automatic resolution for lookup fields, 36
Available Reports view, 377

B

Back button, 301
Bar button, 290
bar charts, creating, 290
billable time for cases, 228

body, record, 23
boldface elements in book, xvi
book conventions, xv
book errata, xxiii
book practice files, downloading, xxi
branding campaigns, relating to marketing
 campaigns, 187, 188
Browse button, 377
bulk data, importing. *See* Import Data Wizard
bulk editing records, 29, 30, 358-361
bulk emails. *See* direct emails
bulk mail, 172-173

C

calculation type in worksheets, 374
Calendar
 24-hour configuration, 260
 appointments displayed in, 88
 configuring, 260
 defined, 88
Calendar button, 74
campaign activities. *See also* activities
 channels for, 199
 creating, 196-199
 defined, 399
 distributing, 202-205
 distribution method, selecting, 198
 email, distributing, 203
 email templates for, 204
 fields commonly tracked for, 196
 marketing lists, 200-202
 opening, 203
 Other channel, 199
 overview of, 195
 promoting to, 207-209
 results, viewing, 212-213
 saving, 198
 status reports on, 214
 viewing, 197
Campaign Activity form, 198
Campaign Activity Status report, 214, 215
Campaign Response activity form, 207
campaign responses, 70. *See also* activities
 canceling, 212
 completing, 212
 converting, 209-211
 creating, 206
 defined, 399
 opening, 210
 promoting campaign activities to, 207-209
 tracking, 206-207
campaign results, 212-213

campaign templates, 189-190
campaigns. *See also* marketing campaigns
    copying records from, 189, 190
    naming, 190
    opening, 188, 197
    quick, 191, 192, 193
    relationships between, 188
Cancel Case button, 232
Canceled status for contracts, 265
Canceled status value, 57-58
canceling
    cases, 230, 232
    contracts, 267
    Quick Find, 32
Case Cancel Confirmation dialog box, 232
case statuses, setting, 232
cases
    Active status, setting, 232
    assigning to CSRs, 223
    assigning to queues, 273
    assigning to users, 223
    associating with accounts/contacts, 222
    autonumbering, configuring, 223
    billable time, entering, 228
    canceling, 230, 232
    closed activities, viewing, 229
    closing, 267
    converting activities into, 78
    creating, 221-222, 231
    defined, 399
    follow-up activities, creating, 227
    marking tasks as complete, 228
    opening against contracts, 266
    options, displaying, 226
    origin, setting, 222
    overview of, 220
    reactivating, 230, 232
    resolving, 228-229, 266
    status options, 229
    status, updating, 228
    subjects, assigning, 224
    tasks, creating, 227
    tracking, 226
    uses for, 220
    viewing, 221
categories. *See also* subject tree
    adding, 337
    fields for, 337
    Outlook , unrelated to, 71
    for reports, 337, 339
    in reports, 340
cell phones. *See* mobile devices
Change Column Properties dialog box, 352
channels for campaign activities, 199

Chart button, 305-306
Chart Designer, 289-291
Chart Pane button, 100, 285, 292
chart (user interface area), 22
charts
    aligning, 285
    bar , 290
    closing, 302
    contextual, 286
    creating, 288-291
    in dashboards, adding, 305
    in dashboards, switching, 311
    entities available for, 288
    list of, 283
    in Microsoft Dynamics CRM for Outlook, 100
    moving, 309
    opening, 143, 292
    pie , 287
    vs. Report Wizard, 319
    saving, 291
    sharing, 292-293
    updating, 144, 286
    uses for, 283
    viewing, 285
    viewing records in, 302
    width, changing, 309-310
Charts tab, 285
child accounts, 399
child records, 63
Choose Contact Groups dialog box, 110
CLEAN UP paragraphs, xvi
Close And Convert The Response dialog box, 210
Close As Lost button, 146
Close As Won button, 146
Close button, 267, 302
close date for opportunities, 139-140
Close Designer button, 291
Close Opportunity dialog box, 146
Close Phone Call button, 77
Close Task button, 75
Close Task dialog box, 75
closed activities, 78, 84
closing opportunities, 144-145
co-branding campaigns, 187-188
codes for marketing campaigns, 180
collapsing chart area, 22
collapsing Get Started pane, 21
columns
    selecting multiple, 26
    sorting, 352
    width, changing, 24
combining records, 62-64
comma-separated files, 384
Comment On This Article dialog box, 248

communication points, 196. *See also* campaign
　activities
Communications Server, integration with, 9
company manuals, 186-187
Completed status value, 58
completing activities, 78
completing tasks, 75
Component Designer dialog box, 305
Configure Sort Order dialog box, 325, 352
contact associated view
　creating contact from, 53
　customizing, 52
　defined, 51
Contact button, 105
Contact link, 51, 54
contact records
　defined, 45
　parent customers, 51
contacts
　account relationships, 51-52
　Add Contacts wizard, 108-109
　attaching email messages to, 117
　attaching files to, 56
　creating, 52, 54, 106, 107
　creating, from contact associated view, 53
　creating, from email messages, 117
　creating, in Outlook, 105
　customizing view for, 52
　defined, 45, 399
　deleting, 120
　editing, 53, 107
　employers, as parent customers, 52
　field mapping, 53, 54
　filtering, 52
　importing from Outlook, 109-110
　linking to parent account, 105-106
　organizing, 109
　overview of, 51
　parent customers, 51-52
　populating, 55
　pre-populating, 53
　primary, specifying, 53
　searching for, 55
　synchronizing, 108
　tracking, 105-106
　updating, 53
　views for, 52
contract lines, 399
contracts
　activating, 265
　Active status, 264-265
　automatic updating of, 263
　auto-numbering, configuring, 261

Canceled status, 265
canceling, 267
case manager, viewing, 265
components of, 257
creating, 260-261
defined, 399
details, specifying, 262
Draft status, 264
editing, 264
examples of, 257
Expired status, 265
Invoiced status, 264
invoicing, 265
line items, adding, 262
line items, examples of, 257
link between original and renewed, 268
On Hold status, 265
opening, 265
overview of, 255-256
placing holds on, 267
reasons for changing, 264
refreshing, 267
resolving cases, 266
specifying resource availability in, 259
start/end date, including, 262
status, updating, 267
templates for, 257-258, 260, 399
conventions of book, xv
Convert Activity button, 78
Convert E-mail To Lead button, 148
Convert E-Mail To Lead dialog box, 148
Convert Lead dialog box, 137
converting campaign activities, 209
converting campaign responses, 209-211
converting leads, 134-135
Copy A Link button, 61
Copy As Campaign action, 190
Copy As Campaign button, 190
Copy As Template action, 190
copying
　campaign records, 189-190
　marketing list members, 167-168
costs of marketing campaigns, tracking, 179
counting records, 24
Create Opportunities button, 170
Create Opportunity For Marketing List Members
　dialog box, 171
Create Quick Campaign Wizard, 191
CRM button, 173
CRM Online Login button, 10
CSRs (customer service representatives), assigning
　cases to, 223
custom activities, 70

customer field, 52
customer loyalty programs. *See* marketing
    campaigns
customer relationships, defined, 400
Customer Service dashboards, 298
Customer Service Representative security role, 241
customer service representatives (CSRs), assigning
    cases to, 223
customer service requests. *See* cases
customers
    defined, 400
    linking to marketing campaigns, 183-184

D

dashboards
    built-in, 298
    charts, 305, 309-311
    closing charts in, 302
    components, adding, 306
    creating, 303-307
    default, setting, 314
    dragging chart objects, 309
    editing, 308-313
    enlarging items on, 301
    fields, adding, 301
    layout, selecting, 304
    lists, adding to, 307
    naming, 305
    navigating, 301
    opening, 142
    overview of, 297
    vs. Report Wizard, 319
    saving and closing, 307
    selecting, 299
    sharing, 315
    view selector, configuring, 311
    viewing, 299
Data Enrichment
    overview of, 395
    updating data with, 395-397
data, importing. *See* Import Data Wizard
data maps, 382, 385
    automating, 388-390
    defined, 400
data records. *See* records
data views
    changing, 24
    selecting, 21
Deactivate button, 59
deactivating cases, 230, 232
deactivating leads, 136-137

deactivating records, 58-59
Decrease Width button, 309
default view, setting, 32-33
Delete button, 120
deleting
    contacts, 120
    knowledge base articles, 245-246
    lookup field values, 37
    marketing list members, 159-160, 163-164
    Microsoft Dynamics CRM for Outlook records, 118
    notes, 87
    Outlook contacts, and synchronization, 119
    tabs, 99
delimiters, 384
deploying Microsoft Dynamics CRM, 8
Details button, 357, 359
dialog boxes
    Add A New Section, 251
    Add Column, 324
    Add Columns, 350, 369
    Add Grouping, 324, 330
    Add To Queue, 273
    Article Approval Confirmation, 242
    Article Template Properties, 250
    Article Unpublish Confirmation, 246
    Assign Accounts, 361
    Assign Queued Items, 273
    Assign To Team Or User, 223
    Case Cancel Confirmation, 232
    Change Column Properties, 352
    Choose Contact Groups, 110
    Close And Convert The Response, 210
    Close Task, 75
    Comment On This Article, 248
    Component Designer, 305
    Configure Sort Order, 325, 352
    Distribute E-Mail Messages To Target Marketing
        Lists, 204
    Distribute Phone Calls To Target Marketing
        Lists, 205
    Download Complete, 369
    Edit Columns, 349, 369
    Edit Multiple Records, 30, 360
    Export Data To Excel, 366, 389, 395
    File Download, xix, 366
    Insert Template, 116
    List Or Chart Properties, 310
    Look Up Records, 36, 73, 184, 186-188, 200, 273,
        293, 316
    New Filter, 125
    New Report, 377
    Outlook Filter, 125
    Provide A Reason, 247

dialog boxes *(continued)*
  Query Properties, 354
  Reactivate The Selected Case, 232
  Renew Contract, 267
  Resolve Case, 228, 267
  Select A Template, 237
  Select Dashboard Layout, 304
  Select PivotTable Columns, 373
  Select Records, 214
  Select Values, 339
  Select Whether To Include Campaign Activities, 201
  Set Personal Options, 40
  System Settings, 337
  Template Explorer, 260
  View Information, 282
  Who Would You Like To Share The Selected Report With?, 332
  Who Would You Like To Share The Selected Saved View With?, 355
  Who Would You Like To Share The Selected User Chart With?, 315
digital edition of book
  accessing, xvii, xviii
  downloading, xix
direct emails
  defined, 400
  sending, 91
direct mail, 172-173
disabled data connection alert, 369
disqualifying leads, 136-137
Distribute Campaign Activity button, 203-204
Distribute E-Mail Messages To Target Marketing Lists dialog box, 204
Distribute Phone Calls To Target Marketing Lists dialog box, 205
distributing campaign activities, 202-205
document libraries, 9
Download Complete dialog box, 369
downloading online edition of book, xix
downloading practice files, xxi
Draft status for contracts, 264
Draft view, 247
dragging chart objects in dashboard designer, 309
due dates, setting
  for planning activities, 182
  for tasks, 74
duplicate checking, 62
duplicate records, merging, 62
duration, task, 227
dynamic Excel reports, 368-371
dynamic marketing lists, 165
dynamic PivotTables, 376
dynamic values, 400

E

eBook version of book
  accessing, xvii
  downloading, xix
Edit button, 308, 329, 339
Edit Columns button, 349
Edit Columns dialog box, 349, 369
Edit Multiple Records dialog box, 30, 360
editing
  bulk data. *See* Data Enrichment
  contacts, 53
  contracts, 264
  dashboards, 308-313
  records, multiple, 29-30
Email A Link button, 61
email activities, 69
email addresses, entering for queues, 270
email campaign activities, distributing, 203
email messages
  attaching to contacts, 117
  categorizing, 113, 115
  creating, 113-115, 148
  importing, with Add Contacts wizard, 111
  linking entities to, 115
  organizing, 113, 115
  for queues, 270
  Regarding field, 113, 115
  sending, 117
  sent, viewing, 117
  templates, inserting, 116
  tracking, 113, 115
  tracking received, 113
email templates, 91, 400
emailing campaign activities, 202-205
emailing links to records, 61
emails. *See* direct emails; email activities; email messages
employers as parent customers, 52
Enlarge button, 301
enlarging dashboard items, 301
entity navigation pane, 23
errata, book, xxiii
Evaluate Members And Update Marketing List dialog box, 162
Exact Words button, 244
examples shown in book, xiii
Excel
  exporting data to. *See* Excel reports; PivotTable reports
  exporting reports to, 328
  worksheets, formatting, 369

Excel reports. *See also* PivotTable reports
  dynamic, 368-371
  static, 364-367
  uploading to Reports area, 377-378
Excel Viewer, 367
expanding
  chart area, 22
  Get Started pane, 21
Expired status for contracts, 265
Export Data To Excel dialog box, 366, 389, 395
Export To Excel button, 365, 395
exporting data to Excel. *See* Excel reports;
    PivotTable reports
exporting reports to other formats, 328

F

fax activities, 69
feedback on book, xxiii
field mapping
  defined, 400
  overview of, 53-54
  when importing data, 385
fields, 47
  in activities, 71
  adding to Advanced Find, 350
  blue plus symbols, 47
  filtering by, 281
  lookup. *See* lookup fields
  red asterisks, 47
  tracking as campaign activities, 196
file attachments. *See* attachments
File Download dialog box, xix, 173, 366
Filter button, 281-282
filtering
  activities, 82-83, 90
  contacts, 52
  records, 31, 280-282
  records in Microsoft Dynamics CRM for
    Outlook, 98
  records on multiple fields, 281
filters
  adding to views, 282-283
  saving, 283
find fields, 36
finding. *See* Advanced Find; Quick Find; searching
follow-up activities, creating, 76
footers, record, 23
form fields. *See* fields
formatting Advanced Find results, 349, 351, 353

G

Get Started pane
  collapsing/expanding, 21
  turning off, 39
global branding campaigns, 187-188
Go Offline button, 122, 125
Go Online button, 122
going online/offline, 7
grid, 21
grouping users into teams, 59-60
groupings in reports, 324, 330

H

headers, record, 23
help
  accessing, xxiv, 41-42
  context sensitivity of, xxiv
  navigating, xxv
  searching for topics, xxv
  table of contents, displaying, xxv
Help button, xxiv, 42
Help menu, xxiv
history, 400
Home button, 35, 301
home page
  navigating to, 35
  setting, 39

I

Import Contacts button, 109
Import Data button, 384
Import Data Wizard. *See also* importing data
  data maps and, 382, 385
  data source, selecting, 384
  delimiters and, 384
  duplicate detection option, 387
  importing data with, 384-385, 387-388
  information required for, 383
  mapping fields in, 385
  overview of, 381-382
  record types for, 382
Important paragraphs, xvi
importing data. *See also* Import Data Wizard
  automatic data mapping, 388-390
  troubleshooting, 391-393
importing email messages, 111

importing Outlook contacts, 108-110
Imports view, 391-393
inactive records
  defined, 57
  reactivating, 59
Inactive status value, 57-58
Increase Width button, 310
index bar, 21, 31
Insert Template button, 116
Insert Template dialog box, 116
Invoice Contract button, 265
Invoiced status for contracts, 264
invoicing contracts, 265

J

jump selector, 23

K

Keyword Search button, 244
keywords for knowledge base articles, 239,
  243-244
knowledge base,
  defined, 400
  overview of, 236
knowledge base articles
  approving, 242, 245
  auto-numbering, 240
  comments, viewing, 248
  components of, 237
  creating, 237-239
  deleting, 245-246
  keywords, 239
  published, viewing, 246
  publishing, 241-242
  Quick Find, 244
  rejecting, 245, 247
  removing, 245-246
  searching for, 243-244
  security privileges and, 241
  submitting for review, 240, 245
  templates, adding sections to, 251
  templates, applying, 238
  templates, creating, 249-252
  unapproved, marking as, 240
  unapproved, viewing, 241
  viewing, 237
  viewing queue, 244
  views, moving between, 245

L

lead sources
  defined, 400
  entering, 134
  origination of, 132
  tracking, 133
leads
  converting, 134-135, 209-211
  converting emails into, 148
  creating, 133-134, 137
  data structure for, 130
  defined, 400
  disqualifying, 136-137
  vs. opportunities, 132
  overview of, 130
  qualifying, 131, 134-135
  tracking, 132
  tracking disqualification, 137
letter activities, 69
linking activities to other records, 71-72
linking directly to records, 61
List button, 307
list members, 400
List Or Chart Properties dialog box, 310
lists in dashboards, adding, 307
lists, marketing. *See* marketing lists
local data groups, 400
locking marketing lists, 154
logging on
  to Microsoft Dynamics CRM, 11-12
  to Microsoft Dynamics CRM Online, 9-10
  with mobile device, 15
Look Up Record dialog box, 73, 168, 273
Look Up Records dialog box, 36, 55, 60, 63, 156,
  173, 184, 186-188, 200, 293, 316
Lookup button, 55, 73, 222, 273
lookup fields
  appearance of, 36
  automatic resolution for, 36
  defined, 400
  deleting values from, 37
  find fields and, 36
  linked records, displaying, 36
  populating, 37-38
  recently used records, selecting, 36
lookups, adding marketing list members with,
  155, 156
loyalty programs. *See* marketing campaigns

M

mail merge, 172-173
Mail Merge On List Members button, 172
Mail Merge Recipients dialog box, 174
Manage Attachment dialog box, 56
Manage Members button, 156, 158, 160, 162, 166
Manage Members dialog box, 156, 158, 160, 162
Manage Members Find dialog box, 166
mapping fields. *See* field mapping
Mark Complete button, 75, 228
marketing, 151
marketing campaigns
    activities included in, 178
    activity due dates, setting, 182
    campaign codes, 180
    copying records from, 189-190
    costs, tracking, 179
    creating, 179-181
    defined, 400
    fields tracked by, 179
    linking lists to, 183-184
    marketing lists, adding, 200, 202
    opening, 182, 188
    overview of, 178
    planning activities, 181-182
    quick, 191-193
    relating to other campaigns, 187-188
    sales literature, adding, 186-187
    statuses, 179
    target products, adding, 185-187
    templates for, 189-190
    tracking, 179
Marketing Dashboard, 299
marketing lists
    accessing, 200
    adding members to, 155-156
    adding to campaigns, 200, 202
    Advanced Find, adding members with, 157-159
    copying members between, 167-168
    creating, 153, 165, 185
    creating from existing lists, 168
    creating opportunities from members, 169-170
    defined, 152, 400
    dynamic, 165
    evaluating members in, 161-162
    finding members for, 157-159
    linking to campaigns, 183-184
    locking, 154
    lookups for, 155
    mail merge and, 172-173
    managing, 200

member types, 152
members, viewing, 158
modifying, 154
opening, 155, 158
query-based, 165
removing from campaign activities, 202
removing members from, 159-160, 163-164
search criteria, removing/adding members with, 161-162
setting up, 152
static, 152-154
target, creating, 184
updating from search criteria, 163
viewing details on, 185
Marketing module, information tracked by, 5
marking activities as completed, 78
marking tasks as complete, 75, 228
mass emails. *See* direct emails
master records, 63
Merge button, 64
merging records, 62-64
Microsoft Communications Server, 9
Microsoft Dynamics CRM
    access points, 6-7
    accounts, searching for, 106
    flexibility of, 6
    help, accessing, 41-42
    information tracked by, 5
    mobile device access, 7
    overview of, 5
    xRM, 6
Microsoft Dynamics CRM for Outlook
    accessing, 98
    address books, 114
    benefits of, 95
    charts, displaying, 100
    creating email messages with, 114
    deleting records in, 118
    filtering, 98
    logging activities in, 100
    pinning tabs, 99
    Quick Find, 98-99
    reading pane, 98
    Reading Pane button, 100
    ribbon, 97
    settings, changing, 101
    Solution folder, 97
    synchronization with, 102-105, 108
    synchronization with, and deleted records, 119
    synchronizing tasks/appointments, 112
    tracking email messages, 113

Microsoft Dynamics CRM for Outlook *(continued)*
  user interface, 97-98
  user interface, personalizing, 100
  versions of, 6, 96
  views, changing, 99
  working offline, 121-122
**Microsoft Dynamics CRM Mail Merge For
    Microsoft Office Word dialog box**, 172
Microsoft Dynamics CRM Online, 8
Microsoft Dynamics CRM Overview dashboard, 299
Microsoft Dynamics CRM workflow.
    See workflow rules
Microsoft Excel. *See* Excel
Microsoft Knowledge Base, xxvi
Microsoft Outlook. *See* Microsoft Dynamics CRM
    for Outlook; Outlook
Microsoft Press Twitter feed, xxiii
Microsoft Press website, xxiii
Microsoft Product Support Services, xxvi
Microsoft SharePoint Server, 9
Microsoft SQL Server Reporting Services, 319-320.
    See also reports
Microsoft Word. *See* Word
mobile devices
  accessing Microsoft Dynamics CRM via, 7, 15
  synchronizing with Microsoft Dynamics CRM, 103
Mobile Express module
  access with, 15
  overview of, 7
multiple selections, 26
My Activities view, 368

N

naming
  campaigns, 190
  dashboards, 305
  quick campaigns, 191
navigating
  dashboards, 301
  help system, xxv
New Account form, 48
New button, 48, 153, 180, 221, 237, 260, 304,
    322, 369
New Campaign form, 180
New Campaign (Template) form, 189
New Chart button, 289
New E-Mail button, 115
New Filter dialog box, 125
New Lead form, 211
New Report dialog box, 377
New Task form, 73

New Template button, 189
notes
  creating, 86
  defined, 67
  deleting, 87
  overview of, 85
  rolling up behavior, 87
  viewing, 56, 87
Notes & Activities link, 56
numbering cases, 223

O

Office ribbon, 20
offline access, 7
offline synchronization filters, 123-125
**offline working with Microsoft Dynamics CRM for
    Outlook**, 121-122
On Hold status for contracts, 265
one-way relationships between campaigns, 188
online edition of book
  accessing, xvii-xviii
  downloading, xix
**on-premise deployment of Microsoft Dynamics
    CRM**, 8
Open Opportunities view, 395
opening
  campaign activities, 203
  campaign reports, 210
  campaigns, 197
  charts, 292
  views, 282
operators for filtering, 345
opportunities
  close date, entering, 139-140
  closed, viewing, 146
  closing, 144-145
  converting activities into, 78
  creating, 139, 169-170
  deactivating, 144
  defined, 400
  vs. leads, 132
  open, viewing, 280
  opening, 146
  overview of, 132
  probability, entering, 139-140
  ratings, entering, 139
  reopening, 146-147
  revenue settings, 138
  saving, 140
  System Calculated, 138

tracking, 138
User Provided, 138
views for, 141
Opportunities tab, 281
Opportunity grid view, 280, 282
organizing contacts, 109
Other channel, 199
Outlook. *See also* Microsoft Dynamics CRM for
    Outlook
    accessing Microsoft Dynamics CRM via, 6, 13-14
    integration with Microsoft Dynamics CRM, 13
Outlook contacts
    creating, 106-107
    deleting, 120
    deleting, and synchronization, 119
    importing, 108-110
    synchronizing, 108
    tracking in Microsoft Dynamics CRM, 105-106
Outlook Filter dialog box, 125
Owner field, 61

P

parent accounts
    creating, 50
    defined, 400
    overview of, 49
Parent Customer field, 51
Parent Customer fields, populating, 37-38
parent customers, 51-52
partner-hosted deployment of Microsoft Dynamics
    CRM, 8
pasting, 61
PDAs. *See* mobile devices
PDF of book, downloading, xix
PDFs, exporting reports to, 328
permissions
    granting, 60
    for saved views, 354
    viewing, 61
personal options, setting, 39-41
personal view, setting, 32-33
phone call activities, 69, 76. *See also* activities
Phone Call button, 76
Phone Calls Created list, 208
Pie Chart icon, 287
pie charts, creating, 287
pinning records/views to recent list, 34
pinning tabs, 99
PivotTable reports. *See also* Excel reports
    calculation type, changing, 374
    creating, 373-375

fields, including in, 373
formatting, 374
overview of, 371-372
PivotTables, dynamic, examples of, 376
planning activities for marketing campaigns,
    181-182
populating contacts, 53, 55
practice files, downloading, xxi
price sheets, 186-187
probability
    for opportunities, 139-140
    searching on, 347
product and pricing sheets, 186-187
product catalogs, 185, 401
products, adding to marketing campaigns,
    185-187
Promote To Response button, 209
promoting campaign activities to responses,
    207-209
prospects, linking to marketing campaigns,
    183-184
Provide A Reason dialog box, 247
Publish Articles security privilege, 241
Published Articles view, 246
publishing knowledge base articles, 241-242
publishing reports, 332-333

Q

Qualify button, 135
qualifying leads, 131, 134-135
queries
    details, viewing, 359
    operators for, 345
    saving, 353
Query Properties dialog box, 354
query-based marketing lists, 165
queues
    actions available for, 269
    cases, assigning to, 273
    creating, 271-272
    defined, 401
    email addresses, associating with, 270
    email configuration, 270
    item details, viewing, 269
    overview of, 256, 269
    records, adding, 270, 273
    releasing users from, 269
    removing items from, 269
    routing items in, 269-270
    viewing, 271
Quick Campaign button, 191

quick campaigns, 191-193
  activity type, selecting, 191
  defined, 401
  naming, 191
  opening, 193
Quick Find. *See also* searching
  accessing, 30
  canceling, 32
  defined, 401
  inactive records and, 31
  for knowledge base articles, 244
  in Microsoft Dynamics CRM for Outlook, 98-99
  overview of, 21
  searching with, 32
  wildcard characters, 31, 37
Quick Find search box, 30
quotes, 401

R

rating opportunities, 139
Reactivate button, 232
Reactivate The Selected Case dialog box, 232
reactivating
  cases, 230, 232
  records, 59
Reading Pane button, 100
Reading Pane in Microsoft Dynamics CRM for
    Outlook, 98, 100
recently visited records/views, 34-35, 39
record footer, 23
record header, 23
records
  activating, 59
  adding to queues, 270, 273
  assigning, 61-62, 361
  body, 23
  converting campaign records into, 209-211
  copying, from campaigns, 189-190
  deactivating, 58-59
  deleting, 118
  duplicate, merging, 62
  editing multiple, 29-30, 358-361
  emailing links to, 61
  filtering, 31, 280-282
  inactive, 57
  jumping to, 23
  master/child, 63
  maximum number, unlimited, 24
  merging, 62-64
  navigating, 24
  number per page, setting, 40

ownership, changing, 61-62
paging through, 24
permissions, viewing, 61
pinning to recent list, 34
reactivating, 59
recently visited, accessing, 34-35
resizing columns, 24
running reports from, 338
selecting, 27-28
selecting multiple, 28, 191, 361
selection indicator, 27
sharing, 59-61
shortcut addresses, 61
sorting, 25-27
status values, 57-58
total count, viewing, 24
tracking icon, 104
tracking pane, 103
updating in bulk. *See* Data Enrichment
URLs for, 61
user interface, 23
view, changing, 24
recurring appointments, 70. *See also* activities
red asterisks, 47
Refresh button, 28, 267
refreshing
  contacts, 267
  dynamic reports, 371
  views, 28
Regarding field, 71-73, 113-115, 401
Reject button, 247
rejecting knowledge base articles, 245-247
relating campaigns, 187-188
releasing users from queue, 269
Remove button, 202
Remove From Marketing List button, 164
Remove Members dialog box, 160, 164
removing marketing lists from campaign
    activities, 202
Renew Contract button, 267
Renew Contract dialog box, 267
renewing contracts, 267
reopening opportunities, 146-147
Reopen Opportunity button, 147
Report Scheduling Wizard, 334-335
Report Wizard, 283. *See also* reports
  benefits of, 322
  vs. charts and dashboards, 319
  creating reports with, 322-326
  modifying reports with, 329-331
  starting, 322
  when to use, 322
Report Wizard button, 322

reporting errors in book, xxiii
reports. *See also* Report Wizard; SQL Server
  Reporting Services
  accessing from toolbars, 338
  categories, 337, 339-340
  columns, adding, 324
  creating, 322-326
  exporting to other formats, 328
  fields, adding to, 329
  filtering criteria, 323, 328
  grouping, adding, 324, 330
  included with SQL Server Reporting Services, 320
  layout, changing, 330
  modifying, 328-331
  properties, entering, 322
  refining output, 328
  refreshing, 371
  running, 214, 327
  running from within records, 338
  scheduling, 334-335
  sharing, 332-333
  sort order, configuring, 325
  viewing, 377
Reports area, uploading Excel reports to, 377-378
requests for service. *See* cases
resizing columns, 24
resolution, automatic, 36
Resolve Case button, 228, 266
Resolve Case dialog box, 228, 267
Resolved status value, 57-58
resolving cases, 228-229, 266
Resource Center, xxvi, 41
Results arrow, 287
Results button, 348
results of campaigns, 212-213
reviewing data import status, 391-392
reward programs. *See* marketing campaigns
ribbon
  in Microsoft Dynamics CRM for Outlook, 97
  overview of, 20
routing queue items, 269
Run Report button, 214, 327
running reports, 214, 327, 338

S

Safari account, registering, xviii
Sales Activity Dashboard, 142, 299
sales literature, adding to marketing campaigns, 186
Sales module, information tracked by, 5
Sales Performance dashboard, 299
sandbox environments, xiii

Save And Close button, 50, 81, 86, 99, 107, 154,
  183, 198, 260, 263, 307
Save As button, 282
Save button, 48, 74, 125, 137, 181, 209, 222, 239,
  252, 261, 291
Save Filters button, 283
saved views
  accessing, 355
  creating, 354
  dynamic results of, 353
  permissions for, 354
  sharing, 353, 355
Saved Views button, 355
saving
  accounts, 50
  Advanced Find queries, 353
  charts, 291
  filters, 283
  opportunities, 140
  views, 282
Schedule Report button, 334
scheduling reports, 334-335
screen shots in book, xiii
Search button, 244
searching. *See also* Advanced Find; Quick Find
  across multiple columns, 31
  for contacts, 55
  for help topics, xxv
  for knowledge base articles, 243, 244
  for marketing list contacts, 157-159
  partial records, 31
  wildcard characters, 31, 37
security alerts for disabled data connections, 369
security model, 59
security privileges, 241, 249
security roles
  book conventions for, xiv
  Customer Service Representative, 241
See Also paragraphs, xvi
Select A Template dialog box, 237
Select Columns button, 373
Select Dashboard Layout dialog box, 304
Select PivotTable Columns dialog box, 373
Select Records dialog box, 214
Select Values dialog box, 339
Select Whether To Include Campaign Activities
  dialog box, 201
selecting
  all, 369
  multiple items, 26, 191, 361
  records, 27-28
Send button, 117
Send Direct E-mail button, 92

sending direct emails, 91
sending email messages, 117
sent email messages, viewing, 117
service activities, 70
service agreements. *See* contracts
Service module, information tracked by, 5
service queues. *See* queues
service requests. *See* cases
services, adding to marketing campaigns, 185-187
Set As Default button, 314
Set As Default View button, 33
Set Parent button, 105-106
Set Personal Options dialog box, 40
Set Regarding button, 115
SET UP paragraphs, xvi
Share button, 292, 332
SharePoint Server, 9
sharing
   accounts, 59
   charts, 292-293
   dashboards, 315
   defined, 401
   records, 59-61
   reports, 332-333
   saved views, 353
   views, 355
   views, permissions for, 354
Sharing button, 60-61
Show Contents button, xxv
simple campaigns. *See* quick campaigns
Simple mode for Advanced Find, 357
smartphones. *See* mobile devices
Solution folder (Outlook), 97
sort order
   changing, 26
   indicators for, 25
   in reports, 325
sorting columns, 352
sorting records, 25-27
SQL Server Reporting Services, 319-320.
      See also reports; Report Wizard
staging environments, xiii
static Excel reports, 364-367
static marketing lists, 152-154
static values, 401
statuses, 57-58
   for activities, 78
   for campaign activities, 214
   for cases, 229
   for marketing campaigns, 179
strategic dashboards, 297
sub-accounts
   defined, 401
   overview of, 49

subject tree
   accessing, 225
   configuring, 224
   example of, 224
subjects, 401
Submit button, 240
submitting knowledge base articles for review, 240, 245
synchronization filters, 123-125
Synchronize button, 108, 120, 125
Synchronize With CRM button, 105
synchronizing with Outlook, 102-105, 108
   automatic timing, 104
   deleted records and, 119
System Calculated opportunities, 138
System Settings dialog box, 337
system views. *See* views

T

tables. *See* Pivot Table reports; PivotTables, dynamic, examples of
tabs, pinning and removing, 99
tactical dashboards, 297
target marketing lists, 184
target products/services for marketing campaigns, 185-187
Target Products window, 186
task activities, 69, 81. *See also* activities
Task button, 227
tasks
   creating, 73
   creating, for cases, 227
   due dates, setting, 74
   duration, setting, 227
   marking as complete, 75, 228
   status, setting, 75
   synchronizing, 112
   viewing, 90
teams, 59-60
Template Explorer dialog box, 260
templates
   applying to knowledge base articles, 238
   for contracts, 257-258, 260
   in email messages, 116
   for emails, 91
   for knowledge base articles, creating, 249-252
   for marketing campaigns, 189-190
   naming, 190
   sections, adding, 251
   security privileges for, 249
   viewing, 250
test environments, xiii

time zone, setting, 40
timing Outlook synchronization, 104
Tip paragraphs, xvi
toolbars, report access from, 338
Track button, 105, 106, 115
tracking
    activities, 70, 78-79
    campaign reports, 206-207
    cases, 226
    email messages, 113, 115
    fields, for campaign activities, 196
    leads, 132
    marketing campaigns, 179
    opportunities, 138
    Outlook contacts, 105-106
    service request activities, 226
tracking icon for Microsoft Dynamic CRM
        records, 104
Troubleshooting paragraphs, xvi
Twitter feed for Microsoft Press, xxiii

U

Unapproved Articles view, 241, 247
unpinning records/views from recent list, 35
Unpublish button, 246
unpublishing knowledge base articles, 245-246
Untrack button, 104
updating
    bulk data. See Data Enrichment
    charts, 144, 286
    contacts, 53
    marketing lists, from search criteria, 163
URL for Microsoft Dynamics CRM site, 12
URLs for records, 61
Use Query button, 167
user interface, 20-23
    personal options, setting, 39-41
    sort order indicators, 25
User Provided opportunities, 138
users, 60-61

V

View Information dialog box, 282
View Records button, 302
view selector, 21, 52

views
    default display of, 32-33
    defined, 401
    exporting to Excel, 365
    filters, adding, 282-283
    in Microsoft Dynamics CRM for Outlook, 99
    modifying, 348
    opening, 282
    for opportunities, 141
    pinning to recent list, 34
    recently visited, accessing, 34-35
    refreshing, 28
    saving, 282, 383-385
    sharing, 355
    sorting records in, 25

W

web client
    defined, 401
    home page. See home page
web clients
    defined, 6
    user interface, 20-23
Who Would You Like To Share The Selected Report
        With? dialog box, 332
Who Would You Like To Share The Selected Saved
        View With? dialog box, 355
Who Would You Like To Share The Selected User
        Chart With? dialog box, 315
wildcard characters in searches, 31, 37
Windows Live ID, 9
Word
    exporting reports to, 328
    integration with, 9
    mail merging with, 172-173
Work On button, 273
workflow rules, 68
working offline with Microsoft Dynamics CRM for
        Outlook, 121-122
Workplace pane
    defined, 401
    overview of, 88
    personalizing, 40
worksheets, dynamic, 368-371

X

xRM, overview of, 6

About Sonoma Partners

This book's authors, Mike Snyder, Jim Steger, and Brendan Landers, are executives at the Chicago-based consulting firm Sonoma Partners. Sonoma Partners is a Microsoft Gold Certified Partner that sells, customizes, and implements Microsoft Dynamics CRM for enterprise and midsize companies throughout the United States and Canada. Sonoma Partners has worked exclusively with Microsoft Dynamics CRM since the version 1.0 prerelease beta software. Founded in 2001, Sonoma Partners possesses extensive experience in several industries, including financial services, professional services, health care, and real estate.

Sonoma Partners is different from other Microsoft Dynamics CRM partners because:

- We write the books for Microsoft. Consequently, we know the product inside and out, and our relationships with Microsoft product teams will save you tons of time and headaches down the line.

- We offer a cost guarantee on all of our deployments. We can do this because of our experience completing more than 400 Microsoft Dynamics CRM deployments.

- We offer clients our unique pre-built intellectual property that consists of a full library of tools, utilities, controls, and solutions that you can plug and play in your deployment—saving clients thousands of hours of development time.

- Sonoma Partners offers pre-built solution templates for professional services, financial services, healthcare, franchise management, and real estate.

In addition to the multiple books we've written for Microsoft Press, we share our Microsoft Dynamics CRM product knowledge through our email newsletter and online blog. If you're interested in receiving this information, you can find out more on our website at *http://www.sonomapartners.com*.

Even though our headquarters is in Chicago, Illinois, we work with customers throughout the United States and Canada. If you're interested in discussing your Microsoft Dynamics CRM system with us, please don't hesitate to contact us! In addition to working with customers who want to deploy Microsoft Dynamics CRM for themselves, we also act as a technology provider for Independent Software Vendors (ISVs) looking to develop their solution for the Microsoft Dynamics CRM platform.

Sometimes people ask us where we got our name. The name *Sonoma Partners* was inspired by Sonoma County in the wine-producing region of northern California. The wineries in Sonoma County are smaller than their more well-known competitors in Napa Valley, but they have a reputation for producing some of the highest quality wines in the world. We think that their smaller size allows the Sonoma winemakers to be more intimately involved with creating the wine. By using this hands-on approach, the Sonoma County wineries can deliver a superior product to their customers—and that's what we strive to do as well.

Mike Snyder

Mike Snyder is co-founder and principal of Sonoma Partners. Recognized as one of the industry's leading Microsoft Dynamics CRM experts, Mike is a member of the Microsoft Dynamics Partner Advisory Council and is a Microsoft Dynamics CRM MVP. He has co-authored several books about Microsoft Dynamics CRM for Microsoft Press that have sold more than 50,000 copies worldwide. Before starting Sonoma Partners, Mike led multiple product development teams at Motorola and Fortune Brands. Mike graduated with honors from Northwestern's Kellogg Graduate School of Management with a Master of Business Administration degree, majoring in marketing and entrepreneurship. He has a bachelor's degree in engineering from the University of Notre Dame. He enjoys ice hockey and golf in his free time.

Jim Steger

Jim Steger is co-founder and principal of Sonoma Partners. He has been developing solutions for Microsoft Dynamics CRM since the version 1.0 beta. Microsoft recognized Jim's leadership in the technical community with the Microsoft Dynamics CRM MVP award in both 2010 and 2009. Jim has co-authored books about Microsoft Dynamics CRM for Microsoft Press since the 3.0 version of the software. Before starting Sonoma Partners, Jim designed and led various global software development projects at Motorola and ACCO Office Products. Jim earned his bachelor's degree in engineering from Northwestern University.

Brendan Landers

Brendan Landers is a consulting director at Sonoma Partners, overseeing all of the company's Microsoft Dynamics CRM consulting projects. He has led numerous Microsoft Dynamics CRM implementation projects for companies in the following industries: professional and financial services, education, healthcare, hospitality, and others. Prior to joining Sonoma Partners, Brendan worked at Information Resources, Inc. as a Director, Quality Assurance and Delivery, where he led several data quality and business intelligence initiatives. He holds a bachelor's degree in management information systems from the University of Iowa.

Microsoft

How To Download Your eBook

Thank you for purchasing this Microsoft Press® title. Your companion PDF eBook is ready to download from O'Reilly Media, official distributor of Microsoft Press titles.

To download your eBook, go to
http://go.microsoft.com/FWLink/?Linkid=224345
and follow the instructions.

Please note: You will be asked to create a free online account and enter the access code below.

Your access code:

QHWQDHL

Microsoft Dynamics® CRM 2011 Step by Step

Your PDF eBook allows you to:

- Search the full text
- Print
- Copy and paste

Best yet, you will be notified about free updates to your eBook.

If you ever lose your eBook file, you can download it again just by logging in to your account.

Need help? Please contact:
mspbooksupport@oreilly.com
or call 800-889-8969.

Please note: This access code is non-transferable and is void if altered or revised in any way. It may not be sold or redeemed for cash, credit, or refund.

Choose the Right Book for You

Plain & Simple
- Easy visual approach shows the simplest ways to get things done
- Full color! with easy-to-follow steps and screenshots
- Just the basics—with no jargon

Step by Step
- Build exactly the skills you want
- Take just the lessons you need, or work from cover to cover
- Get ready-made practice files and a complete eBook

Inside Out
- The ultimate, in-depth reference for intermediate to advanced users
- Features hundreds of timesaving solutions, troubleshooting tips, and workarounds
- Includes eBook and custom resources

Resources from Microsoft Press

Plain & Simple

Windows® 7
Plain & Simple
978-0-7356-2666-9

Microsoft® Office 2010
Plain & Simple
978-0-7356-2697-3

Microsoft Access® 2010
Plain & Simple
978-0-7356-2730-7

Microsoft Excel® 2010
Plain & Simple
978-0-7356-2727-7

Microsoft Outlook® 2010
Plain & Simple
978-0-7356-2734-5

Microsoft PowerPoint® 2010
Plain & Simple
978-0-7356-2728-4

Microsoft Word 2010
Plain & Simple
978-0-7356-2731-4

Microsoft SharePoint® 2010
Plain & Simple
978-0-7356-4228-7

Step by Step

Windows 7
Step by Step
978-0-7356-2667-6

Microsoft Office
Professional 2010
Step by Step
978-0-7356-2696-6

Microsoft Access 2010
Step by Step
978-0-7356-2692-8

Microsoft Excel 2010
Step by Step
978-0-7356-2694-2

Microsoft Office Home
and Student 2010
Step by Step
978-0-7356-2721-5

Microsoft Outlook 2010
Step by Step
978-0-7356-2690-4

Microsoft PowerPoint 2010
Step by Step
978-0-7356-2691-1

Microsoft Project 2010
Step by Step
978-0-7356-2695-9

Microsoft SharePoint
Designer 2010
Step by Step
978-0-7356-2733-8

Microsoft Word 2010
Step by Step
978-0-7356-2693-5

Inside Out

Windows 7 *Inside Out*
978-0-7356-2665-2

Microsoft Office 2010
Inside Out
978-0-7356-2689-8

Microsoft Access 2010
Inside Out
978-0-7356-2685-0

Microsoft Excel 2010
Inside Out
978-0-7356-2688-1

Microsoft Outlook 2010
Inside Out
978-0-7356-2686-7

Microsoft Project 2010
Inside Out
978-0-7356-2687-4

Microsoft Word 2010
Inside Out
978-0-7356-2729-1

Other Titles

Windows 7: The Best of
the Official Magazine
978-0-7356-2664-5

Beyond Bullet Points:
Using Microsoft Office
PowerPoint 2007 to Create
Presentations That Inform,
Motivate, and Inspire
978-0-7356-2387-3

Take Back Your Life! Using
Microsoft Office Outlook 2007
to Get Organized and Stay
Organized
978-0-7356-2343-9

Microsoft Office Excel 2007:
Data Analysis and Business
Modeling
978-0-7356-2396-5

Coming Soon!

Microsoft PowerPivot for
Excel 2010: Give Your
Data Meaning
978-0-7356-4058-0

microsoft.com/mspress

What do you think of this book?

We want to hear from you!

To participate in a brief online survey, please visit:

microsoft.com/learning/booksurvey

Tell us how well this book meets your needs—what works effectively, and what we can do better. Your feedback will help us continually improve our books and learning resources for you.

Thank you in advance for your input!

Stay in touch!

To subscribe to the *Microsoft Press® Book Connection Newsletter*—for news on upcoming books, events, and special offers—please visit:

microsoft.com/learning/books/newsletter

Lightning Source UK Ltd.
Milton Keynes UK
UKOW06f0744040913

216486UK00001B/5/P